The Spiritual Work of RACIAL JUSTICE

194 576-7365

A Month of Meditations with Ignatius of Loyola

504
900
1180

The Spiritual Work of
RACIAL JUSTICE

A Month of Meditations
with Ignatius of Loyola

Patrick Saint-Jean, S.J.

The Spiritual Work of Racial Justice
A Month of Meditations with Ignatius of Loyola

Copyright © 2021, Anamchara Books.

ANAMCHARA BOOKS
Vestal, NY 13850
www.anamcharabooks.com

All Scripture quotations, unless otherwise indicated, are taken from the Holy Bible, New International Version of the Bible.® Copyright © 1973, 1978, 1984, 2011 by Biblica, Inc.® Used by permission. All rights reserved worldwide.

Print ISBN: 978-1-62524-836-7
eBook ISBN: 978-1-62524-837-4

Contents

In the sixteenth century, Ignatius of Loyola adopted this symbol as the seal of the Society of Jesus. IHS (the first three letters of Jesus' name in Greek), the three nails (representing the crucifixion), and the sunburst (representing the Light of the World) are all ancient images of Christ.

FOREWORD

by the Jesuit Antiracism Sodality (JARS) Midwest

General Congregation 36 of the Society of Jesus asked an important question: *Why don't the Spiritual Exercises change us as much as we would like?* This refreshing admission that we all miss the mark came from the highest teaching authority of the Society of Jesus. Documents from the General Congregations are meant for Jesuits, as well as for the men and women who labor in the vineyard of its wide and varying ministries around the world, including elementary schools, high schools, colleges, universities, parishes, social centers, and immigration and refugee work, among others.

Patrick Saint-Jean, S.J., offers a guide for all who desire to be more deeply impacted by the Spiritual Exercises. Even though the Exercises occur in four movements or weeks, they may take longer than a calendar month or year to truly absorb and pray over. Indeed, they may take an entire lifetime. Similarly, the work of antiracism is lifelong. A month can only provide a start to any project, let alone one as daunting as staring the sin of racism in the eye.

Still, this year could be the opportunity we have been waiting for to walk with Jesus and ask ourselves many important questions: *How has the COVID pandemic impacted me? How has the past year of protests impacted me? Have I ever confessed the sin of racism or the sin of omission? Can I hear the cry of Black Lives Matter or Stop Asian Hate as though it were coming from God?*

The point of the Spiritual Exercises is not to wallow in our own sin or focus on the ways we have failed Jesus. The point is to encounter Jesus, grow closer to Jesus, and follow Jesus. So when we sit at the feet of our crucified Jesus, we ask, "What have I done for Christ? What am I doing for Christ? What will I do for Christ?" If Christ's face is that of someone who is experiencing the pain of racism, will it change us?

What Patrick Saint-Jean offers is a voice that is often missing. He invites us to be companion on the spiritual journey of reconciliation that racial justice requires.

— *Emmanuel Arenas, S.J.*
  Thomas Bambrick, S.J.
  Aaron Bohr, S.J.
  Billy Critchley-Menor, S.J.
  Patrick Hyland, S.J.
  Joshua Peters, S.J.
  Damian Torres-Botello, S.J.

INTRODUCTION

I was raised by faithful, dedicated people who were as passionate about activism as they were about God. They taught me that the life of faith cannot be separated from the work of justice. Our love of God and God's love for us must flow through us into the world. This is what Jesus teaches us in the Gospels.

Although my family are Southern Baptists, their perspective proved to be fertile ground for the teachings I discovered in the Society of Jesus (which is also known as the *Jesuits*). When I first encountered the Jesuits, I realized they offered me a path to a life of faith-in-action. Since then, the Society of Jesus has become my home here on earth, as well as the road that leads me to my eternal home. It gives me a structure for building a faith that is both deeply spiritual and functionally practical.

But you need not join the Jesuits to learn from their founder, Ignatius of Loyola! You don't need to be a Catholic either. Back in the sixteenth century, Ignatius left all of us a roadmap for the spiritual path, one that works as well today as it did five hundred years ago. He called his roadmap the *Spiritual Exercises,* a carefully thought-through plan for interlacing the life of Christ with our own lives. These exercises are based on Ignatius's own experiences as he grew spiritually, but he was certain they could be equally applied to others' lives. He believed the Spiritual Exercises were a gift directly from God, and that God wanted them to be shared as widely as possible.

In this book, we will use the Spiritual Exercises as our framework for exploring the ways Christ calls us to the work of antiracism. This book's premise is that antiracism is not an optional aspect of the spiritual life, but rather that it is essential to becoming all that God calls us to be. The goal, however, is not that we will reach a state of antiracist perfection, for this is an ongoing process for our entire life. Engaging in antiracist work is not about perfection but rather a constant quest for grace to see each other as Christ sees us. It asks that we hold antiracism as an intentional aspiration each and every day.

If you feel drawn to this book, ask yourself, "What do I hope to get from this book? Do I want to be perceived as 'woke' so that others will think better of me? Or do I genuinely want to allow myself to be changed?" Ignatius recommended, "Ask God for what I want and desire." In other words, think about what you hope to gain from this book, and then ask God to open your heart to that grace. And then ask, "Am I ready to do the work required? Am I willing to look past my blind spots? Do I have the humility to listen to others' perspectives?" The Ignatian approach does require work. It involves a sincere commitment to prayer and the hard effort of self-knowledge.

In Toni Cade Bambara's novel *The Salt Eaters,* a healer asks, "Are you sure, sweetheart that you want to be well? . . . Just so's you're sure, sweetheart, and ready to be healed, cause wholeness is no trifling matter. A lot of weight when you're healed." The weight of healing, I believe, is the responsibility we take on to be constantly vigilant for the presence of racism in our lives. It is our commitment to be a unified Body of Christ, allowing ourselves to experience one another's pain and working for the well-being of all members of that Body. Ask yourself, "Am I ready for that weight?" If the answer is yes—if you are choosing to commit to both inner and outer healing—then I welcome you to the journey that lies ahead!

Ignatius taught that freedom and choice are essential aspects of spiritual development. His concept of freedom meant detaching from all that might limit us or hold our minds captive. A truly free choice, according to Ignatius, requires that we set aside our own preferences and preconceptions, as well as the pressures of our society. We carefully examine our motives and desires. Like antiracism, however, freedom is not something that can be achieved once and for all, nor can we manufacture it through sheer willpower. Instead, the Spiritual Exercises are meant to help us progressively enter into ever-greater freedom. As author Charlotte C. Prather put it, "At each point [in the Spiritual Exercises], a new dimension of freedom . . . is needed in order to be able to choose the end (love) which has been seen and embraced from the beginning."

The Spiritual Exercises are not structured like a story. They are much more like reading a car manual; they're a how-to set of directions for drawing close to God so that we can be freed to see our lives differently and make a difference in the world around us. Because the Exercises themselves are only a manual, the actual experience we have as we use them will be a joint creation between ourselves and God. The Exercises teach us how to pray, using two methods: meditation, which, from an Ignatian perspective, is an exercise of our minds; and contemplation, which springs from our emotions and imaginations.

The book is designed to be used over the space of a month, with a reading for each day, followed by a journaling exercise and a prayer—but feel free to adapt it in whatever way works best for you. The "weeks" and "days" of the Spiritual Exercises are not to be measured by external, sequential divisions. Instead, each day's meditation is offered as a doorway into eternal time, *Kairos* time, the perfect moment when eternity intersects with the here and now, when conditions are right for God to take action in our world.

This is not the sort of book to be read straight through. Instead, it is intended to be slowly digested, allowing the Spirit to speak through the pages and transform your inner and outer being. Plan to set aside at least a half-hour to forty-five minutes for each "chapter." Spend time in prayerful reflection with each section of the chapter. You may want to read one chapter a week, instead of one a day. Maybe you'll want to ignore calendar time altogether and simply follow your own heart's timing. You also might want to read this book in a group or with a friend. As Ignatius of Loyola learned, companions are good to have when we are seeking to grow spiritually. At the very least, I suggest that you have someone with whom you can share the fruit of your prayers and discuss how Christ is encountering you on this pilgrimage of racial healing

However you decide to approach this book, please take enough time with each chapter to truly interact with it. Before you begin, have a notebook ready for journaling your responses to the questions that are placed after each day's reading. After Ignatius's conversion, he journaled faithfully, filling many copybooks with notes from his spiritual life. He encouraged his followers to do the same, keeping a daily written record of the spiritual insights that came to them during prayer and throughout the day. This record could then be reviewed in the future as a reminder of wisdom that might otherwise be forgotten in the busyness of life.

The journal sections at the end of each chapter can also be used as a form of "Examen." The Examen is a prayer tool that Ignatius devised. It can be adapted to life's various demands, but it generally follows this basic outline:

1. Place yourself in God's presence, thanking God for the love that surrounds you.

2. Pray for insight into the ways God is acting in your life.

3. Review the past day, recalling specific moments and your emotional reactions.

4. Reflect on what you did, said, or thought on each of those occasions. Did you feel closer to God—or further away?

5. Look toward the future, thinking about how you might collaborate more deeply with God's plan for your life and the world around you.

Most of us have busy lives that often interfere with our intentions to devote time to a spiritual project such as the one this book offers. As Ignatius noted, "The devil often acts in such a way as to curtail the time set apart for meditation or prayer." Ignatius, however, believed that busyness need not interfere with our spiritual growth. When some students wrote to him saying their studies were so demanding they did not have time to pray, they must have been surprised when he responded that he saw no need for them to spend extra time in prayer. Instead, he advised them to give themselves completely to their studies, while at the same time they sought intimacy with God even in the midst of their busy lives—while walking, while talking with others, while going about their lives' many tasks. The one thing he asked of them was that they take some brief time during each day to apply the Examen to their hearts.

This intentional check-in with your own heart needs only a few minutes. While showering, while driving, while waiting in line, or while falling asleep, you can ask yourself, "What role has racism played in my life today? Have I seen God in a person of color today? Have I been answering God's call to justice today?" This tiny daily exercise will help you apply the book's lessons in practical, ordinary ways.

Each "Week" in this book concludes with a prayer for a particular grace—a gift from God that will endure beyond your reading, so that it finds an ongoing place in your life. These small prayers acknowledge that as much as we might want to, we often struggle to achieve a new outlook or emotion. We need God's help.

Grace, as Ignatius understood it, is something that happens inside us rather than in the outer world. He would advise us to not ask, for example, for the grace of a certain candidate being elected to office, but rather for the grace to see more clearly which candidates will contribute most powerfully to Divine justice. Or we might ask for the grace to embody God's love to everyone we meet—but we wouldn't ask for the grace to get a raise at work (even if we intend to give away the extra money).

Ignatius defined his Spiritual Exercises as a form of activity that makes us stronger (just as physical exercises do). Each person, counseled Ignatius, will engage in these exercises in unique ways and at different levels, depending on where they are at in their lives. Through the Spiritual Exercises, everyone, however, will become freer from their unhealthy attachment to self, so that they can open themselves to a deeper understanding of life.

Each person's spiritual growth, Ignatius believed, is essential to transforming the world. Our inner state influences our outer actions—and what we do or don't do, say or don't say can have a ripple effect that spreads throughout reality, touching a multitude of people in ways we will never know. Jesuit theologian Roger Haight describes Ignatian spirituality as championing "a radical commitment to this world and the people in it, on the conviction that the very actions that carry out that commitment are responses of love to the God of love that is within it all."

Jesus preached a message of inclusion where all people are freed from the chains of division, exclusion, hatred, and violence. His life embodied this message. In the days ahead, we will use his life as our model, allowing the Spiritual Exercises to lead us step by step through his time on earth.

In his autobiography, Ignatius of Loyola referred to himself as *the pilgrim*. Like all pilgrims, he had undertaken a long journey, a lifelong spiritual pilgrimage in which he learned to find and serve God in ordinary life. In the Spiritual Exercises, Ignatius invites us to take this same journey.

And so, with Ignatius of Loyola as our guide, let us open our hearts to Divine love, examining our hearts for anything that stands in the way of justice.

My Lord God,
I have no idea where I am going.
I do not see the road ahead of me.
I cannot know for certain where it will end.
nor do I really know myself,
and the fact that I think I am following your will
does not mean that I am actually doing so.
But I believe that the desire to please you
does in fact please you....
Therefore will I trust you always
though I may seem to be lost and in the shadow of death.
I will not fear, for you are ever with me,
and you will never leave me to face my perils alone.

—THOMAS MERTON

WEEK ONE

The Sin of Division

Many of us are uncomfortable with the word sin. It reminds us of a hell-and-brimstone perspective on Christianity. It smacks of a narrow and legalistic Victorian morality. But that is not the biblical understanding of sin. Instead, the word used in the Bible's original languages meant, literally "to miss the mark," as when an archer fails to hit a target with her arrow. We might also think of sin as anything that makes us deviate from the image of God we are meant to embody and carry out into the world. In this sense, then, sin is like a disease that robs us of our God-given health and wholeness. It not only deprives us as individuals but it also destroys our society as a whole.

Think about the coronavirus that slammed our world with a seismic force, shaking us both individually and as a global community. This disease touched nearly every level of our lives, spiritually, emotionally, physically, and socially. Meanwhile, as COVID-19 assaulted every nation on Earth, a different virus, that of division, has plagued our world with violence and injustice.

Divisions are sins, according to Saint Paul, who called for unity when he wrote, "I appeal to you, brothers and sisters, in the name of our Lord Jesus Christ, that all of you agree with one another in what you say and that there be no divisions among you, but that you be perfectly united in mind and thought" (1 Corinthians 1:10). People who claim the name of Christ may nod along with this verse, but at the same time, many of them demonstrate complacency and implicit participation in an unjust system that sustains personal interests, upholds privilege, and deepens divisions in our communities (including our faith communities).

The sin of division is much the same as the coronavirus. It harms both individuals and societies. It makes us sick at heart; it isolates us from one another; and it damages bodies and takes lives. The sin of division normalizes racism, sexism, and homophobia. It erects boundaries between us as human beings, even as it blocks our vision of God. It robs us of the power and health we are meant to experience, both individually and as communities. It pushes us off course, so that we fail to hit the target of unity and love that God intends for our world.

Historians tell us that racism as we know it today did not begin until the fifteenth or sixteenth centuries, when the first Africans were brought against their will to North America. Nevertheless, the sin of division is an ancient one. Jesus recognized it in his society and spoke out against it; so did his followers in the years that followed his death. Somewhere along the way, however, Christianity lost sight of just how destructive division is. And as Christianity helped to give birth to racism, the ugly virus of division flourished and grew.

The virus can be seen as early as the first century CE, when Christians severed their ties with the Jewish people—and started humiliating, denigrating, and fighting them. As Christianity spread, so did the virus. In the Middle Ages, Christians claimed that the Jews' role in the crucifixion of Jesus consigned them to a spiritually enslaved and inferior status. Myths of Jewish violence against Christians contributed to the hatred many people felt for Jews (just as today, myths about Blacks being criminals have driven whites' fear, hatred, and violence). In the fourteenth century, popular opinion blamed the Jews for the Black Death epidemic (as today, many people have blamed Asians for the coronavirus), and anti-Semitic violence erupted throughout Europe.

As the centuries passed, the pandemic of division continued to spread. Pope Nicholas V, in his 1455 document *Dum Diversas*, noted that he did not recognize Blacks as full humans. Christopher Columbus arrived in the "new" land and then, in the name of the Christian faith, enslaved and killed the brown-skinned people he found there. The papal bulls in the 1493 *Inter Caetera* officialized, even sacralized, this terrible sin.

Then, in the sixteenth century, Ignatius of Loyola brought a new perspective to Christianity. After his conversion in 1521, he was heard to say on more than one occasion that he would like to have been born of Jewish blood because he would then be closer to Christ. Ignatius had an inclusive approach, and he gladly accepted candidates of Jewish ancestry into his order, making sure there was no discrimination among the brothers. One of the Jesuits' founding fathers was of Jewish blood, and in its early decades, men of Jewish ancestry substantially influenced the Society of Jesus. According to Ignatius, all people carry within them the image of God.

Unfortunately, Ignatius's original teachings were buried beneath the racism of the centuries that followed. In North America, both the Catholic and Protestant churches were staunch supporters of the division that undergirds racism. The Jesuits themselves did not escape the virus of division. Instead, Christianity contributed to the growth of racism.

In Frederick Douglass's biography, he tells the story of his "master," Thomas Auld, who became a Christian at a Methodist camp meeting. Douglas had hoped that Auld's conversion would make him "more kind and humane"; instead, wrote Douglass, "If it had any effect on his character, it made him more cruel and hateful in all his ways." Auld put on a good show; he prayed "morning, noon, and night" and attended every revival meeting he could find—but at the same time, Douglass wrote, "I have seen him tie up a lame young woman and whip her with a heavy cowskin upon her naked shoulders, causing the warm red blood to drip; and, in justification of the bloody deed, he would quote this passage of Scripture—'He that knoweth his master's will, and doeth it not, shall be beaten with many stripes.'" Douglass's experience was all too common in the nineteenth century, leading him to believe that most Christians were frauds. He wrote that there was "the widest possible difference" between the "slaveholding religion of this land" and "the pure, peaceable, and impartial Christianity of Christ."

Although the Catholic Church and Pope Leo XIII denounced slavery in 1890, this made little difference to the racism in the white church. Now, more than a century after Douglass's death, we are still struggling with that "slaveholding religion." Surveys conducted by the Public Religion Research Institute found that white Christians—including evangelical Protestants, mainline Protestants, and Catholics—are almost twice as likely as whites without a religious affiliation to say police violence against Black are "isolated incidents," rather than evidence of a pattern. White Christians are also about 30 percentage points more likely to say monuments to Confederate soldiers are symbols of Southern pride rather than symbols of racism, and white Christians are about 20 percentage points more likely to disagree with this statement: "Generations of slavery and discrimination have created conditions that make it difficult for Blacks to work their way out of the lower class." In his book *White Too Long,* Robert P. Jones, the head of the Public Religion Research Institute, made the case that "the more racist attitudes a person holds, the more likely he or she is to identify as a white Christian." Jones goes on to say: "If you were recruiting for a white supremacist cause on a Sunday morning, you'd likely have more success hanging out in the parking lot of an average white Christian church—evangelical Protestant, mainline Protestant, or Catholic—than approaching whites sitting out services at the local coffee shop."

As a Black Christian, I too have experienced the sin of division within my own faith community. Not too long ago, in my parish, which is in a predominantly white suburban congregation, I had a conversation about worship music with one of my white sisters in Christ. When I commented that I preferred African spirituals to "Amazing Grace" (which was written by a white slaveholder), she responded that I didn't belong in her church. Apparently, there was no room in her mind for my perspective.

This is only one relatively small instance of the sense of "otherness" I often experience among my fellow Christians. I find myself on uneasy ground. Do I speak out against the sin of division? Or do I remain silent in order to not reinforce the perception that I am different from everyone else? If I take a stand, will I further distance myself, socially and emotionally, from my white brothers and sisters?

And yet I remain convinced that division is a sin. I believed we are called to pray against the division that murdered George Floyd, Breonna Taylor, and so many others. Even more, however, we are called to look into our own hearts. Are we willing to allow Christ to truly transform us, so that we no longer perceive others through the lens of division? Can we labor together with Christ for unity?

In this first week of meditations with Ignatius of Loyola, he invites us to examine the role sin has played in our own hearts and lives. But first, he gives us a vision of what ourselves and the entire world are meant to be, without the division of sin. This is called the "Principle and Foundation" of the Spiritual Exercises. It places every part of the Exercises within the context of love— God's love for us and ours for God and for all creation. In the modern-language version written by David Fleming, S.J.:

> The goal of our life is to live with God forever. God, who loves us, gave us life. Our own response of love allows God's life to flow into us without limit.
>
> All the things in this world are gifts of God, presented to us so that we can know God more easily and make a return of love more readily.

As a result, we appreciate and use all these gifts of God insofar as they help us develop as loving persons. But if any of these gifts become the center of our lives, they displace God and so hinder our growth toward our goal.

In everyday life, then, we must hold ourselves in balance before all of these created gifts insofar as we have a choice and are not bound by some obligation. We should not fix our desires on health or sickness, wealth or poverty, success or failure, a long life or a short one. For everything has the potential of calling forth in us a deeper response to our life in God.

Our only desire and our one choice should be this: I want and I choose what better leads to God's deepening his life in me.

As we choose to allow God's life to deepen within us, we are ever more deeply transformed. And as we change, so will our society.

There is no room for division in Christ's Body. Let us work to eradicate this terrible virus from our world, so that God's life will flow into us and out of us, unhindered and without limit.

Just as a body, though one, has many parts
but all its many parts form one body,
so it is with Christ.

—1 CORINTHIANS 12:12

DAY 1

Time Out

Finding a Space to
See from a New Perspective

Come with me by yourselves
to a quiet place.

—JESUS (MARK 6:31)

To withdraw from creatures
and repose with Jesus in the Tabernacle
is my delight; there I can hide myself and seek rest.
There I find a life which I cannot describe,
a joy which I cannot make others comprehend,
a peace such as is found only
under the hospitable roof of our best Friend.

—IGNATIUS OF LOYOLA

ORIENTATION, DIS-ORIENT
RE-ORIENT

> *If I truly want to be part of the solution,*
> *I need to explore those parts of me*
> *that are most unwholesome, embarrassing, unflattering.*
> *... My goal is to dismantle the insidious thoughts*
> *that reinforce a hierarchy based on race,*
> *education, and other markers of privilege*
> *that separate me from others.*
> *These thoughts, fed by implicit bias,*
> *are more common than I find easy to admit.*
> *Although I know not to believe everything I think,*
> *I also know that thoughts guide attention,*
> *and attention guides actions.*
> *Until I bring to light and hold myself accountable*
> *for my own racist tendencies, I am contributing to racism.*

—DEBORAH COHAN

Ignatius of Loyola was not one of those saints blessed with holiness from the time they are young children. Although he was a Catholic who observed the practices of his faith, his attention was often distracted from God. He dreamed of a life full of romance, adventure, and excitement.

Born in 1491, Ignatius grew up among family members who valued their commitment to king and country. His father was famous for his deeds of valor, and his older brother had sailed with Columbus across the Atlantic Ocean. Some of his other brothers had been in the military, and Ignatius longed to follow in their footsteps by proving himself in battle. While he was still a teenager, he became a soldier.

This period of Ignatius's life was filled with fighting, gambling, fancy clothes, and sexual adventures. With his attention so taken up by these activities, he had little time to think about God. The Divine Voice may have been speaking to him, but Ignatius's life was simply too noisy. He couldn't hear the still, small voice of God.

And then one day in 1521, Ignatius was forced to step back from his busy life. As he fought with an army of fellow Spaniards against the French, a cannonball struck his hip. It went straight through his leg, shattering the bone, and then down to his other knee. The army medics set the bones as best they could, and then they sent him home to Loyola to convalesce. The doctors there told him his injury had been badly treated; now, if he wanted to walk again, the bones would have to be rebroken and reset. In his autobiography, Ignatius described the procedure as "butchery."

When his legs finally mended, one leg was shorter than the other, and he had a lump of bone that stuck out below his knee. Even now, after so much pain, Ignatius's thoughts were still focused on his plans to return to his old life. Worried about how his deformed leg would look in the tight-fitting stockings and boots that were fashionable at the time, he told the doctors to saw off the bump of bone. Then he chained a cannonball to his short leg and spent hours every day letting it dangle from his leg, hoping the weight would stretch his leg back to its normal size. All this was done without any anesthesia.

During the long bed-ridden months, Ignatius grew bored, so he asked his family to bring him something to read. He was hoping for tales of brave knights who fought for the hands of beautiful ladies and had adventures in distant lands. Instead, the only two books in the house were a life of Christ and a collection of saints' stories. Still, these books must have seemed like a better option than lying on his bed staring at the ceiling. Ignatius began to read.

And then, during the quiet lonely hours as he turned the pages, Ignatius started to think new thoughts. He found a new perspective from which to view his life, and he became ashamed of his vanity, pride, and lust. The voice of God's Spirit was audible now, and he decided to commit himself to a pilgrim's life of spiritual adventures. He was no longer interested in worldly adventures that fed his pride. Now he saw with new eyes.

Hopefully, most of us will not need to experience the physical agony Ignatius of Loyola did—but we all need times when we retreat from life. These are periods of quiet when we clear out the noise and clutter of our daily lives and make a space for God to enter. For the last five centuries, the Spiritual Exercises have been used as a tool for intentionally doing this. They provide us with a guidebook for stepping back and looking at ourselves in new ways.

During this time when we choose to retreat from our ordinary lives, the "discernment of spirits" plays an important role. This is a term for something Ignatius experienced as he lay on his bed, convalescing from his injuries. In the quiet of his bedroom, he noticed different "movements" taking place within his thoughts as he imagined his future. With nothing else to occupy him, Ignatius paid close attention to what was happening in his interior being. He wrote in his autobiography that he began to notice distinct differences in his feelings.

He did not consider nor did he stop to examine this difference until one day his eyes were partially opened and he began to wonder at this difference and to reflect upon it. From experience he knew that some thoughts left him sad while others made him happy, and little by little he came to perceive the different spirits that were moving him; one coming from the devil, the other coming from God.

Ignatius came to believe that as we pay attention to the inner "motions of the soul," we gain a deeper understanding of the paths God wants us to take in our outer lives. These interior movements include thoughts, emotions, desires, repulsions, attractions, and imaginings. Spending time in quiet reflection helps us become more sensitive to our own hearts, so that we can hear God talking to us from deep within ourselves.

Ignatius referred to the contrary motions of our hearts as "good spirits" and "evil spirits." Discerning the difference between the two is a way to understand the voice of God speaking in our hearts. Today we might refer to these opposing forces as negative or destructive thoughts versus positive or life-giving thoughts.

Ignatius called the feelings that these thoughts aroused *consolation* and *desolation*. Spiritual consolation inspires us with Divine love so that we feel energized to serve God and reach out in love to those around us; we feel encouraged and empowered, connected both to God and to all creation. Spiritual desolation, on the other hand, brings a heavy feeling of confusion to our hearts; we feel anxious, cut off from God and others, preoccupied with doubts, temptations, and our own egos. In Ignatius's words, negative feelings like this "leave one without hope and without love."

Spiritual Tools — Spiritual Evil

However, spiritual consolation is not necessarily "good," nor is desolation necessarily "evil." Sometimes an experience of desolation can lead to a deeper intimacy with God and a new understanding of our role in building a better world. By the same token, feelings of peace and happiness can sometimes act as buffers, protecting us from the reality of the world's pain as we avoid answering the call of Divine justice. This is why we need to set aside time to reflect on our feelings and thoughts. In doing so, we will be able, with practice and God's help, to discern the direction in which the Spirit is tugging us.

The discernment of spirits is a useful tool when it comes to identifying the sin of racism in our hearts and lives. As Ibram X. Kendi noted in *How Not to Be a Racist,* "being an antiracist requires persistent self-awareness, constant self-criticism, and regular self-examination." He went on to say, "Being antiracist is an ongoing process of discernment and praxis, requiring honest reflection on who we are and who we want to be." Ignatius of Loyola's Spiritual Exercises give us tools to do just that.

As you read this book over the next month (or however long it takes you), you too, like Ignatius on his sickbed, are withdrawing from your normal busy life. You are choosing to quiet the noise, both outside you and inside you, so that you can listen to your own heart. You will also have the opportunity to hear God speaking to you through the voices of people of color. Some of what you hear may be painful; it may cause you to experience desolation. But this is an opportunity to let the Spirit of God enter more deeply into your inner being and outer life. Ultimately, the Divine presence always leads us to peace, wholeness, joy, and love.

This is a process that requires utter honesty. As Ignatius counseled, "We must speak to God as a friend speaks to his friend . . . , now asking some favor, now acknowledging our faults, and communicating to God all that concerns us, our thoughts, our fears, our projects, our desires, and in all things seeking God's counsel."

Are you ready to hear what God has to say to you?

Journal

Ibram X. Kendi said, "Racist ideas make people of color think less of themselves, which makes them more vulnerable to racist ideas. Racist ideas make White people think more of themselves, which further attracts them to racist ideas." As you think back over the past few days, ask the Spirit to open your eyes to any racist ideas that have entered your mind. Here are some possible examples:

- I feel nervous when I see a Black man because I suspect he may be a danger to me.

- I am particularly impressed by the intelligence of a person of color because I assume that whites are generally more intelligent than people of color.

- I minimize or disbelieve the experiences of people of color, insisting that their experiences must be similar to my own.

- I mistake a person of color for a service worker.

- I criticize an Asian person for being quiet or a Black person for being noisy, assuming that my own culture is the "normal" one to which others must conform.

In your journal, jot down each racist idea you recognize in yourself. Do these ideas make you think less of yourself? Or do they inflate your sense of your own importance and superiority? Note whether it brings you consolation or desolation. Does it make you feel closer to God or further from God?

This exercise cannot be done quickly, since many of us have become numbed and blinded to the racism all around us. You will need to spend time in prayer, consciously opening yourself to the Spirit's light. Remember, these racist ideas are everywhere, and none of us are immune to them; having them does not make you a "bad" person. The goal of this exercise is to help you begin to discern the "spirits" that are at work within you.

If after a half hour or so of prayer and reflection, you are still not able to identify any racist ideas that you've had, you may want to take the online Implicit Association Test (https://implicit.harvard.edu/implicit/selectatest.html) for race, which measures attitudes and beliefs you are unwilling or unable to recognize. After you have taken the test, note the results in your journal, and then try again to identify some of the racist ideas that influence you, even without you knowing.

For Further Reflection

If I believe that only bad people are racist,
I will feel hurt, offended, and shamed
when an unaware racist assumption of mine is pointed out.
If I instead believe that having racist assumptions
is inevitable (but possible to change),
I will feel gratitude when an unaware racist assumption
is pointed out; now I am aware of
and can change that assumption.

—ROBIN DIANGELO

Prayer
— Repent /
confess

Pardon me, O perfection of my God,
for having preferred imperfect and evil ideas to you! . . .
Pardon me, O holiness of my God,
for having so long stained your vision's purity with my sins.
Pardon me, O mercy of my God,
for having rejected for so long your mercy's voice.
In deep sorrow and contrition, I cast myself before you.
Have mercy on me.

—IGNATIUS OF LOYOLA

DAY 2

Our Broken World

Systemic Racism

Learn to do right; seek justice.
Defend the oppressed.

—ISAIAH 1:17

If it happens that your soul is attached
or inclined to a thing inordinately,
you should move yourself,
putting forth all your strength,
to fight back against
that which you are wrongly drawn to.

—IGNATIUS OF LOYOLA

If I am not aware of the barriers you face,
then I won't see them,
much less be motivated to remove them.
Nor will I be motivated to remove the barriers
if they provide an advantage to which I feel entitled.

—ROBIN DIANGELO

n the First Week of the Spiritual Exercises, Ignatius invites us to look at the history of sin. In doing this, he
implies that sin is not only a question of individual wrongdoing.
Instead, we are all born into a long and ancient story of spiritual brokenness, one that has molded the very structure of our
society. As we reflect on this reality, Ignatius then encourages us
to realize that we are a part of that history. It shapes our individual stories.

When Ignatius wrote *The Spiritual Exercises,* he included a
section that's known as the Two Standards Meditation. In this
meditation, Ignatius, always a believer in the spiritual power
of the imagination, asks us to envision a battlefield where the
forces of evil are opposing Christ's force for love. Each group
has a "standard"—a flag or banner—that allows their side to be
clearly recognized.

In the Two Standards Meditation, Ignatius teaches us that
evil is sometimes hard to recognize; we may not fully realize the
banner under which we've taken our stand. Privilege and pres-
tige, said Ignatius, can lead us away from the love of Christ. It
can lead us into sin.

This has a direct application to the sin of racism. We can't point out specifically the individuals to blame for the racism in our world, because it has become so pervasive throughout our society that it is everywhere. The effects of decisions made centuries ago are still persisting in our world today. And now, at the same time that people of color suffer because of this, white people benefit from it. The forces of evil are at work, just as Ignatius described, creating a world of perceived superiority versus perceived inferiority, of privilege versus discrimination.

The word for this division is *systemic racism*. It is as pervasive in our society as the air we breathe. For white people, it may be nearly invisible; it is something they just take for granted. For people of color, is the experience of our daily lives. It affects our education, our medical care, our professional opportunities, our housing, and our legal rights.

White people often push back against the idea that they are privileged. "I worked hard for everything I have," I've heard people insist. "Nothing was given to me. You don't know what challenges I had to overcome to reach where I am today." No one is denying that white people have faced hardships of their own; however, they have never had to live in an entire system that was weighted against them. Whether they realized it or not, the playing field has always been slanted in their favor. They start out ahead of people of color simply because of the lack of pigment in their skin.

The statistics back this up. For example, a 2015 study from the Department of Health and Human Services found that a baby is more than twice as likely to die during childbirth if the mother is Black—and a Black mother is three to four times more likely to die during childbirth than a white mother. A report

TRUTH -TELLING
— Re-pness

published by the Proceedings of the National Academy of Sciences in 2016 reported that almost 75 percent of the medical professionals who participated in the study believed that Blacks had higher pain tolerance than whites, with the result being that Black people were significantly less like to receive adequate pain management medication. In 2020, another study, this one published in the *Journal of General Internal Medicine,* found that Black people were more than three times as likely to die from COVID-19. The results from these three studies have nothing to do with Black people being genetically disposed to certain conditions or being somehow less healthy than whites. The individual medical professionals involved would likely deny that they were racist or that they practiced discrimination in their treatment of people of color. But what these studies demonstrate is the effects of systemic racism.

Other statistics tell the same story. According to the Bureau of Labor, unemployment among Blacks has consistently been 5 to 10 percent higher among Blacks than whites for the past fifteen years, and there are 10 percent fewer Blacks than whites in professional and management jobs, while there are nearly 20 percent fewer Latinos than whites. This in part can be explained by overtly racist hiring practices, but it's not as simple as that. A 2017 Harvard University study found that when Blacks and Asians "whitened" their professional resumes by using more "American" names (for example, Jason instead of Jamal or Amber instead of Aadya) and also obscured any information indicating their ethnic identification, they got significantly more callbacks for interviews. In addition, since many companies get employment referrals from their existing employees, this can also perpetuate white workforces. A survey given by the Public

Religion Research Institute found that three-quarters of white employees have *no* friends who are people of color.

And then there's income, where systemic racism places more limits on people of color. The 2018 US Census reported that the average Black or Latino worker made just over 60 percent of what the average white worker made, and this income gap has remained about the same since 1970. Twice as many Blacks and Latinos as whites are living at poverty levels, and 62 percent of Black children grow up in poor neighborhoods, compared to only 4 percent of white children. The Pew Research Center estimated that white households are worth about twenty times as much as Black households, and while only 15 percent of whites have zero or negative wealth, more than a third of Blacks do

Reports on educational differences reveal the same reality. Even though American schools were desegregated in 1954, about half of all students still attend either predominantly white or nonwhite schools, according to a 2019 report from the nonprofit group EdBuild—and for every student enrolled, the average nonwhite school district receives $2,226 less funding than a white school district. Black high-school students are almost half as likely as whites to be enrolled in advanced-placement courses. All this means that since nonwhite schools have fewer resources and educational opportunities, fewer students of color will have what they need to go on to college. (Which also contributes to the differences in employment and income between whites and people of color.)

The effects of systemic racism are seemingly endless. People of color are also more likely than whites to be denied mortgage loans, which in turn means they are also less likely to own their own homes. Blacks are more likely to be arrested than whites (even for the same or similar crimes), they are more likely to be denied bail, and they face harsher sentencing than whites. Black men are more than five times as likely to be imprisoned as white men. All these factors are aspects of systemic racism at work in our society.

Recently, while I was talking with a white friend, she mentioned that she enjoys driving and feels annoyed rather than nervous if a police officer stops her. "It must be nice," I responded. "I'm constantly afraid while I'm driving, constantly cautious. I don't want to get pulled over. I don't want to lose my life if an officer misinterprets something I say or do." This too is an effect of systemic racism. It's the reason why white children are raised to think of police officers as their friends, people to whom they can go if they're in trouble—while Black parents have "the talk" with their children, warning them to remain calm, watch their facial expressions, and speak respectfully if they encounter the police (because to do otherwise could prove fatal).

Systemic racism is also the reason why my voice often goes unheard in meetings of my peers, as though I am both invisible and inaudible. If you were to ask the people at that meeting if they are racist, each one would deny it; and yet there is a basic underlying assumption in the room that says my ideas and contributions are in some way inferior or less important than those of my white counterparts.

Systemic racism is so pervasive that it's become normalized; we take it for granted. It's just the way things are. One thing that makes it so difficult to tackle is that it not only gives people of color a disadvantage, but it also gives white people advantages they are reluctant to surrender. The loss of their privilege can be perceived as a threat, giving rise to accusations of "reverse prejudice." It's easier by far to blame racial inequalities on individuals' personal failures and shortcomings than to accept that no one did anything to deserve these inequalities; they are simply the natural consequences of centuries of unequal treatment.

The economy also reinforces systemic racism and makes it that much more difficult to fight. In the eighteenth and nineteenth centuries, many state and national economies could not have survived without slave labor; today slavery has been outlawed, and yet our industrial agricultural system depends on an underclass of near-slave labor, people of color from Mexico and Central America. Without this labor pool, our current food system would collapse. The system as it exists today requires that these workers lack the right to protections that most of us take for granted. This economic dependency on systemic racism is a powerful incentive to ignore it, to look away and pretend it's simply not practical to try to dismantle it.

And yet people continue to protest, "I'm not a racist." I know they mean they are not white supremacists. They wouldn't join the Ku Klux Klan or commit a hate crime; most of them wouldn't even tell a racist joke or use racial slurs. Nevertheless, they participate in an unjust social system.

Many of us have worked from the assumption that racism is something that happens between individuals. It's far harder to perceive the mammoth, overarching systems that grant more power to white people than people of color. Because these systems are so pervasive, almost too big for us to see, they also interact with individuals, causing them to demonstrate racism without their conscious awareness.

This means that our individual failures and the failures of our society as a whole are so interwoven that it will take painful effort to separate them. It will require Divine help. As Louis M. Savary writes in *The New Spiritual Exercises:*

> Because social sins and personal sins are tied together so inextricably, it is inadequate to say that in his crucifixion Christ died only for our personal sins. What is much more realistic is that Jesus of Nazareth very consciously died bearing the weight of the social sins of organized society, those very sins he openly struggled to confront during his ministry. We might call them, collectively, the sins of humanity. Of course, our personal sins are bound up in those social evils and have contributed to their continued existence.

Amy Cooper's behavior in Central Park is an example of this interaction between personal and social sins. In the summer of 2020, when a Black birdwatcher named Christian Cooper asked Amy Cooper (no relation) to put her dog on a leash, she called the police and claimed an African American man was threatening her life. Although Ms. Cooper prided herself on being a liberal, progressive, and tolerant person, her actions were based on an assumption she had absorbed from a structurally racist society—that a Black man is inherently dangerous simply because he is Black. At the same time, Ms. Cooper also assumed certain things about the criminal justice system—that because she was a white woman, the police would be on her side, not Mr. Cooper's. As Mikulich, Cassidy, and Pfeil point out in their book, *The Scandal of White Complicity,* "I may be consciously committed to all people being equal, and to universal principles of justice and fairness, but encountering a black man I may have feelings in my body of aversion, fear, avoidance and discomfort" that are difficult to acknowledge.

Systemic racism creates enormous blind spots, areas where clear vision can be almost totally obscured. Ignatius challenges us to look past the blur of systemic racism, so that we can perceive what is truly going on in our world. Systemic racism is a destructive force that negates our humanity. It is in direct opposition to the Divine force of love and justice.

In the Two Standards Meditation, Ignatius asks us first to focus on "Satan." (This is the word Ignatius uses for what he defines as the "enemy of our human nature.") Ignatius describes an evil strategy that traps human hearts with wealth, privilege, and pride. When we fall prey to this snare, we value material things over spiritual. The goal we work toward is success as our society defines it. We pride ourselves on our superiority and achievements. With our eyes blinded by these priorities, we are then in a position where we can be led far astray in other ways. We lose sight of the active love to which God calls us, a love that reaches out to all creation.

Then, Ignatius directs our vision toward Christ as he stands humbly in opposition to the forces of evil. Listen, Ignatius tells us, as Christ tells his followers to go out into the world and lead everyone to freedom. The flag Christ carries bears the symbols of humility, self-giving, and the liberty to be what God created us to be. Those people who align themselves with Christ's banner see everything around them as a gift from God. They realize that possessions have little importance compared to the love to which we are called. Refusing to identify with our society's standards of privilege and superiority, they are committed to a life of serving others with unconditional love.

Angela Davis once said: "In a racist society, it is not enough to be non-racist, we must be anti-racist." Author and activist Ibram X. Kendi has explained this concept further, pointing out that *everyone* is taught to believe they are not racist. "I am the least racist person there is anywhere in the world," stated one of our most racist leaders. The colonizers of America didn't believe they were racist, and even white supremacists today insist that they are "not racist." This means that proclaiming yourself to be "not racist" isn't enough. It allows you to sit back and passively support systems and policies that promote racial inequality. As an antiracist, however, you actively engage in the fight against racism. There is no middle ground, says Kendi, no place where you can take a neutral stance.

Where will you take your stand? Under the banner of injustice and inequality—or under Christ's banner of love?

Journal

From the following list, pick at least three or four statements that are true for you. Then journal your thoughts and feelings in response to each statement. How does each statement relate to systemic racism? Imagine you are having a conversation with Ignatius of Loyola about these statements. What do you think he would have to say? How might he help you to determine if you are truly living your life under Christ's banner? Write your imaginary conversation into your journal.

- I live on land that formerly belonged to Native Americans.

- I went to a school district where the textbooks and other classroom materials reflected my race as normal, heroes and builders of the United States, and there was little mention of the contributions of people of color to our society.

- I have received a job, job interview, job training or internship through personal connections of family or friends.

- I work in a job where people of color made less for doing comparable work or did more menial jobs.

- I live in a neighborhood that has better police protection and municipal services than that where people of color live.

- I see people who look like me in a wide variety of roles on television and in movies.

- The house, office building, school, or other buildings and grounds I use are cleaned or maintained by people of color.

- I don't need to think about race and racism every day. I can choose when and where I want to respond to racism.

For Further Reflection

When white terrorists bomb a black church
and kill five black children,
that is an act of individual racism,
widely deplored by most segments of the society.
But when in that same city ...
five hundred black babies die each year
because of the lack of proper food,
shelter and medical facilities,
and thousands more are destroyed
and maimed physically, emotionally and intellectually
because of conditions of poverty and discrimination
in the black community,
that is a function of institutional racism.

—STOKELY CARMICHAEL

Prayer

Confession

Have mercy on me, O Lord.
I have blinded my eyes.
In spite of the clear evidence
of deeply embedded racism all around me,
I have looked the other way.
Too many have died. Too many have suffered. . . .
Too many injustices. And still I looked the other way.
Have mercy on me, O Lord.
I have hardened my heart. . . .
I have cared too little. I have grieved too little.
Have mercy on me, O Lord.
I have silenced my tongue.
My voice has not been raised in prophetic rebuke and anger.
My feet have not stepped out for justice
alongside those who have more courage than I.
And in my silence I am an accomplice to bigotry.
Forgive me, O Lord.
I have sinned against you
and against those who suffer the evil of racism. . . .
Empower me, O Lord.
I need your strength to step beyond blindness,
indifference and fear; to step toward those
whom I have sinned against.

—MARK YOUNG

DAY 3

The Divine Image

Seeing God in All Humanity

*God shaped human beings
in God's own image,*

—GENESIS 1:27

*We ought to consider not only God,
but also others for God's sake.*

—IGNATIUS OF LOYOLA

*There is no dichotomy between [humans] and God's image.
Whoever tortures a human being,
whoever abuses a human being,*

.

whoever outrages a human being,
abuses God's image.

—OSCAR ROMERO

[handwritten: Historical Analysis]

A lthough 1521 is celebrated as the year of Ignatius's conversion, his spiritual transformation took time. He did not instantly rise to a condition of sainthood. In fact, his military fervor and quick temper lingered with him. This is obvious in a story he tells about himself in his autobiography.

A year after his conversion, Ignatius was riding a mule to the shrine at Monserrat when he encountered a Moor—a man with black skin, who may have been a Muslim. As the two men rode along together, they fell into a conversation about the Virgin Mary. The Moor remarked that although he believed Mary was a virgin when she conceived Jesus, he found it hard to swallow that she remained a virgin for the rest of her life. Ignatius insisted that she did, and when the Moor refused to change his opinion, Ignatius became increasingly indignant.

After the two men parted, Ignatius rode on, still thinking about their conversation. As he did so, he became more and more outraged. He worked himself up into such a fury that he began to fantasize about turning around, chasing down the Moor, and killing him. Perhaps, he reasoned, that was what he should have done in the first place. He should have had the courage to defend the Virgin's honor.

He had just enough sense left to realize that murder might not be a good idea. Still, his violent fantasy would not leave his mind. Finally, he decided to leave the decision up to his mule. When he reached a fork in the road, one road leading into town and the other going into the hills, he dropped the reins and let the mule go whichever way it wanted. If the mule took the road toward town, Ignatius made up his mind to seek out the Moor and stab him—but if the mule took the road into the hills, Ignatius would let the Moor live.

The mule took the road into the hills. The Moor was spared, and Ignatius did not become a murderer.

When Ignatius included this story in his autobiography, he understood what the reader would see: a man still ruled by both his sense of honor and his hot temper, a man who was ready to take another's life because of a religious disagreement. This earlier version of Ignatius certainly did not see the image of God in the Moor. Instead, he perceived this Black man's beliefs and culture to be so "other" as to make him unworthy of life. If not for the mule, the Moor might have been wiped off the face of the earth, all in the name of religion.

Ignatius had enough humility to use himself as an object lesson about spiritual blindness. He stated that his goal in telling the stories included in his autobiography was "in order that it may be seen how God was dealing with his soul, still blind, though greatly desirous of serving Him in every way it knew how." Later, after his stay in Montserrat, Ignatius went on to Manresa, where he spent several months; during this time, as sat beside the river outside town, "the eyes of his understanding began to be opened; not that he saw any vision, but he understood and learned many things . . . with so great an enlightenment that everything seemed new to him."

The decision to follow Christ does not automatically make us able to see with the eyes of Christ. We too need the eyes of our understanding opened so that we are able to see God more clearly. As we gain greater clarity, we will begin to look into the eyes of other humans, and we will see God looking back at us. We will be enlightened by the Image of God shining out of every human being we encounter.

And yet this form of spiritual blindness persists in our world. Recently, a political commentator and former Senator made this public statement about America: "We birthed a nation from nothing; I mean, there was nothing here." Praising the pioneer spirit of white folks, he looked straight through the people who were already in the Americas when white settlers arrived. These spiritually rich cultures weren't merely unworthy in Mr. Santorum's eyes; they were invisible. They didn't even exist. He looked at the population of some 7 to 18 million indigenous people who lived in North America before whites settled the continent—and he saw absolutely nothing. In fact, he saw with the same blindness that most whites had centuries ago when they encountered North America's native people, a blindness that allowed millions of human beings to be wiped off the face of the earth.

Few of us would admit to wanting to murder another human being. And yet we allow a societal system to exist that literally kills people of color, through lack of good medical care, unequal legal rights, and the effects of poverty. This is a curse on people of color that lives side by side with white Christianity. As James wrote in his epistle, "With the tongue we praise our Lord and Father, and with it we curse human beings, who have been made in God's likeness" (3:9).

In the Gospel of Matthew, Jesus says that to even speak disrespectfully of another human being is a form of murder (5:21–22). How much more serious then it must be, in Jesus' eyes, to treat an entire group of human beings as though they are unworthy of respect and care. The Hebrew scriptures affirm that God "shows no partiality" and Divine love is extended to the "stranger" (Deuteronomy 10:17,18). All humans carry the Image of God; we are all equally worthy of respect, love, and protection. As Archbishop Desmond Tutu affirmed,

> Each person is not just to be respected but to be revered as one created in God's image. To treat a child of God as if he or she was less than this is not just wrong, which it is; it is not just evil, as it often is; not just painful, as it often must be for the victim; it is veritably blasphemous, for it is to spit in the face of God.

We have been spitting in God's face for a long time. Slavery was just the beginning. The racism that undergirded slavery did not end with Abolition.

In 1906, for example, Ota Benga, a man from the Congo, was put on display at the Bronx Zoo. People could walk by and stare at him, just as they did at the giraffes and elephants. The exhibit was meant to confirm that people of African descent were nothing more than a form of primates, the "missing link" between humans and apes.

Soon after this, American eugenicists began using false biological distinctions between human beings to justify federally funded coerced sterilization that sought to limit "undesirable" populations. While some states' eugenics programs were driven

ECUMENICAL

by anti-Asian and anti-Mexican prejudice, Southern states used sterilization in an attempt to reduce Black populations. Unnecessary hysterectomies performed by medical students on Southern women of color were called "Mississippi appendectomies." A third of the sterilizations were done on girls younger than eighteen; in at least one case, the girl was only nine years old. And lest you think this is long-ago practice with no relevance today, consider that the forced sterilization of Native American women persisted into the 1970s and '80s, with young women receiving tubal ligations at the same time they were undergoing other surgeries. And as recently as 2020, women of color in prison were still being forced to undergo sterilizations.

The reasoning behind this? The fewer babies born to people of color, the "safer" America will be. Instead of seeing God in the eyes of all humans, whites looked at people of color and saw danger. They saw something undesirable, something unworthy of existing. Something they would rather not see at all. Frantz Fanon wrote about how this affects people of color: "A feeling of inferiority? No, a feeling of nonexistence."

The spirituality of Ignatius of Loyola invites us to see the sin of racism as what it is—the murder of the Image of God in our fellow humans. It asks that we look at no human being as less than ourselves but rather that we see the full reality of one another, as sisters and brothers, all sharing in the Divine DNA. If when we look at another human being, we see danger, inferiority, or nothing at all, we are denying God.

Right now, you may be protesting, *But I never engaged in forced sterilizations. I don't believe in eugenics.* But I ask you: Have you ever seen a person of color in a hotel and assumed they were a housemaid? Or taken for granted that a person of color wandering through a garden must be a groundskeeper? If so, you may not have meant any harm by these assumptions—but you failed to see the Divine Image when you looked at these individuals. Instead, you saw someone you assumed must be a worker, not a peer or an equal.

I have had this supposition made about me. When I was in the first stage of my formation as a Jesuit—what we call the novitiate—we sometimes invited friends and benefactors to come and share a meal with us. Since I love to cook, I enjoyed the opportunity to show off my skills, but on one particular occasion, I was running late. People were already eating the first course, while I was still scurrying to produce more food to feed our hungry guests. As I was working, one of our guests came into the kitchen. "Which restaurant do you work at?" she asked me.

I smiled and shook my head. "No, ma'am, I'm a novice here."

She could not believe me. "I have been coming here for years," she said, "and I've never seen a Black novice. So please—be honest. Tell me what restaurant you work at. Your food is delicious, and I'd love to go to the restaurant."

I shut my eyes for an instant, then took a deep breath. "I am a second-year novice here," I said.

"Fine," she said. "I know you're lying to me. Thank you anyway for your hard work. Your food is delicious."

Did this woman think she was being racist? I'm sure she didn't. She merely looked at a Black man and assumed he had to be a kitchen worker rather than a Jesuit in training. In her mind, people of color are workers, there to serve "normal" people (white people). She thought she was being gracious by complimenting my food.

CULTURAL AESTHETICS
SOCIETAL "Norms"

↑ DOESN'T SHY AWAY
from THE 'DEVIL ↓

After this experience, I found myself less eager to cook. When I saw this woman in the future, I avoided her. I also avoided the kitchen. I felt diminished in some way. I knew that when the woman looked at me, she saw someone different from herself. She did not recognize the Image of God in me.

The first chapter of Genesis tells us that human beings were created in God's image, and God declared that we are good. Unfortunately, the temptation in the Garden of Eden is still alive today—the temptation to refuse to accept our human goodness, its reflection of the Divine. When we fail to perceive the inherent dignity of each person, we are listening to the lies of the Deceiver, the evil force Ignatius referred to as the "enemy of our human nature."

In the Gospel of Matthew, Jesus told his disciples a story about an imaginary scene in the afterlife. In the story, he says to a group of people who come before him, "I was hungry and you gave me nothing to eat. I was thirsty and you gave me nothing to drink, I was a stranger and you did not invite me in, I needed clothes and you did not clothe me, I was sick and in prison and you did not look after me."

The people gathered in front of Jesus answer, "Lord, when did we see you hungry or thirsty or a stranger or needing clothes or sick or in prison, and did not help you?"

Jesus replies, "Truly I tell you, whatever you did not do for one of the least of these, you did not do for me."

Theologian and author Kelly Brown Douglas suggested that the question asked of Jesus today might be, "Lord, when did we see you dying and on the cross?" And Jesus would answer, "On a Florida sidewalk, at a Florida gas station, on a Michigan porch, on a street in North Carolina. As you did it to one of these young black bodies, you did it to me."

When we fail to see God in one another, we not only fail to reach out to each other in love; we can also excuse cruelty, even death. In doing so, we are also rejecting Jesus. We are crucifying him all over again. As Mother Teresa said, "I see Jesus in every human being. I say to myself, this is hungry Jesus, I must feed him. This is sick Jesus. . . . I must wash him and tend to him." Can we look at people of color and say, "This is Jesus, I must protect him. This is Jesus, I must stand up for his freedom"?

Jesuit author James Martin wrote, "Instead of seeing the spiritual life as one that can exist only if it is enclosed by the walls of a monastery, Ignatius asks you to see the world as your monastery." This means that we encounter holiness everywhere we turn, including in the faces of people of color. The Divine Spirit cries out to us from their bodies and in their experiences.

I am reminded of a story told by another Jesuit author, Anthony DeMello. (Pretty much the same story is told near the end of the Disney Pixar movie, *Soul.*) It goes like this: A small fish swims up to a whale. "Excuse me," he says, "can you tell me where to find this thing called the ocean?"

The whale answers, "It's right here. It's where you are right now."

"This?" asks the little fish. "This is only water. I want the ocean." And he swims away disappointed.

Many of us are spiritual seekers, searching for connection with the Divine. And all the while, God is right in front of us, all around us—present in the faces of our fellow human beings.

If you were to look into my face, would you see the Image of God in my eyes?

Journal

Have you ever noticed that white people often describe people of color by their pigmentation, rather than by any other characteristic? Sociologist Michael Emerson, who has written many books on racism, sometimes gives his students this assignment: For the next twenty-four hours, any time you refer to someone who is white, preface it with the word *white*. So if you are telling someone about your minister, say "my white minister." If you are talking about your friend, say "my white friend." If you are talking about your neighbors, refer to them as "my white neighbors."

As an experiment, try this out for yourself. After the twenty-four hours are over, write about the experience in your journal. Was it difficult to do? How did it make you feel? Did doing this make you more sensitive to the times when you speak of another person as "Black" or by some other "racial characterization"?

Do you think labeling people of color by their pigmentation has anything to do with seeing the Image of God in them? Why or why not?

For Further Reflection

When will we learn
that human beings are of infinite value
because they have been created in
the image of God,
and that it is a blasphemy to treat them
as if they were less than this.

—DESMOND TUTU

Prayer

Help me see, Divine One.
Remove the scales from my eyes.
Show me your light shining forth
from each human being I encounter.
May I look for your presence
in those the world ignores and mistreats.
Teach me to affirm you where you are present,
in each human life.
I have been blind too long.

DAY 4

Our Disordered Hearts

Racism as a Barrier to God's Love

For your selfish human nature
wants what is contrary to the Spirit,
and the Spirit wants what is contrary to your selfish nature.
They are in conflict with each other,
keeping you from carrying out your good intentions.

—GALATIANS 5:17 (AUTHOR'S TRANSLATION)

The evils of vanity and vainglory
arise from ignorance and blind self-love.

—IGNATIUS OF LOYOLA

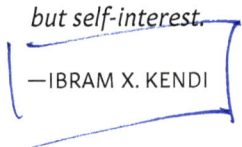

My research kept pointing me to the same answer:
The source of racist ideas was not ignorance and hate,
but self-interest.

—IBRAM X. KENDI

When religious historians tell the story of Ignatius of Loyola before his conversion, they usually emphasize his vanity, his devotion to romance and adventure, and his military ambition. They often leave out the fact that Ignatius's life was not going all that well for him before his conversion. He was not the happy-go-lucky womanizer he is often pictured. The cannonball that injured him so badly in 1521 did not shatter an otherwise successful life; instead, it was a final blow to a young man who had already endured much heartache.

Ignatius's mother had died when he was only seven; his father died when he was sixteen. One of his older brothers lost his life in battle, while another one went to sea and never returned home. He grew up in a family that observed religious traditions but failed to enforce moral boundary lines. His father was a womanizer who had had several illegitimate children, and his grandfather's behavior was so reckless and immoral that two floors of the family castle were demolished as a punishment from the Crown.

Ignatius grew up both spoiled and lonely. He brawled, getting into serious trouble, but was able to use his privileged position to escape any consequences. His father, before his death, had sent Ignatius to live in the household of one of King Ferdinand's provincial governors, and there Ignatius remained for many years. Like most young men of his class, he had little education beyond learning how to be a good soldier, an accomplished horseman, and a gallant courtier. By the time of his injury at the battle at Pamplona, his foster father had fallen from favor with the king. Ignatius was left with only his own vanity to serve as an anchor in life. His injury in battle took even that from him, leaving him broken in body with his soul adrift.

After his conversion, however, Ignatius's priorities began to change. He perceived that his own emotions had been "disordered"—in other words, out of balance, unhealthy, pulling him away from his true God-given identity. As soon as he was healed enough to walk, he set off for Jerusalem, seeking the physical geography of Christ even as his heart was searching for a spiritual path. When his travels led him to someone in need, Ignatius gave the man his fancy clothes. Then, in an all-night vigil before the Black Madonna in a church in Montserrat, Ignatius hung up his sword and dagger. With these actions, he demonstrated that he was separating himself from his old priorities. He was allowing his desires and goals to be rearranged—reordered by Christ.

At the beginning of *The Spiritual Exercises,* Ignatius wrote an ancient prayer called the Anima Christi. The prayer includes these words: "Permit me not to be separated from you." Ignatius had learned that vanity and self-serving passions had come between him and Christ. They had also come between him and his fellow humans. "Disordered affections" separate us from one another as much as they separate us from the Divine.

Racism is a form of disordered affection, an imbalance in our priorities that puts us out of sync with the Divine Spirit at work in our world. Theologian M. Shawn Copeland wrote, "Racism spoils the spirit and insults the holy; it is idolatry." In other words, it not only makes divisions between human beings, but it also has the power to separate us from God.

Most of us are probably familiar with the first of the Ten Commandments: "Thou shalt have no other god before me." The sin of worshipping another god—otherwise known as idolatry—is a Commandment we often skim over. After all, most of us probably don't prostrate ourselves before a statue or say prayers to Zeus. Rabbi Abraham Joshua Heschel, however, defines an idol as "any god who is mine but not yours, any god concerned with me but not you." When we allow racism to exist within our Christianity, our god is no longer the living, loving Force who sustains the universe. We may think we are devoted to the same God who Jesus called Father, but instead, we are worshipping something lifeless and loveless, an empty god—an idol.

"Racism is a faith," wrote theologian George D. Kelsey, ". . . a form of idolatry. It is an abortive search for meaning." Kelsey went on to explain that the concept of a "superior race" arose out of the need to justify human selfishness in the form of political and economic power. White people needed to find an excuse for their oppression and exploitation of people of color, and so they came up with a belief system about the very order of being itself, an idea that was totally contrary to the actual tenets of both the Hebrew and Christian scriptures. "The god of racism," said Kelsey, is the white race itself, which has set itself up to be "the ultimate center of value," possessing an inherent right to power that reduces the lives of people of color.

The god of racism now permeates our political, social, medical, and educational institutions. Theologian Bryan Massingale challenges us to see this force at work even within our churches, where "idolatry lies in the pervasive belief that European aesthetics, music, theology, and persons—only these are standard, normative, universal. . . . That only these can mediate the divine and carry the holy." He concludes that "idolatry is divinizing what is not God."

Racism makes us see white as "normal." It equates whiteness with being human, the standard against which all people are measured. Author Richard Dyer noted that racism enables white people to "construct the world in their own image . . . set[ting] standards for humanity by which they are bound to succeed and others bound to fail." Centralizing whiteness in this way, said Dyer, is an act of idolatry that worships the created instead of the Creator.

"Keep away from anything that separates you from God, anything that might take God's place in your hearts," cautioned the author of First John (5:21). He was underlining the fact that although an "idol" is something external, the force that gives an idol its power lies within us. Although racism is very real at the systemic level, it is also the external embodiment of our own disordered hearts.

We may think we are immune to racism's demands, but it nevertheless enforces a reality where some people are worth less than others, a system that perpetuates inequality and suffering. And at the same time, it separates us from connection with the true God, the God of Love and Life. The work of antiracism requires that we work at both levels: fighting the external social forces while at the same time we rearrange our own internal priorities.

Racism is a state of the heart as well as a systemic problem. Its roots lie in the separation of our inner selves from Divine love. As we discussed in the reading for Day 3, we forget that we bear the image and likeness of God, and as a result, we become blind to our own Divine life and to the Divine Image present in others. As we begin to see with the Light of Christ, we also begin to perceive what needs to be reordered within our lives. Sooner or later, we find ourselves at the point Ignatius did after his injury, a place of vision and enlightenment where we are challenged to rearrange our inner desires.

This is the purpose of the Spiritual Exercise. As Ignatius said, these exercises are the "means of preparing and disposing your soul to rid itself of all its disordered affections, and then, after their removal, of seeking and finding God's will in the ordering of your life." After Ignatius's conversion, during his long period of prayer in Manresa, he came to understand his spiritual journey as a process of reorientation. He was called to intentionally turn away from his disordered passions—his self-centeredness and his illusions of grandeur—to a new place of humility, a place of openness to God.

Ignatius referred to this place as a state of indifference. By this he didn't mean apathy or lack of interest but rather a detachment from all his fears, false assumptions, and selfish desires. In this unencumbered state, he was free to receive God's call to a new life of healthy interaction with others, a life of service and love.

For those of us living in the twenty-first-century world, the work of antiracism is an essential part of our call to detachment from ourselves. It asks us to remove the idol of racism from our lives so that we can connect more intimately with both God and others.

How will you answer this call? Only you can say.

Journal

One of the spiritual tools Ignatius recommended is referred to as a *colloquy*. He defined it like this: "Colloquy is made, properly speaking, as one friend speaks to another . . . now asking some grace, now blaming oneself for some misdeed, now communicating one's affairs, and asking advice in them." A colloquy has no structured form; it is a form of prayer that is simply an intimate conversation with God. It is an opportunity to allow the Spirit to be expressed through you.

Like Carl Jung, the twentieth-century psychoanalyst, Ignatius was a great believer in the power of the imagination as a spiritual tool. For your journaling exercise today, use a Jungian technique called *active imagination* to engage in a colloquy with Jesus. First, ask the Spirit to guide this practice. Then, without effort or extra thought, allow yourself to write down both sides of a conversation between yourself and Jesus. Allow your pen to flow across the paper without stopping to edit or criticize your words. Focus on one or two of the following questions as you write this conversation:

- Is there any way in which racism interferes with my ability to follow Jesus' command to love God and love others as myself? Is racism coming between me and God?

- Can I honestly consider myself to be antiracist? Or am I holding on to an identity of "not racist"?

- Where does my own selfishness intersect with racism?

- Have I ever stood by and said nothing while I witnessed a person of color suffer the consequences of some form of racism?

For Further Reflection

To respond with love to a world
which seems to have gone wrong
in fundamental ways, a broken world,
we must get free to love—we need to find
a way to love better and over the long haul.

—DEAN BRACKLEY, S.J.

Prayer

I recognize, Holy One,
that racism exists not only in social structures
but also in my own individual thoughts,
attitudes, actions, and inactions.
I ask your forgiveness.
Give me eyes to see into my own heart.
Show me where my priorities need to be reordered.
Dethrone the idol of racism from my soul,
so that I may contribute to the work of antiracism.
Let nothing come between my heart and yours.

DAY 5

Repentance

Detaching from White Privilege

Repent, then, and turn to God,
so that your sins may be wiped out,
that times of refreshing may come from the Lord.

—ACTS 3:19

Penitence should include contrition of heart,
confession of the lips, and satisfaction in act.

—IGNATIUS OF LOYOLA

God calls us all to a future where the first are last
and the last are first (Matthew 20:16).
Such a future does not reflect
a reversal of privilege and penalty.

Rather, it is a time when there is no first or last
because everyone is treated and respected
as the equal child of God that they are.
It is left for faith communities to "repair the breach"
between the present injustice and God's just future.

—KELLY DOUGLAS BROWN

"**R**epent for the Reign of Heaven is near." These were the words John the Baptist spoke as he prepared the way for the transforming message of his cousin Jesus (Matthew 3:2). But what did John mean? And what did repentance have to do with the Reign of God? How are the two connected? These are questions that Ignatius also struggled with.

When we think about the meaning of the word *repent,* we often limit our understanding. We imagine that it's merely an emotional response of sorrow for our sins. Dictionary.com reinforces the focus on our emotions, giving this definition as the primary meaning of *repent*: "to feel sorry, self-reproachful, or contrite for past conduct; to regret or be conscience-stricken about a past action." Definitions like this imply that when we find our priorities disordered and our lives off target, it's enough to simply feel bad about it. But is that what John the Baptist was saying? Or was he calling us to take action in a way that was consistent with the overarching structure of the Reign of Heaven? And if so, how do we do that?

After Ignatius's conversion, he was genuinely sorry for the selfishness and emptiness of his previous life. He wanted to express his contrition in action—but he was not quite sure how to go about doing that. Eager to do something, though, he began a program of strict, even tortuous self-denial. He went days without food; he walked barefoot on the coldest winter days; and he wore a shirt made of animal hair against his skin. Sometimes, he also wore a nail-studded belt with the points turned inward. He allowed his long hair, of which he had once been so vain, to become matted and filthy.

All this self-deprivation gave him a gaunt and haggard appearance that frightened anyone he encountered—but did it do anyone any good? And it still did not seem to Ignatius to be enough to truly express his repentance. He tried to confess each and every one of his sins, but he found he had committed so many he could not count them all. A priest suggested he make a written list, which he began to work on.

Then, however, during his months of retreat at Manresa, as he took notes on his spiritual journey, he came to a new understanding of repentance. His Spiritual Exercises arose out of this time of reflection. Although Ignatius, like many spiritual people in the Middle Ages, continued to see the value of physical self-denial (in the form of fasting, for example), for the most part, the Spiritual Exercises point to a more practical course of action, one that focuses on both the inner and outer work of repentance. Ignatius wrote in the First Week of the Exercises:

> Penance is that virtue by which we destroy sin in ourselves and make reparation to God for our offences. In sin there is an interior and an exterior element, a turning away from God and a turning to creatures. Hence, satisfaction should reach both elements, and should consequently be both interior and exterior.

The Greek word that most versions of the Gospels translate as "repent" is *metanoia,* which means "to change our thinking and our purpose." The *Oxford Dictionary* says that metanoia is a change in the way we live our lives, brought about by spiritual transformation. In other words, it has to do with both our interior and exterior lives, just as Ignatius realized. This inner and outer change is a necessary step for ushering in what John and Jesus referred to as the Reign of Heaven—a way of being and interacting where oppression and injustice have been replaced with respect and equality, and where those who have been marginalized and ignored are heard, seen, and honored.

In Austin Channing Brown's book, *I'm Still Here: Black Dignity in a World Made for Whiteness,* she wrote, "The ideology that whiteness is supreme . . . permeates the air we breathe—in our schools, in our offices, and in our country's common life. White supremacy is a tradition that must be named and a religion that must be renounced." In other words, white supremacy—the system that privileges white people and oppresses people of color—demands repentance. We must reject it from within ourselves, just as we work to destroy it in the external world. Jesus challenged us to "produce fruit in keeping with repentance" (Matthew 3:8). Along the same lines, Ignatius wrote, "Since, therefore, exterior penance is the fruit of that which is interior, we may well doubt the worth of our interior penance, if it has not strength enough to put forth this exterior fruit." True repentance means we not only change our hearts and minds; we also change the way we live our lives. If we seek to build the Reign of God here on earth, we will make the world a safer place for people of color.

Meanwhile, acts of violent racism seem to be constantly in the news. Often, my heart feels as though it cannot contain the pain. During just two months of 2021, March and April, six Asian women were killed in a shooting rampage; police killed Adam Toledo, a thirteen-year-old Latino boy; and Daunte Wright, a twenty-year-old Black motorist was shot during a traffic stop. Meanwhile, the trial of George Floyd's killer, Derek Chauvin, was going on, keeping that horrendous event at the center of my consciousness. I remembered Breonna Taylor, a Black woman who was shot eight times when police officers invaded her home in 2020. I called to mind Stephon Clark, an unarmed Black man who died in 2018 after being shot at least seven times in his grandmother's backyard in Sacramento. I mourned the memory of Philando Castile, a Black man who was killed by police in 2016 while reaching for his driver's license. I wept as I recalled the seemingly endless list of names: Walter Scott, a Black man shot in the back five times by a police officer in 2015, after Scott had been pulled over in South Carolina for having a broken light on his car; Tamir Rice, a twelve-year-old Black boy killed by Cleveland police in 2014 for brandishing a toy gun; Eric Garner, who died the same year while police held him in a chokehold. I was sickened when I read a 2019 study published by the Proceedings of the National Academy of Sciences that gave these disturbing statistics: Black men are about 2.5 times more likely to be killed by police over the course of their lives than are white men. Black women, indigenous men and women, and Latinx are also significantly more likely to be killed by police. Some of the past decade's mass shootings targeted people of color: after a man fatally shot twenty-two people at a Walmart store in El Paso in 2019, he called his act "a response to the Hispanic invasion of Texas"; in 2015, a white supremacist killed nine Black people in a church in Charleston, South Carolina.

I know not only people of color mourn when they read these stories; whites do also. But injustice is not confined to these isolated and blatantly racist incidents. The disturbing headlines we read in the news are the fruit of our collective way of being together, a way of life that is shaped by the all-pervading miasma of racism. We may not have committed conscious or deliberate acts of racial hatred, but we cannot declare our innocence if we are complicit with the overarching fog of injustice that permeates our world.

Social scientists who study racist behaviors have come to realize that many people who perpetuate racial inequities do so unintentionally. Though they may have worked hard to evict conscious racial stereotypes from their minds, their thinking has nevertheless been warped by the racist ideology so omnipresent in our society. And sometimes—especially when people make decisions at speed, as police officers often do—that unconscious racism overrules conscious convictions.

Philosopher Barbara Applebaum wrote in her book, *Being White, Being Good*, "White people can reproduce and maintain racist practices, even when, *and especially when*, they believe themselves to be morally good." Ignatius recognized a similar truth: "How greatly mistaken are those who, while thinking themselves to be full of the spirit, are eager for the government of souls!" Sometimes white folks pat themselves on the back for how liberal and progressive they are, unaware that at the same time they benefit from a societal hierarchy that subordinates people of color.

Sociologist Peggy McIntosh used the term "invisible knapsack" to describe the privilege white people bring with them wherever they go. She spent months delving into both her interior and exterior life before she came up with an inventory of privileges she carried with her simply because of her white skin. The items in her knapsack were advantages most white people take for granted, things like:

- Wearing a hooded sweatshirt without worrying you'll be perceived as threatening.

- Moving into a new neighborhood without being concerned your neighbors won't accept you because of the color of your skin.

- Not worrying if you go to the Emergency Room that the color of your skin will cause you to receive inadequate treatment.

- Being able to protect your children most of the time from people who don't like them.

As Francis E. Kendall explained in *Understanding White Privilege,* for whites, "Purely on the basis of our skin color, doors are open to us that are not open to other people."

In the Spiritual Exercises, Ignatius challenges us to confront our hidden attachments, to become aware of the unconscious motivations that drive us. His concept of the spiritual journey was that it leads to ever-greater freedom from the "disordered affections" we discussed in Day 4. These attachments, said Ignatius, hinder us from being able to judge our lives accurately, and they get in the way of a life lived in harmony with God and others.

Ignatius understood that we need "discernment"—the ability to see clearly so that we can make Spirit-led decisions that shape the way we live our lives. These decisions take place every day, in countless large and small ways, determining how we make use of the physical world, the people we connect with, the values we hold, the projects we take on, and the attitudes that shape our choices.

The English word *discernment* comes from a Latin word that meant "to sift, to separate." Ignatius used the word to talk about the insight needed to separate life-giving desires and actions from those that contribute to a world out of harmony with God's plan. Discernment is ongoing, a daily practice that invites us to examine ourselves and our motivations ever more deeply. As we focus on racism, discernment is the first step toward repentance—toward changing the way we think and live.

The next step, according to Ignatius, is "indifference," the detachment from our rights and privileges that creates a new freedom. As we recognize that all of life is a gift—not something to be taken for granted, not something that is owed to us—we replace our attachment to our privilege with a sense of gratitude.

In the First Week of the Spiritual Exercises, Ignatius included what's known as the "Meditation on Three Classes of People." He used this meditation to help people on spiritual journeys identify where they stood in terms of their "attachments." We can also apply the meditation to the work of antiracism.

The First Class, Ignatius said, want to free themselves from their unhealthy attachments, but they put off doing anything about it. Finally, they die, never having addressed their own selfishness. If we apply this to the struggle against racism, these would be the people who sincerely believe racism is evil—but they never do the hard work of examining their own lives to see how their attachment to privilege is contributing to an unjust world. They allow themselves to remain in comfortable ignorance. "A fault that might easily be overcome at its first appearance," wrote Ignatius, "becomes unconquerable through passing of time and habitual giving way."

The Second Class of people, according to Ignatius, also want to be free of selfish attachments, but they convince themselves they can spiritually rid themselves of selfishness while still keeping everything they want. These would be the people who condemn racism and want to think of themselves as antiracist—but enjoy their own privileges too much to actually give them up. "Let's be practical," they say to themselves. "It's not possible to change the way things are." But, as Ibram Kendi said, "Critiquing racism is not activism. Changing minds is not activism. An activist produces power and policy change, not mental change." Kendi is talking about what Ignatius referred to as the "fruits" of repentance. Ignatius had this to say to people who have convinced themselves they are antiracist, despite their lack of action: "Self-love does a great deal; frequently it deludes our mind's eye so as to make us think things impossible that, if we saw them clearly, would evidently appear easy and even necessary." Ignatius also said, "In judging of what you are to choose, you should consider not the plausibility of appearances, but look forward to the end." This class of people may think of themselves as followers of Christ, but they have allowed the idol of racism to replace the true God in their hearts.

Ignatius's Third Class are people willing to truly give up their attachments. "They seek only to will and not will as God our Lord inspires them," wrote Ignatius,

> and as seems better for the service and praise of the Divine Majesty. Meanwhile, they will strive to conduct

themselves as if every attachment to it had been broken. They will make efforts neither to want that, nor anything else, unless the service of God our Lord alone move them to do so. As a result, the desire to be better able to serve God our Lord will be the cause of their accepting anything or relinquishing it.

In the work of antiracism, these are the people who seek to discern the path of justice every day. They are open to changing both their attitudes and their behaviors. They search for and hear the Divine Voice speaking to them—through the books they read, through the people they connect with, through their own daily self-examination. They are willing to repent and do whatever is necessary each day to build a more just world in any way they can, and they can do so because they are supported by the love and energy of the Divine Spirit.

Which class do you belong to? You may need to ask God to give you the discernment to see. You can't repent until you become truly self-aware. "Rare indeed are the people who know all their weaknesses of all kinds," said Ignatius, "unless God specially reveals them." We all have blind spots, particularly when it comes to racism. We need the Spirit's help to truly see, to truly repent, to truly change our hearts and lives.

Only then will we be able to participate in building God's Reign of justice.

Journal

On social media, take some time to seek out posts by people of color. Intentionally follow people who are different from yourself. Open yourself to hearing their perspectives. Then write in your journal about your reactions. Ask yourself:

- What new things have I learned?

- How do I feel as I see these posts? (For example, do I feel defensive? Embarrassed? Sorrow? Surprised? Compassion?)

- In what ways can I identify with these people? In what ways am I different?

- Am I able to perceive white privilege any more clearly than I did before?

For Further Reflection

Racism is not merely one sin among many;
it is a radical evil that divides the human family
and denies the new creation of a redeemed world.
To struggle against it demands
an equally radical transformation,
in our own minds and hearts
as well as in the structure of our society.

—U.S. CATHOLIC BISHOPS, PASTORAL LETTER ON RACISM, 1979

Prayer

To the Creator of all races and peoples,
who loves each of us for our uniqueness,
we offer our prayers of petition:
for an end to discrimination in all its forms, we pray:
Lord of all nations, hear our prayer.
That each person may be respected
and valued as a child of God, we pray:
Lord of all nations, hear our prayer.
That each of us may acknowledge our part
in mistakes and sins pertaining to discrimination
and racism, we pray:
Lord of all nations, hear our prayer.
Almighty God, source of our life,
help us to see each other as you see us:
your sons and daughters loved into being
and sustained by your parental care.
Keep watch over our hearts
so that the evil of racism will find no home with us.
Direct our spirits to work for justice and peace
so that all barriers to your grace
which oppress our brothers and sisters will be removed.

— AUGUSTINIAN SECRETARIATE FOR JUSTICE AND PEACE

DAY 6

The Grace of Divine Love

We Are Beloved Sinners

God demonstrates his own love for us in this:
While we were still sinners, Christ died for us.

—ROMANS 5:8

I will give thanks to God our Lord that...
up to this very moment He has shown Himself
so loving and merciful to me.

—IGNATIUS OF LOYOLA

Love is creative and redemptive.
Love builds up and unites.

—MARTIN LUTHER KING JR.

During those early days of his conversion, Ignatius was tormented by the memory of his sins. As we described in the reading for Day 5, at first the only way he knew how to repent was by punishing his own body, trying to erase his guilt with painful ascetic practices. He made his confession to a priest more than once, but he was obsessed with the thought that he had failed to mention some hidden, unremembered sin. During his first months at Manresa, he spent seven hours a day on his knees in prayer, and still, he found no relief from the shame that consumed him.

His self-hatred was destroying him. At times, he thought about killing himself by jumping out a window; only the fear that this would be a sin stopped him. Instead, he made up his mind to neither eat nor drink unless he was in danger of dying. Luckily, a priest put a stop to this after the first week, but now Ignatius was tempted to simply give up his spiritual journey. He wrote in his autobiography that he was filled with disgust for the life he was leading—and no wonder! He was denying himself food and sleep, he wasn't washing or putting on clean clothes, and he was spending long, boring, and uncomfortable hours doing nothing but pray.

As we consider this period in Ignatius's life, we might ask ourselves: What was the picture he had in his head of God? Clearly, the God he imagined was a fearful and wrathful deity, a judgmental God of wrath. Like most of us, his image of God was probably based on his experience growing up. His dominant but remote father would have taught him little about unconditional love, and the early loss of his mother robbed him of a chance to experience a more tender parental relationship. His only adult understanding of love was wrapped up in the trappings of romance and chivalry—a form of love that emphasized loyalty and sacrifice rather than unconditional acceptance. All this would have warped the way he thought about God. As Jesuit author James Martin wrote, "To some of us the humiliation of failure seems to open a wide gulf between God and us. We imagine that God turns away from us in disgust." This is where Ignatius found himself.

But then the Divine Light broke into his depression and guilt. He realized that God would never turn away from him. His despair and self-hatred were from the "Evil One," not God. He finally understood that although he had sinned, God's love was real and present in his life. He was a "beloved sinner."

During the First Week of the Spiritual Exercises, Ignatius asks us to realize that we are sinners. That realization is the first step to our transformation; we cannot change until we understand that we need to change. But then Ignatius puts our sin— our failure to live in harmony with God—within the context of Divine love. Only when we know the extent of our brokenness can we begin to comprehend the depth and breadth of God's love. As Jesuit author Gerald M. Fagin has said, "We are not as good as we thought, but we are much more loved than we ever imagined."

Fagan also wrote that this part of the Exercises is "diagnostic."

It explores whether a person has truly grasped at an interior level the experience of God's creative and sustaining love. . . . Even those advanced in the spiritual life need to experience anew that foundational experience of God's love before progressing further in the Exercises. Until people can claim that gift of God's love on a personal level, they cannot hear God's words of forgiveness or the call in freedom in the rest of the Exercises. To enter into the meditations on sin in the first week of the Exercises without a genuine experience of God's love can be a destructive experience. A person cannot come to honest self-knowledge without first knowing they are loved.

Once we are secure in God's love, Ignatius said, then we can "embrace salvation." Evangelical definitions have sometimes robbed the word *salvation* of its entire meaning. The salvation Jesus described in the Gospels, the salvation that Ignatius saw as the goal of the Spiritual Exercises, is not the eternal bliss of the afterlife. Instead, it happens here, now, in our current lives. It is a state of healing and health, of wholeness and well-being, both individually and also within the entire network of relationships to which God calls us.

In fact, the two are inseparable: we cannot achieve individual healing and well-being if our relationships with others are unhealthy or unjust. Salvation is an experience of relationship, both with God and with others. We can find completeness only within this interactive web of life-affirming love. No one is left out of this web, no one is marginalized. All are needed and necessary.

Divine love does not minimize sin. This means we cannot dismiss our complicity with racism simply because we are forgiven sinners, unconditionally loved by God. But self-hatred is a dead-end street. Love is the road to new possibilities. Love empowers us to act.

I have to confess that when I first came to America, the racism I experienced here shook me deeply. In Haiti and Europe, I had never encountered racism that was so overt, so in my face. This was particularly painful when I encountered racial microaggressions even from within the Jesuit community. I responded by withdrawing. As I came to doubt my own identity, I became unwilling to connect with others; I wanted to protect myself from further hurt. Like Ignatius during the early days of his conversion, I sank into depression. But eventually, God's mercy reached me, just as it did Ignatius during his time at Manresa.

I realized that *all* of us are beloved sinners. God's forgiveness calls us to also forgive others. Divine love means we can reach out to one another in love. We can begin to build relationships anchored in trust rather than fear. We can admit our failures and seek each other's support as together we struggle to build a more just world. As we do so, we will find our true identities, fulfilled in our connections with God and one another.

Racism seeks to establish identity apart from these connections. Ironically, some of us may also cling to antiracism as an identity—but that can be just another form of what Ignatius called attachment. If I delight in pointing out the racism in others in order to bolster my own self-image as an antiracist, then I too am guilty of the sin of division, as well as the sin of idolatry, for I have set myself up as superior to others. "When, as is but human, errors are committed by others," Ignatius reminds us, "you should see in them, as in a mirror, some deformity that needs removing in yourself." And Jesus put it like this:

> Why do you look at the speck of sawdust in your brother's eye and pay no attention to the plank in your own eye? How can you say to your brother, "Let me take the

speck out of your eye," when all the time there is a plank in your own eye? You hypocrite, first take the plank out of your own eye, and then you will see clearly to remove the speck from your brother's eye. (Matthew 5:3–5)

It would be comforting to believe that racism is something perpetrated by other people, not ourselves. The work of antiracism, however, requires that we acknowledge that we are sinners; racism dwells within us all. Racist thinking molds and shapes the minds and actions of everyone within our culture. Even people of color are not immune, for we too internalize this thinking, even though doing so contributes to our own marginalization. As James Baldwin commented, "You know, it's not the world that was my oppressor, because what the world does to you, if the world does it to you long enough and effectively enough, you begin to do to yourself."

And yet God's love continues to work in us all. This is the reality that saved Ignatius from despair. It is what allowed him to construct a theology of hope, a spirituality that expresses itself in active love.

Love doesn't give up. Love sees possibility even in the midst of our racist world. And love works to make that possibility real.

Journal

Ignatius understood that if we want to work to change the world, we need God's unconditional love as our foundation and guiding principle. Keeping that in mind, write in your journal the answers to these questions:

- What is my image of God?

- How might my image of God relate to my relationship with my parents?

- How does my image of God need to be expanded?

- Does my self-worth spring from my knowledge of God's love—or am I depending on racism or any other attachment to give me a sense of identity?

- If I truly believed God loved me unconditionally, how might I act differently?

- What connections are there between Divine love and the work of antiracism?

For Further Reflection

Your true identity is as a child of God.
This is the identity you have to accept.
Once you have claimed it and settled in it,
you can live in a world that gives you
much joy as well as pain.
You can receive the praise
as well as the blame that comes to you
as an opportunity for strengthening your basic identity,
because the identity that makes you free
is anchored beyond all human praise and blame.
You belong to God, and it is as a child of God
that you are sent into the world.

—HENRI NOUWEN

Prayer

Only in love can I find you, my God.
In love the gates of my soul spring open,
allowing me to breathe a new air of freedom
and forget my own petty self.
In love my whole being streams forth
out of the rigid confines of narrowness
and anxious self-assertion,
which make me a prisoner of my own poverty and emptiness.
In love all the powers of my soul flow out toward you,
wanting never more to return,
but to lose themselves completely in you,
since by your love you are the inmost center of my heart,
closer to me than I am to myself.

—KARL RAHNER, S.J.

DAY 7

The Grace of Community

The Unity of Christ's Body

You are no longer foreigners and strangers,
but fellow citizens with God's people
and also members of his household.

—EPHESIANS 2:19

It is not enough that I should serve God by myself:
I must help the hearts of all to love him
and the tongues of all to praise him.

—IGNATIUS OF LOYOLA

When my brothers try to draw a circle to exclude me,
I shall draw a larger circle to include them.

Where they speak out for the privileges of a puny group,
I shall shout for the rights of all [hu]mankind.

—PAULI MURRAY

I n 1528, Ignatius moved to France to study at the University of Paris. There, he gathered around him six companions, all fellow students at the university. These were friends who shared his sense of mission, his commitment to actively serve God. Together, they encouraged and supported one another as they traveled along the spiritual path. On August 15, 1534, they formalized their small community by taking religious vows, calling themselves the *Compañia de Jesús*—the Society of Jesus. Six years later, the Pope granted them official approval to become a religious order.

As the order grew, Jesuits—as they were now known— became an active community that spread across Europe and beyond. As they did so, they were following the instructions Ignatius had given them: to "seek the greater glory of God" and the good of all humanity. Everywhere they went, they built schools, colleges, and seminaries. In 1541, Ignatius sent his good friend and fellow Jesuit, Francis Xavier, all the way to India. "Go, set the world on fire," Ignatius told him.

Today, some people think of Ignatian spirituality as a path that focuses mostly on the individual. Because of Ignatius's emphasis on interior self-examination, we might forget that as he grew spiritually, his relationship with God reached out beyond himself. His inner connection to God flowed out from him, forming a network of human relationships that eventually grew into a community that spanned the globe, all united by the mission of service to God and humanity. Ignatius understood that the true good of each individual is ultimately dependent on the good of everyone.

To be fully human, bearing the image of Christ as we are created to do, we too must reach out beyond ourselves, just as Ignatius did. As Pope Francis has said, "Faith is truly a good for everyone; it is a common good." We have been speaking in this book of the spiritual "journey," which is one way of looking at the life of faith, but Pope Francis reminds us, "Faith is not only presented as a journey, but also as a process of building, the preparing of a place in which human beings can dwell together with one another. . . . Precisely because it is linked to love, the light of faith is concretely placed at the service of justice, law and peace."

"Social justice" was not a term that Ignatius used, but his followers have always been active in working to make the world better. In the twentieth century, Pedro Arrupe, the Jesuit Superior General from 1965 to 1983, explicitly linked Ignatian spirituality to the promotion of social justice. "Only by being a man or woman for others does one become fully human," said Father Arrupe. He put this belief into action in his own life: during World War II, he cared for victims of the Hiroshima atomic bomb blast; later, moved to compassion by the plight of Vietnamese refugees, he created the Jesuit Refugee Service; and he led the Jesuits into practical work with the poor, especially in Latin America.

In doing these things, Arrupe was continuing the spiritual legacy of Ignatius of Loyola, who said, "Workers for the salvation of souls ought so to labor as to make themselves acceptable not only to God but also to [human beings]; and regulate their zeal for the divine honor by their neighbor's progress." In other words, we can judge our own spiritual growth by how well our "neighbor" is doing. If those around us are suffering because of the way we are living, we should not be patting ourselves on the back for our spiritual maturity! This means that racism and spiritual growth cannot exist for very long in the same space. Ignatius also said, "If you wish to live among and mix with your fellows securely, you must esteem it a matter of the first importance to be equally affected to all and partial to none." There is no room for white privilege in the Body of Christ.

Community is essential to our spiritual growth. We need to both give and receive within a living network in order to achieve the salvation that Ignatius described. "God created the world to be a fabric," theologian Tim Keller wrote, "for everything to be woven together and interdependent." Archbishop Desmond Tutu expressed a similar thought: "You can't be human all by yourself." And this sense of interconnection leads to the awareness that "what you do affects the whole World. When you do well, it spreads out; it is for the whole of humanity."

In the fourth century, Gregory of Nyssa spoke about the Divine community as the fullness and completion of humankind. According to Gregory, the community to which we all belong reaches across space and through time; this is a notion that many people of color understand and affirm, for we feel the presence of our ancestors beside us. Gregory called his concept of Divine community the *pleroma,* a Greek word that has to do with totality, fulfillment, and completion. For Gregory, the full community of all humanity is necessary for the Body of Christ, which only in its totality truly reflects the Divine likeness and beauty. Each member is needed and necessary.

Author Kimberly Flint-Hamilton summarizes Gregory's view: "Only in universal freedom can the fullness of *pleroma* unfold, with each individual human being contributing. Slavery, racism, and oppression in general, are completely incompatible with the will of God." For Gregory, no true human unity or even any perfect unity between God and humanity can exist without the real and lived solidarity of all human beings. It is the complete community, with absolutely no one left out, that is the true image of God.

Jesuit theologian and scientist Pierre Teilhard de Chardin also wrote about this same concept of *pleroma*, saying:

> Our individual mystical effort awaits an essential completion in its union with the mystical effort of all other [humans]. The divine milieu which will ultimately be one in the Pleroma, must begin to become one during the earthly phase of our existence. . . . It is impossible to love Christ without loving others. . . . And it is impossible to love others (in a spirit of broad human communion) without moving nearer to Christ.

Teilhard understood love as being not simply an emotion or even a Divine attribute. Instead, he believed it was a practical, hardworking energy we experience in our everyday life. It is the Breath of God that feeds the entire Body of Christ, the human community. Love is not something sentimental or abstract, said Teilhard, but rather it is the power that moves us toward our true fulfillment and identity in Christ.

As we breathe the same breath, the breath of love, we are united in one body—*Corpus Christi,* as Ignatius would have said. It is like the constant movement of inhalation and exhalation, one dependent on the other. As Ignatius also wrote in the Spiritual Exercises, "Love consists in an interchange."

And yet sometimes, despite our best intentions, it's hard to find our own place in this living, breathing community. It is difficult to perceive the spiritual reality hidden in our all-too-imperfect world. "A healthy community must preserve itself and look to its welfare by cutting off its corrupt members in good time," advised Ignatius, "before their rottenness reaches to the parts that are sound." Racism is a rottenness that has corrupted the human community.

The struggle to take my place as a member of the Body of Christ is one I often experience. Recently, while preaching from the pulpit, I mentioned the fight for Black Lives Matter. That afternoon, as we sat around the dinner table, a young man—a white man who works hard to be seen as "woke"—asked me, "Why are you so concerned with the question of race in this country? You're not even from here. Does it ever occur to you that this is an American issue, something for Americans to deal with? Not an outsider?"

"What if I were to ask you the same question?" I replied. "What would you answer?" I meant, since he *was* born in America, was he also concerned about racism? But perhaps I did not make myself clear. I cannot know my brother's intention when he asked me his questions.

I couldn't shake the feeling, however, that I was once again being pushed back because of the color of my skin. I disengaged from the conversation, feeling confused and disconnected, and went back to my room. *When am I going to feel at home?* I was thinking. *What do I have to do to belong?*

Although I was born in Haiti, my ancestors arrived in 1719 in what would become the state of Florida. They were from the African region known as Senegambia, and it had not been their choice to immigrate to North America. Slave traders had forced them onto a ship named the *Aurore*.

A year later, my many-times-great grandparents walked from Pensacola, Florida, to the new city of Baton Rouge in Louisiana. According to the Archives of the Diocese of Baton Rouge, they were baptized into the Catholic Church on April 18, 1725. Eventually, my ancestors ended up with a middle-class Polish slave owner from New Jersey. In 1876, their descendants traveled on a medical mission to Haiti. And so, a century or so later, I came to be born in Haiti.

The color of my skin marks me as a person of color, and my accent marks me as an immigrant. I have been living in America for years now; my ancestors lived here for more than a hundred and fifty years; but still, I am considered an outsider. I suffer from the myth that immigrants come to this country to take jobs, bring drugs, and commit crimes. Like many people of color, I remain lost and confused, unsure of where I belong.

I want to point to my years of education, my professional standing, my intelligence, as though these things will make people more likely to accept me. I'm still following that same old adage that Black parents tell their children: "If you want to succeed, you'll need to be twice as good as white folks"—twice as smart, twice as talented, twice as hardworking.

A 2015 report from the National Bureau of Economic Research found that this idea is more than an old platitude. The study indicated that across the board, Black workers are monitored far more closely than white employees. Because Black workers are scrutinized so closely, any errors they make are more likely to be noticed. And then, according to the researchers, it's more likely a Black employee will be let go for those errors than a white one would be. Blacks don't get a second chance. When they do keep steady employment, they're not promoted as often as white workers, and they get fewer raises. So it's not just our imagination that we need to work at least twice as hard to be accepted.

Meanwhile, despite all my hard work, I continue to grapple with my identity within the American community. I am constantly asked questions like these: "Where are you from?" (My current answer: "Omaha, Nebraska.") "Are you legal?" ("Yes. Are you?") "When was the last time you went home?" ("I live in my home in Omaha.") "What are you?" ("I am human. Did you think I might be canine?") The people who ask these questions don't think they are being rude. They don't realize their questions are a form of microaggression, that their words are a way to force me out of the same community to which they belong. I want to fight for my community—the people I interact with every day, the people I love. I want to work hard to make it better, to build the Body of Christ in the place where I live. But do I have the right if I do not truly belong?

And yet America has always been known as the land of hope. I refuse to believe this is only a fantasy, a pretty lie we like to tell about ourselves. Despite the ongoing suffering of the entire BIPOC community (Blacks, indigenous, and people of color), I still have hope that America will become a better version of herself. In the midst of our recent traumas—COVID-19, the deaths of George Floyd and others, the protests and political unrest—I hear a new call to community. As Desmond Tutu said, "Hope is being able to see there is light despite all the darkness."

This deep sense of hope is what convinces me I am truly part of a community. I do belong. Civil rights activist Josephine Baker once said, "America belongs to [Blacks] just as much as it does to any of the white race . . . , in some ways even more so because they believe in hope." As a person of color, I know how to pray and work for hope—and hope is essential to the life of any community. Hope is what calls us ever deeper into God's Reign of justice.

"Hope," said Coretta King, "is never really won, you can earn it and win it in every generation." My ancestors carried hope with them when they arrived in this land in 1719; they carried it with them still when they traveled to Haiti; and now, I bring it with me back to America and to the Ignatian community where I find my identity. My faith and my sense of hope keep me anchored, despite the confusion that racism often brings to my heart. "Faith," said Pope Francis, "helps us build our societies in such a way that they can journey towards a future of hope."

Martin Luther King Jr. spoke often about his hope for the "Beloved Community," a society based on justice, equal opportunity, and love between all human beings. According to Dr. King, this is the goal for which God created us. "The end is reconciliation; the end is redemption; the end is the creation of the Beloved Community," he wrote.

> It is this type of spirit and this type of love that can transform opponents into friends. It is this type of understanding goodwill that will transform the deep gloom of the old age into the exuberant gladness of the new age. It is this love which will bring about miracles in the hearts of [humanity].

As Ignatius knew, inner miracles give fruit to outer service; the two movements work together hand in hand. In Paul's epistles to the Corinthians, he makes clear that having the "mind of Christ" requires that we actively live within the "Body of Christ." This means we make a commitment to intentional love, an involvement in the world's affairs that carries us beyond our personal interests. In today's world, this is the call to the work of antiracism.

Together we can accomplish far more than we can alone. The work of people joined by community relationships can achieve things that the individual members of the community cannot do on their own. Together, we can, as Ignatius said, "set the world on fire." This is the hope I cling to.

Will you join me?

Journal

According to a recent study done by the Public Religion Research Institute, in a scenario where each person has a hundred friends or close acquaintances, the average white person has just one Black friend, one Latinx friend, one Asian friend, and one mixed-race friend. The average Black person has eight white friends, two Latinx friends, and zero Asian friends. How many friends do you have who are people of color? Think about what you might do to change this, and then write out a plan in your journal.

Building cross-racial relationships does not mean you find people of color and insist they be your friends. Instead, you might intentionally change your daily routines to expose yourself to more racially diverse environments in which you may be the minority. This might be something as simple as going to a different gym, switching your usual coffee shop or favorite restaurant, attending a multicultural church, or reaching out to people of color already in your life.

These are a few suggestions to keep in mind as you carry out this exercise:

- Be humble. Be aware of how much you don't know. Don't be afraid to look stupid.

- Accept that you may feel uncomfortable.

- Listen. Be open to other opinions and points of view.

- Don't be afraid to discuss race issues. Race should not be the elephant in the room!

- If a person of color lets you know you've been offensive in some way, don't get defensive or make excuses. Trust their insight even if you don't understand. Be quick to apologize. Be sincere. (Keep in mind what Ignatius had to say about this: "It is a great help to progress to possess a friend who is privileged to point out to you your failings.")

- Ask for and receive feedback.

Be sure to record in your journal your experiences, reactions, and insights. Describe how your concept of the Body of Christ is changed by this activity.

For Further Reflection

We need other human beings to help us to be human.
The solitary isolated human being
really is a contradiction in terms.
We are made for interdependence, for complementarity.
I have gifts which you do not have
and you have gifts that I do not have.
… We have our own gifts and that makes us unique,
but the first law of our being
is that we are made for interdependence.
We are made to exist in a delicate network
of interdependence with our fellow human beings
and with the rest of God's creation.

—DESMOND TUTU

Prayer

Love of Christ, breathe in me.
Unite me with your human Body.
Reveal anything in me that blocks the flow of your love.
Show me practical ways
I can work to make your Body stronger.
Bring new people and relationships into my life.
May we together set the world on fire,
making love and justice come alive.

The Grace I Keep

I ask for the grace of an open heart.
May this openness lead me
into new friendships with people of color.

WEEK TWO

Christ as a Person of Color

In 2013, Fox News host Megyn Kelly made this statement: "Jesus was a white man, too . . . he's a historical figure. That's a verifiable fact." Unfortunately, Kelly is not the only one who holds this viewpoint. For centuries, most people have imagined Jesus with a white face. This Middle Eastern man is even portrayed with blond hair and blue eyes.

Some people like to remind us that Jesus transcends race. In a spiritual sense, he is all humanity, regardless of skin tone. While this is true (just as the statement "All lives matter" is true), it misses the reality of Jesus' life in a particular place and time. Although the universal Christ mystically goes beyond all human concepts of race, Christ also descended as Jesus of Nazareth into the context of this world's division and injustice.

In the Second Week of the Spiritual Exercises, Ignatius invites us to get to know Jesus when he was a human being. The grace we seek during this phase of our spiritual journey is captured in a prayer often repeated by Jesuits: "Lord, grant that I may see thee more clearly, love thee more dearly, and follow thee more nearly." Ignatius encourages us to use our imaginations to enter as completely as we can into Jesus' human experience. If we imagine Jesus as being white, we will miss out on who he really was.

Jesus was not born as the son of the Roman emperor. His family were not among the noble and elite Romans who controlled the politics of his world. Instead, he was a child of an oppressed group of people, a people colonized by the Roman Empire. When we picture a Jesus who has European features, skin, and hair, we are not understanding the full meaning of his life. We are connecting Jesus to the powerful rather than the oppressed and marginalized. We are even allowing *Christ* to be synonymous with *white supremacy.*

Christ is alive in every human being—but especially in those who have been pushed to the edges of our society, who have been shoved down and victimized. In his book *The Cross and The Lynching Tree*, James Cone wrote, "The cross places God in the midst of crucified people, in the midst of people who are hung, shot, burned, and tortured."

During his time on earth, Jesus experienced the political and economic oppression of the Roman Empire. Most whites today may have a hard time identifying with that aspect of his life, since they have never experienced that kind of oppression. If they want to better understand the life of Jesus, they might look more closely into the lives of people of color. As Cone explained, people of color know more experientially what it means to bear the cross of Christ.

This idea turns the white savior complex upside down. It takes away the sense of superiority white philanthropists may feel, the condescension of the superior person reaching down to help an inferior. White followers of Christ need to recognize the spiritual authority of people who have experienced the cross firsthand. People of color do not need whites to "save" them. Just the opposite: whites need the Jesus who is present in people of color. "God's reality is . . . to be found wherever people are being empowered to fight for freedom," James Cone wrote. "Life-giving power for the poor and the oppressed is the primary criterion that we must use to judge the adequacy of our theology, not abstract concepts."

During this week of the Exercises, we will focus on identifying with Jesus, both the Jesus of the Bible and the Jesus who continues to live in all who are marginalized. This is the way of salvation—the path to the Reign of Heaven where justice reigns.

> *The gospel of Jesus is not a rational concept*
> *to be explained in a theory of salvation,*
> *but a story about God's presence*
> *in Jesus' solidarity with the oppressed,*
> *which led to his death on the cross.*
> *What is redemptive is the faith*
> *that God snatches victory out of defeat,*
> *life out of death, and hope out of despair.*

–JAMES H. CONE

DAY 1

The Call to Build the Reign of Heaven

Hearing Jesus in the Voices of People of Color

*Today, if you hear God's voice,
do not harden your hearts.*

—HEBREWS 3:15

Our ears should be wide open to our neighbor.

—IGNATIUS OF LOYOLA

*It is impossible to experience a person's life,
or to be compassionate,
if you do not listen to the person
or if you do not ask questions.*

—JAMES MARTIN, S.J.

Ignatius of Loyola heard the call of God. Although Ignatius did have a few mystical visions, for the most part, he listened to the Divine Voice as it spoke to him through everyday reality. As he progressed along his path of contemplation united with active service, his spiritual ears grew sharper. He also continued to use the tools he described in the Spiritual Exercises to help him hear accurately. Paying close attention to the motions of his heart—both "consolation" and "desolation"—he was able to discern where God was leading him.

As we move from the First Week into the Second Week of the Spiritual Exercises, Ignatius directs our attention to what is known as the "Kingdom Meditation." In the first scene of this meditation, Ignatius asks us to imagine an earthly leader who invites people to join him in an undertaking that will benefit all humanity. This leader is willing to sacrifice everything for the good of the people, and he asks that those who choose to follow him do the same. He makes clear that the work will not be easy; there will be pain and suffering before there is triumphant rejoicing.

Next, Ignatius presents us with a picture of Jesus, the human being who entered into this world's physical work, suffering, and oppression in order to build the Reign of God on earth. The Jesus who stands before us in this imaginary scene has risen from the dead, but he knows his work on earth is not yet complete. As we look at him, he says, "I want to destroy all sin, all oppression, all division. I want to build the Reign of Heaven. Will you join me in this great enterprise? If so, you must be willing to work hard. You must accept that you may need to suffer, just as I suffered. This is the only way to build God's Reign."

As we consider Jesus' invitation to join his reclamation project of the Earth, Ignatius advises us to ask for sharper spiritual ears, so that we can more clearly hear Jesus' call. This call is unique for each of us as individuals, but it always asks us to step outside our own small bubbles. It challenges us to take action in the real and messy world of politics, economics, and social welfare. "Self-denial and sacrifice," said Ignatius, "prayer and labor, virtues and good works after the example of Christ, are but means to strengthen this kingdom in ourselves and extend it to others." Our personal salvation can only come to fruition within God's larger plan of salvation for the entire world.

Ignatius believed that no one is exempt from hearing the call of Jesus. Most people, he thought, (people of "good will" and "sound judgment") respond to this call at least at some level. If we want to totally identify with Jesus, however, entering into the most intimate relationship with him that's possible, we will need to offer ourselves wholly to God's work on earth. This means we will set aside our selfish attachments. We will put all our resources—spiritual, emotional, intellectual, and physical—into Jesus' hands for him to use. We will join him in his work to make the Reign of Heaven real, here and now.

This requires a major upheaval in the way we look at the world. The boundaries of God's Reign are not confined to our own souls; this Reign enfolds all creation. Ignatius challenges us to break through the narrow confinement of our egos and begin to think on a far more global scale. This is the "work" to which Jesus calls us.

Martin Luther King Jr. is a shining example of somehow who heard and responded to the call of Jesus as it came to him through the oppression of his own people. The "Beloved Community" was the term he used for the Reign of Heaven. The King Center, which today works to further advance Dr. King's goals, gives this definition for the Beloved Community:

> a global vision in which all people can share in the wealth of the earth. In the Beloved Community, poverty, hunger and homelessness will not be tolerated because international standards of human decency will not allow it. Racism and all forms of discrimination, bigotry and prejudice will be replaced by an all-inclusive spirit of sisterhood and brotherhood.

The Beloved Community, says the King Center on its website, is a call to a healthy society, one that's built on inclusiveness, where everyone shares in the Earth's bounty—"a society in which all are embraced and none discriminated against."

For some time now, many white Christians have insisted that this wasn't what Jesus meant when he spoke about the Reign of Heaven. Instead, they say, he was referring to the afterlife, or at least to some far-distant future. Although Jesus clearly says the Reign of Heaven is among us (Luke 17:21) or "at hand" (Matthew 3:2; 4:17), the white church has often turned the concept into a system of eternal rewards and punishments: Believe in Jesus the same way we believe in him, and you'll go to heaven when you die; don't believe the way we do, and you'll go to hell. When this is your foundational belief, you're excused from doing the hard work of feeding the hungry, visiting those in prison, and healing the broken. Instead, you can focus all your energy on persuading people to believe the way you do.

The question white theologians have traditionally asked is, "When will the Reign of Heaven happen?" They were not concerned with practical questions like *where* it might happen or *how*. Again, this allowed them to focus on the "spiritual world," while they ignored the real-world problems of poverty, injustice, and environmental degradation.

In an interview with *Sojourners* magazine, Osage theologian George Tinker said that from an indigenous perspective, "The kingdom of God has got to be right here. In other words, it becomes a metaphor for creation." He went on to say:

> Jesus' call to repent, to return to the kingdom, is a call to come into a proper relationship with the rest of creation, and with the Creator. A proper relationship recognizes that I am simply a part of the creation, one of God's creatures along with the other two-leggeds, the four-leggeds, the wingeds, and the other living, moving things—including the trees, the grass, the rocks, the mountains.

From this perspective, the Reign of Heaven encompasses the entire cosmos. The Divine plan, with all its projects and actions, is at work everywhere. All of physical reality is laboring to come into wholeness in Christ. The Divine Voice comes to us from every corner of the world, especially anywhere there is injustice, inequality, and oppression, for these are God's call to action.

During Ignatius's time at Manresa, in the vision he had while sitting beside the river Cardoner, he saw all creation coming down from God and returning to God. He understood then that this was the meaning of the Incarnation—and this was the work of Christ in the world, a work we are all called to share. If we commit ourselves to join Jesus' ongoing project, we may not have a vision like Ignatius did, but we will see with new eyes and listen with new ears. We will see reality in a new way.

This reality demands that we begin to perceive the interconnections between us all, including between our separate vocations. We each have individual calls, but these should be cooperative rather than competing. The work I do should support and contribute to the work you do—and vice versa.

For a long time, the environmental movement has been perceived as an alternate issue to the racism issue. People could devote themselves to one cause or the other but not to both. Environmentalists have been traditionally white, and social activists have been more likely to be people of color. Their causes have competed with one another for attention, each one insisting that theirs is the priority, the defining problem of our age.

But the Reign of Heaven includes *all* creation. Everything interacts with everything. You can't separate out one strand without pulling on all the other threads in this living web of relationship.

And the reality is this: environmental issues have a disproportionate impact on people of color. The five-year water crisis in Flint, Michigan—where an entire Black community was forced to function without clean drinking water—is just one example of this. Across America, the communities where people of color live are often exposed to lead, industrial emissions, vehicle exhaust, and other contaminants. A similar reality exists around the world: people of color are more likely to be exposed to polluted air, water, and soil. Climate change also has a greater impact on people of color, particularly in low-lying coastal and island communities that are vulnerable to rising sea levels. The Amazon's indigenous people are threatened by the massive deforestation going on there; water pollution in India is a major health problem; and the expanding deserts of Africa cause famine and relocation. In the environmental battle, clearly, people of color are often on the frontline. And meanwhile, they have fewer resources to address the crisis, meaning it inevitably magnifies their existing poverty and suffering.

At the end of Week One, we spoke of the concept of *pleroma,* the idea that all humanity shares in the Body of Christ. Another translation of this Latin word has to do with being in the same boat. In reality, all humanity is in the boat called Planet Earth. Ultimately, if this boat sinks, no one will survive.

This is not how we've been taught to look at reality, though. Instead, we perceive that different groups have their own boats. This leads to a social model built on competition rather than cooperation. We tend to focus on what is good for our "boat" and not be as concerned for those we think are sailing a separate ship. We may feel bad if we realize people are drowning, but their cries for help seem far away; we turn off the news, forget about the online article we just read, and focus on our own small lives. We go back to paddling our own little watercraft, unaware of the true reality that's all around us.

Martin Luther King's vision of the Beloved Community was all-inclusive. When he responded to the call of his people, he reminded them again and again that their goal was not merely the right to sit at the front of the bus. Their goal was much bigger: a new society that would sweep the entire Earth into its embrace. Dr. King's work was to build a world where all are lifted up and where all benefit. This is the work of Jesus that Ignatius was describing in his Kingdom Meditation.

Our world doesn't make it easy to hear this call, though. Our ears are stuffed full with distractions: all our many responsibilities, not to mention our phones and laptops. We need to take time out, so that we can be "patient in listening to all people," as Ignatius advised. This requires being willing to truly hear what is being said, without any need to defend our own egos. Ignatius included in his Spiritual Exercises this "Presupposition": as Christ-followers, we "must be disposed to receive in a favorable sense and to take in good part every word susceptible of being so received and understood, rather than to take it in a rigorous and objectionable sense." We must be "more ready to justify than to condemn" when we listen to others.

As we listen for the voice of God, we may also need to examine what assumptions are interfering with our ability to hear. When Jesus was a child visiting the Temple, he heard the call of God there. Answering that call meant he allowed it to take priority over his family's voices. He didn't listen to their expectations of where he needed to be and what he should have been doing. He heard God speaking—and he answered.

What might God be saying to you in this moment? Can you hear the Divine Voice speaking to you through people of color?

Journal

Take a few moments to imagine you are sitting with Jesus during his time on earth. Picture the setting: the dust on the ground, the scent of the air, the color of the sky. Imagine the texture of his robe, the shape of his hands, his dark eyes and brown skin. Then have a "colloquy" with Jesus. Ask him:

- How did you perceive God's voice calling to you when you were in the Temple? Was it an emotion, a thought, an inaudible voice?

- How did you feel when you realized God was calling you?

- How did you feel when your parents came back for you?

- Later in your life, did you hear God's call when you were with the people who came to you for healing? Did the lepers, the sick women, the beggars speak to you with God's voice? What did that feel like?

Write Jesus' answers to these questions in your journal. (Remember, Ignatius taught that it was perfectly okay to let our imaginations play as we talk with Jesus.) Then hear Jesus ask you these questions:

- Where in your life do you hear me calling you?

- Can you identify sources of "consolation"—a sense of joy and peace—in your life at this moment?

- Is there anything that gives you "desolation"—a sense of sadness or distance from me?

- Can you tell what these feelings are saying to you?

- Where might God be attracting your attention?

- How can you live my call more deeply? How does it apply to the work of antiracism?

- Are you willing to get to know me better as you listen to the experiences of people of color?

Again, write your answers in your journal.

For Further Reflection

Race and racism is a reality
that so many of us grow up learning to just deal with.
But if we ever hope to move past it,
it can't just be on people of color to deal with it.
It's up to all of us ... to do the honest,
uncomfortable work of rooting it out.
It starts with self-examination and listening
to those whose lives are different from our own.

It ends with justice, compassion, and empathy
that manifests in our lives and on our streets.

—MICHELLE OBAMA

Prayer

Give me ears to hear your voice, Jesus.
May I be willing to hear you calling to me
as I listen to people of color.
Show me when I am being defensive
or unwilling to step free of my
attachments and assumptions.
Bring me ever closer to you,
so that together we can work to build the Reign of Heaven.

DAY 2

White Jesus

How Christianity Has Contributed to Racism

For many shall come in my name,
saying, I am Christ;
and shall deceive many.

—MATTHEW 24:5 KJV

My life is firmly grounded in the fact
that the reality of being a person
is seen fully in Jesus Christ.
… I want the truth of Christ's life
to be fully the truth of my own.

—IGNATIUS OF LOYOLA

*The basic fact is that Christianity as it was born
in the mind of this Jewish teacher and thinker
appears as a technique of survival for the oppressed.
That it became, through the intervening years,
a religion of the powerful and the dominant,
used sometimes as an instrument of oppression,
must not tempt us into believing that it was thus
in the mind and life of Jesus....
Wherever his spirit appears,
the oppressed gather fresh courage;
for he announced the good news
that fear, hypocrisy, and hatred...
need have no dominion over them.*

—HOWARD THURMAN

On January 6, 2021, I watched in disbelief as I saw the US Capitol stormed by a hoard of shouting white men. In the crowd, I saw banners that proclaimed, "Jesus saves." A screaming man with an upraised fist had a cross emblazoned on his T-shirt. The scene on my television screen shifted, and now I saw flags whipping in the wind above the rioters' heads; among the Confederate flags, I caught a glimpse of the Christian flag. Next, I noticed a black-garbed figure with skeleton hands clutching the Bible to his chest. In another shot, I saw a woman carrying a poster-size image of a white Christ wearing a red MAGA hat. Feeling sick to my stomach, I turned off the television.

I knew that the images I'd just seen were not *my* Christianity. None of my Jesuit brothers would have joined the angry mob in Washington; none of them would dream of pairing Christ so blatantly with racism. I also knew that most Christians probably wouldn't place a MAGA hat on their image of Jesus. Nevertheless, many of them would still picture him as a white man.

As much as it pains me, I cannot escape the fact that Christianity was the cradle in which racism grew. Centuries ago, the church rationalized land theft from indigenous peoples and the enslavement of Africans with the belief that God was on the side of white Christians. In 1493, Pope Alexander VI introduced the Doctrine of Discovery, which essentially declared that Europeans could claim whatever land they found. This doctrine dehumanized the native people who were already on these "undiscovered lands," while it declared that European culture was superior to any other culture in the world. (The justification for this was that the native people of other lands were not Christian.) Explorers encountered other cultures with this attitude firmly in place: "These people are savages because they are not Christian; therefore I can take their lands." The church colluded with the idea that God had destined white people to remake the world in their own image. Then, in 1792, U.S. Secretary of State Thomas Jefferson claimed that the European Doctrine of Discovery was international law that also applied to the American government. The ideology that would one day be titled "Manifest Destiny" was already at work, as white Christians soothed their uneasy conscience with their belief in their own God-given exceptionalism.

Ignatius spoke of false Christians' ideas as "poison," "creeping daily like a gangrene." I hope he would have been able to recognize the rottenness that took hold of Christianity during the centuries of colonization and conquest that led to the building of our world today. Theologian Kelly Brown Douglas has said that whites' belief in their superiority is America's original sin, spawning both slavery and the unjust treatment of indigenous people, both today's racism and the fear and resentment of immigrants. This sin is the idolatry we discussed earlier; in effect, white Christians created their own false god—a white god—and this warped all their other beliefs.

And yet America prides itself on being a Christian nation. The Declaration of Independence based the rights it guaranteed on the fact that these are "God-given"; at the same time, it referred to the original inhabitants of North America as "merciless Indian savages." America's founders spoke passionately of the equality of "all men"—and yet the Constitution defined Black Americans as only three-fifths of a person. Clearly, to be "human" meant to be white (and male).

Until the nineteenth century, however, Jesus was usually portrayed as a dark-eyed, dark-haired Jew. Then, in the early 1800s, the American church was increasingly troubled by a number of issues. It struggled with the morality of taking more and more land from Native Americans, while at the same time, the tension around slavery was mounting. In these decades, white churches began printing and distributing pictures of a white Jesus. His image became a wordless source of unity and comfort for many troubled Americans.

Christian ministers went beyond this nonverbal image, stating in no uncertain terms that the enslavement of human beings was justifiable from a biblical point of view. The Reverend James Henley Thornwell, a Harvard-educated scholar who memorized most of the entire Bible, regularly preached the message of white supremacy from his pulpit in Columbia, South Carolina, where he was the pastor in the years leading up to the Civil War. "As long as that [African] race, in its comparative degradation, co-exists side by side with the white," Thornwell told his congregation in 1861, "bondage is its normal condition." Christians need not feel guilty about enslaving other human beings, Thornwell said. "The relation of master and slave stands on the same foot with the other relations of life. In itself, it is not inconsistent with the will of God. It is not sinful." The Bible, insisted Thornwell, sanctioned "slavery as any other social condition of man."

After the Civil War, as Americans struggled with Reconstruction even as they worried about the growing number of Asian and Jewish immigrants, white Jesus became even more important to the identity of white folk. Artists began to portray the Savior as not only fair-skinned but also blond and blue-eyed. This was nonverbal propaganda; it allowed whites to absorb the message that the Divine was like them. White-skinned people were good, like Jesus; brown-skinned people were dangerous and sinful, the opposite of Jesus.

Authors Skot Welch and Rick Wilson refer to white Jesus as "Plantation Jesus." They make the statement that this concept of a white Jesus was what allowed good Christian folk to go to church on Sundays—and then put on the robes of the Ku Klux Klan the rest of the week and bomb, beat, torture, and murder Blacks. "Plantation Jesus was the reason that churches and Sunday schools sometimes dismissed early to participate in . . . lynchings, which happened in every American state except two." Of course not all white Christians participated in lynchings, but the silence of the white church allowed the violence and murder to continue from 1880 to 1968. As historian Jemar Tisby has reminded us, "The refusal to act in the midst of injustice is itself an act of injustice. Indifference to oppression perpetuates oppression."

Many white Christians did not identify themselves with the Ku Klux Klan, but they too worshiped a form of white Jesus. They implicitly believed that because Jesus was white, whites had the corner on God. Meanwhile, from its beginning, KKK members considered themselves good Christians, demonstrating how easily white Christianity could accommodate itself to racism. One Klan leader stated, "As the Star of Bethlehem guided the wise men to Christ, so it is that the Klan is expected more and more to guide men to the right life under Christ's banner." In the opening prayer of Klan rituals, the order proclaimed: "The living Christ is a Klansman's criterion of character, and to Him we look for light, love, and life." Perhaps Ignatius had something like these so-called Christians in mind when he said, "Charity and kindness unwedded to truth are not charity and kindness, but deceit and vanity. "

As the Civil Rights Movement dawned, white Jesus was still very much present. On Sunday, May 14, 1961, a crowd of angry white people in Alabama attacked a Greyhound bus carrying Freedom Riders (protestors against segregationist laws). The mob threw rocks and bricks through the windows and then tossed a firebomb into a broken window. As smoke and flames filled the bus, the attackers barricaded the door. "Burn them alive!" someone in the crowd shouted. In response to this act of racist violence, Montgomery's most prominent pastor, Henry Lyon Jr., condemned the Freedom Riders' cause. "Ladies and gentlemen," he announced at a community gathering, "for fifteen years I have had the privilege of being pastor of a white Baptist church in this city. If we stand a hundred years from now, it will still be a white church. I am a believer in a separation of the races, and I am none the less a Christian."

Lyon waited for the applause to die down before he continued: "If you want to get in a fight with the one that started separation of the races, then you come face to face with your God. The difference in color, the difference in our body, our minds, our life, our mission upon the face of this earth, is God given." Not all white churches took such an outspoken and overt stand in support of racism, but as Jamar Tisby points out, "At a key moment in the life of our nation, one that called for moral courage, the American church responded to much of the civil rights movement with passivity, indifference, or even outright opposition."

White Jesus is still alive and well today, though his worshippers may express themselves differently than they did in the past. They disguise their faith in white supremacy beneath politically correct phrases. "Christian complicity with racism in the twenty-first century looks different than complicity with racism in the past," Jamar Tisby concedes in his book *The Color of Compromise*. He goes on to say that today's version:

> looks like Christians responding to "black lives matter" with the phrase "all lives matter." It looks like Christians consistently supporting a president whose racism has been on display for decades. It looks like Christians telling black people and their allies that their attempts to bring up racial concerns are "divisive." It looks like conversations on race that focus on individual relationships and are unwilling to discuss systemic solutions.

Tisby concludes, however, that "perhaps Christian complicity in racism has not changed after all. Although the characters and the specifics are new, many of the same rationalizations for racism remain."

Given all this, you would think that Black people would have unanimously turned away from Christianity. Instead, many Black people, including my own ancestors, went directly to the Jesus of the Gospels. They found there a Jesus who looked like them—a person with brown skin, a victim of oppression. They discovered a Jesus whose message was love, affirmation, and freedom, a Jesus who came to take his stand with any who are oppressed. This was the Jesus the Apostle Paul described, the Jesus whom Paul advised us to imitate, saying:

> Have the same mindset as Christ Jesus: Who, being in very nature God, did not consider equality with God something to be used to his own advantage; rather, he made himself nothing . . . he humbled himself by becoming obedient to death—even death on a cross! (Philippians 2:5–8)

In the historical Jesus, we find the embodiment of God's love for justice. In his life on earth, we come face to face with a Divine Being who experienced the pain of rejection, of poverty, of political oppression—and yet rose above them all with his message of liberation and love. This is the true message of Christ. "Racism is the ultimate denial of the Gospel," said Archbishop Desmond Tutu, "and it cannot be but that all believers would oppose vehemently this false gospel that would have people place their hope of salvation in a pseudo-gospel."

"Above all," Ignatius tells us, "remember that God looks for solid virtues in us, such as patience, humility, obedience, abnegation of your own will—that is, the good will to serve God and our neighbor in God." Ignatius points us to a spirituality that has nothing to do with white Jesus, a false god of superiority, intolerance, and injustice.

In the Second Week of the Spiritual, Ignatius asks us to focus on humility. He defines humility at its deepest, most authentic level as total identification with Jesus:

> I so much want the truth of Christ's life to be fully the truth of my own that I find myself, moved by grace, with a love and a desire for poverty in order to be with the poor Christ; a love and a desire for insults in order to be closer to Christ in his own rejection by people; a love and a desire to be considered worthless and a fool for Christ, rather than be esteemed as wise and prudent according to the standards of the world.

Ignatius's words challenge us with this question: Can we see Jesus in the lives of those who have been oppressed? Are we willing to serve the true Jesus, a person of color?

Journal

How do you picture Jesus? Write an honest description in your journal. Ask yourself:

- Is my picture of Jesus historically accurate? Why or why not?

- How have my ideas about Jesus' appearance been shaped?

Next imagine that you have just been introduced to Jesus—and he is a Black man. Are you surprised? Write in your journal about your reaction to a Black Jesus.

Now picture yourself having a conversation with this black-skinned Jesus. Write in your journal what he has to say to you. At the end of your conversation, consider whether you feel you have come to know Jesus in a new way.

For Further Reflection

The coming of Christ means a denial
of what we thought we were.
It means destroying the white devil in us.
Reconciliation to God means
that white people are prepared
to deny themselves (whiteness),
take up the cross (blackness)
and follow Christ.

—JAMES CONE

Prayer

Jesus, forgive me if I have ever worshipped
a false version of you.
I want to be open now to your full reality.
Give me the humility to seek you out
in the experiences and insights of people of color.
Show me where I am still clinging
to any notions of superiority.
Help me be willing to learn new things
from those whose experiences
have been different from mine.
Reveal yourself to me in new ways, I pray.

DAY 3

Outsiders and Insiders

People of Color in a White World

Humanity despised and rejected him.
He knew what it was to suffer;
he understood grief and brokenness.
He was one of those people others refuse to look at.
We not only despised him;
we failed to even think about him.

—ISAIAH 53:3 (AUTHOR'S TRANSLATION)

I am at wondrous peace with the world
so long as I do not make war on it ...,
but let me go forth to the camp,
and you will see the whole city rise up against me
while I fight on every side.

—IGNATIUS OF LOYOLA

*It dawned on me with a certain suddenness
that I was different from the others...
shut out from their world by a vast veil.*

—W.E.B. DUBOIS

Before his conversion, Ignatius worked hard to fit in with the elite class of his day, a group of people who enjoyed good food, fine clothes, and constant entertainment. When it came to the high-ranking nobility of his day, Ignatius longed to be an insider, someone accepted and admired.

After his conversion, he disengaged himself from these people. Now, he identified himself with the poor—but he did not stay quietly in the background of life for very long. Soon, he began to preach informally to anyone who would listen to him. In doing so, he brought on himself the attention of the Spanish Inquisition.

Historians speculate why the Inquisition was so interested in Ignatius. One theory is that it was because he was a spiritual advisor to "women of doubtful reputation." The Inquisition also suspected he was too closely connected to people of Jewish blood. At any rate, his actions put him at odds with the accepted morality of his day. Twice, he was imprisoned and questioned at length about his beliefs. Although he was eventually acquitted both times, he was forbidden to preach for the space of three years.

Obviously, Ignatius did not allow himself to be permanently silenced, but even after the organization of the Society of Jesus, he and his followers faced interference and opposition from the Spanish monarchy, as well as from other religious orders.

Many religious institutions of the day were imposing "purity-of-blood" rules to exclude anyone with Jewish ancestry. Ignatius, however, welcomed Jewish converts, and several of the early prominent Jesuits, including the order's second superior general, came from Jewish families. Ignatius refused to identify himself with the antisemitic oppression and hatred that was so common in sixteenth-century Spain.

One day, as Ignatius was sitting around the dinner table with his followers, he remarked that he wished he too came from Jewish ancestry, because then he would have the same blood as Jesus. Following Jesus was far more important to him now than fitting into society, even though his identification with Jesus put him in direct conflict with the dominant culture around him.

Ignatius was well aware of what was going on. In a letter to one of his followers, Isabel Roser, he wrote:

> You speak of the enmities, the intrigues, the untruths which have been circulated about you. I am not at all surprised at this, not even if it were worse than it is. For just as soon as you determined to bend every effort to secure the praise, honor and service of God our Lord, you declared war against the world, and raised your standard in its face, and got ready to reject what is lofty by embracing what is lowly, to accept indifferently honor and dishonor, riches and poverty, affection and hatred, welcome and repulse, in a word, the glory of the world or all the wrongs it could inflict on you. If we wish absolutely to live in honor and to be held in esteem by our neighbors, we can never be solidly rooted in God our Lord.

The man who had once wanted so much to be accepted as an insider had willingly become an outsider. He was no longer welcome in the society he had once inhabited.

People of color feel a similar lack of welcome in a white-dominated society. We are outsiders even in our own country. Our outsider status is deeply rooted in American history.

After Emancipation, as Blacks moved to cities to look for work, many white people were uncomfortable welcoming them as neighbors into their communities. The common practice was for Blacks to be relegated to the less desirable sections of a city—"across the tracks," for example. The "Black sections" of a city came to be known for their poverty and crime. They were considered unsafe places for a white person to venture.

What most whites failed to recognize was that people of color felt equally unsafe in white spaces. The 1970s and 1980s brought "fair housing" laws, school integration, and "affirmative action," allowing many people of color to be assimilated into the middle class—and yet we are always aware that we have ventured into a white world. Meanwhile, many people of color still live in segregated neighborhoods, while their children attend schools that are largely nonwhite.

As a Black man, I am all too aware when I drive or walk through a white neighborhood that I am more likely to be surveilled by police. The possibility of being stopped, questioned, harassed, or even arrested is very real to me. Recent events have proven to me that it can be dangerous to drive while Black, to walk while Black, to shop while Black.

When people of color venture into white spaces, they are often perceived as a threat (as Christian Cooper was when he was birdwatching in Central Park). According to sociologist Elijah Anderson, the "ghetto is always in the background" of white people's minds, shaping how they see any person of color they encounter. "Today, black people inhabit all levels of the American class and occupational structure," Anderson notes.

> They attend the best schools, pursue the professions of their choosing, and occupy various positions of power, privilege and prestige. But for the ascendant black upper middle class, in the shadows lurks the specter of the urban ghetto.

We still struggle to be seen as insiders rather than outsiders.

This is something that challenges me personally. I claim a sense of belonging in my religious order, the Jesuits. Our bond as a group of brothers—sinners, yet loved by Christ—is stronger than the division and racial discrimination that still lingers in our midst. Our love for each other is genuine; when we meet, we always celebrate each other's presence. And yet I never know when I will suddenly plunge out of that sense of belonging into the awareness that I am a person of color in a white world.

This happened to me yet again in early 2021 when I joined a group of Jesuits for a conference in Michigan. On the last day of the conference, we had a meal together, enjoying the chance to catch up on each other's lives. Afterward, I was in the kitchen washing dishes, when one of my brothers called to me, "Patrick! There's a police officer outside by your car. You'd better move your car so you don't get a ticket."

With my hands wet with dish soap and my heart racing, I ran outside. At the same time, I was saying to myself: *Okay, Patrick, stay calm. Go sit in your car, put your hands on the wheel, don't make any sudden moves. When the police officer talks to you, say, Yes, sir. No, sir. Thank you, sir.*

When I reached my car, I found a Black police officer there talking to a white man. I opened my car door and got inside, then waited for the officer to come speak to me. He asked me for my driver's license, took my information, and then gave me back my license. "You're okay," he said.

"Thank you, sir," I answered and got out of my car.

When I did so, the white man ran at me, jabbing my chest with his finger. "This n****r killed my grass, Officer!" he shouted. "If you hadn't been here, I would have killed him. He killed my grass!"

The police officer and I exchanged glances. "That's okay, Patrick," he said. "Get back in your car and move it. Let me take care of this."

While all this was happening, one of my Jesuit brothers came outside to see what was going on. For some reason, he did not join me, but instead, went back inside without saying anything. Though I was grateful for the presence of the Black police officer, I felt very alone.

As I opened my car door, I could hear the white man still shouting: "That n****r killed my grass!" I looked down at the grass beneath my car's tires. It was brown and dry, as grass normally is near Lake Michigan in early March. I could not have killed the grass because it was already dead. I noticed a sign that said parking was allowed on this stretch of the road; the land belonged to the city, not to the white man who was still yelling, "I should have killed him."

"The evil man is ready to suspect others," wrote Ignatius, "like a man attacked by giddiness who thinks that all things are whirling round him, not from any fault of theirs, but because of the disturbed humors of his own head." This white man definitely had disturbed humors. He saw me only as a Black man who had dared to park his car in front of a white man's house. I wasn't carrying a gun. I had done nothing threatening. I had not even raised my voice. And yet he suspected me of being so dangerous that I deserved to be killed. My only crime was that I was an outsider, a person of color who had ventured into a white space.

In the Second Week of the Spiritual Exercises, as we focus on the life of the historical Jesus, we see a person who also was an outsider from the moment of his birth. According to the Gospel of Luke, when Jesus' parents journeyed to Bethlehem, they were denied a room. Jesus was born outside the safe spaces of his society, in a stable. "He came to that which was his own, but his own did not receive him," the Gospel of John tells us (1:11).

The Nativity story is foundational to the message Jesus brought. Again and again throughout the Gospels, we see him identifying with those who are out of place, marginalized, and ignored. He touches people his culture considered unclean; he breaks the taboos of his people and spends time with a woman of Samaria; he converses with Greeks and others outside his own ethnic group; and even as he is dying, he talks to the criminal who is on the cross beside him. He dies as a marginalized person "outside the city gate" (Hebrews 13:12)—outside the acceptable boundaries of his society.

Throughout his life, Jesus listened to outsiders and affirmed their identities. He validated their lives, even as he also identified himself with them. He speaks to us through the Gospel stories, telling us that those who are marginalized have important truths to tell, truths that insiders may never have had the chance to learn. Those who are unwelcome and unwanted have experienced firsthand the meaning of Jesus' life. They recognize their vulnerability and their dependence on one another; they know that their deepest identity cannot come from material wealth, education, social status, or physical health. The insiders of this world have much to learn from them.

Throughout the Gospels, Jesus describes the Reign of Heaven, a place where outsiders become insiders in the best meaning of that word. He invites us to join him in a reality where no one is excluded. He calls us to let go of our privilege and superiority and instead, find our identities with those who have been disenfranchised, pushed out, and rejected.

As one of Jesus' most loyal followers, Ignatius of Loyola recognized that he was called to be an outsider in his society. Only from this position could he work for all to become insiders in the Divine Reign. "Let us, then, go to him outside the camp," wrote the author of the Book of Hebrews, "bearing the disgrace Jesus bore. For here we do not have an enduring city, but we are looking for the city that is to come" (13:13–14).

The racist society in which we live will not endure. The new city—the holy society that God calls us to build—will be founded on justice, equality, and love. In Jesus, those who were "once far off have now been brought near" (Ephesians 2:13). The outsiders are welcomed, respected, and protected.

That is the goal I work toward. I hope it will be your goal too.

Journal

In some sense, we have all experienced the feeling of being an outsider. Write in your journal about a time when you felt rejected and ignored. How does this experience help you to better relate to people of color?

Next, use your imagination to spend some time sitting in the stable with Baby Jesus. Picture him as a Black baby. Hold him in your arms. Think of all the spaces you move in during the course of your everyday life. Imagine yourself carrying this Black child with you into each setting. What work will need to be done to ensure that he is safe in each place? Consciously welcome him into each setting. Promise him that you will work to ensure he is safe and loved wherever he goes. Describe all this in your journal.

For Further Reflection

This nation needs to be a family,
and a family sits down for its dinner at a table,
and we all deserve a place together at that table.

—JOHN LEWIS

Prayer

Embracing God,
You grace each of us
with equal measure in your love.
Let us learn to love our neighbors more deeply,
so that we can create
peaceful and just communities.
Inspire us to use our creative energies
to build the structures we need
to overcome the obstacles
of intolerance and indifference.
May Jesus provide us the example needed
and send the Spirit to warm our hearts for the journey.

—U.S. CONFERENCE OF CATHOLIC BISHOPS

DAY 4

Epiphany

The Revelation of God in Children of Color

Jesus said, "Let the little children come to me,
and do not hinder them,
for the kingdom of heaven belongs to such as these."

—MATTHEW 19:14

May we always care for our children,
not counting the cost,
so that they may . . . always know their infinite worth.

—POPE FRANCIS

Now is the time to make justice
a reality for all of God's children.

—MARTIN LUTHER KING JR.

In the Second Week of the Spiritual Exercises, Ignatius asks us to consider the Epiphany. According to the Gospel of Matthew, "Wise Ones" (perhaps today we would call them shamans) followed a star from faraway lands to Bethlehem, where they met the Child Jesus and gave him gifts of gold, frankincense, and myrrh. The story is important because it indicates that from the very beginning, the Incarnation was intended not only for the Jews but for all people. As Ignatius came to understand, Christ not only reaches out to all people, but he is also revealed in all people.

According to the Gospel story, the Wise Ones came from the East, which could have meant anything from Persia to China. As early as the eighth century, however, one of the Wise Ones was described as a Black man. By the fifteenth century, the story of the "three kings" was considered to symbolize the world's three known continents—Europe, Africa, and Asia—indicating that Christ's message was global in scope. Throughout the early years of the Renaissance, artists portrayed the Black Wise One as a man with a noble bearing. His image had a regal self-possession and authority, a sense of gravitas and grace. His humanity is clear.

The Epiphany story is also about the fear of a privileged people (represented by Herod), threatened by the coming of a child who could upset the status quo. Herod tries to enlist the Wise Ones in his agenda of oppression—but they choose to protect the Divine Child from Herod's violence. Instead of reporting to Herod the whereabouts of the Child, they take another path home. As I think about this story, I find myself asking: What would our world look like if we too chose a path that protected

God's children? What would it take for us to make the safety of children our priority?

The Maasai, one of the most well-known African tribes, value their children as the center of their culture. When Maasai people greet each other, they begin with the phrase, "How are the children?" The response is always: " All the children are well." This exchange not only affirms the community's peace and safety, but it also implies that the well-being of children comes first. The Maasai cannot be well as a people unless their children are well. The rest of the world could learn from this value system. Somewhere along the way, we forgot that our children must be treasured, protected, and entrusted with our future.

Desmond Tutu once told a story about the effects of apartheid on children. Black families were dumped, he said, "as you dump rubbish . . . in poverty-stricken barren resettlement camps." When he visited one of these camps, he encountered a little girl with her sister and widowed mother. "Does your mother get a grant or pension?" he asked the little girl.

"No," the little girl replied.

"What do you do for food?" Tutu asked.

"We borrow food."

"What do you do when you can't borrow food?"

"We drink water to fill our stomachs."

Tutu pointed out that at the time, South Africa was one of the world's largest exporters of food products. "Children were starving not because there was no food," he said, "not accidentally, but by deliberate government policy." Tutu went on to say that he told this child's story again and again so that the world would "never forget the totally unnecessary suffering inflicted on God's children in the name of racism."

I tell it here so that we should never suffer from a convenient amnesia and ever reckon that racism could somehow be a benign thing, that it could be made respectable. Racism is ghastly and evil and immoral and we must stand up against it and oppose it with every fiber of our being.

In our own country, many children of color continue to suffer the effects of racism, often in the form of violence and police brutality. In 2020, six-year-old Gianna Floyd witnessed her father's brutal murder in Minneapolis; later that year, in Wisconsin, Jacob Blake's four youngsters saw their father shot seven times in the back as he walked away from policemen. If Maasai tribespeople came to our continent, they could not honestly say that the children are well. We are failing them.

In my home country of Haiti, during the years I was a child, Francois Duvalier (Papa Doc) and his son Jean Claude Duvalier (Baby Doc) led a dictatorial regime rife with violence. My own father, a minister in the Duvalier regime, became a target of the opposition movement. However, when members of the resistance arrived at our home before dawn one day, planning to torture or kill my father, they saw me, a three-year-old, so they spared my dad and departed. Not all children in Haiti were so fortunate, but I am grateful for the consciences of these resistance fighters.

But where is our conscience today? Are we concerned that our children are confronted every day with the reality of death, that senseless killings and suffering due to racial injustice have become the norm in our land? How do these visuals impact our children?

Most children of color in the United States encounter racism in their daily lives. Researchers have found that the psychological and physical injuries due to exposure to race-based adversity, discrimination, and stress are harmful to children's development and well-being. Events that can cause racial trauma in children include threats of harm and injury, hate speech, and humiliation and shaming. Children also experience racial trauma when they hear about or witness another person's suffering. Negative experiences can cause lifelong psychological damage in young people, and this in turn results in a traumatized society.

The damage racism causes children isn't only psychological. A 2020 study published in the *Pediatrics* journal found that Black and Hispanic children between the ages of twelve and seventeen are significantly more likely to die from police shootings than their white peers. The research, conducted over sixteen years, found that Black children were six times more likely to be shot to death by police than white children, while Hispanic children's risk of death was almost three and a half times higher than that of white children.

Violence is not the only thing that puts our children at risk. Black infant mortality rates are more than twice as high as those of whites, and Black babies are more than three times more likely to die from complications due to low birthweight, thanks to multiple factors that include poverty, less availability of good prenatal care, and poorer medical care in general for minority families (sometimes shaped by unacknowledged biases on the part of medical personnel). One study found that a Black baby born in Wisconsin is more likely to die than a baby born in the developing nations of Colombia, Jamaica, Venezuela, or Tunisia. In 2021, the Centers for Disease Control and Prevention released a report that the vast majority of children dying from COVID-19 are Hispanic, Black, or Native American. Another study reported in *Pediatrics* in 2020 found that children of color are more than three times more likely to die after a surgery. Children are even more fragile than adults when they lack adequate health care, nutrition, and shelter.

Racism's destruction is not confined to children of color; white children also suffer, though in different ways. As James Baldwin wrote, "Children have never been very good at listening to their elders, but they have never failed to imitate them." White children absorb racism from the adults in their lives. As a case in point, Kyle Rittenhouse a seventeen-year-old from Illinois, shot several people with a semiautomatic rifle in the name of "protecting" a business from protestors from the Black Lives Matter Movement. A decade earlier, Deryl Dedmon, a Mississippi teenager, and his friends (a group of white teenagers) robbed and repeatedly beat a Black man named James Craig Anderson; when they were done, Dedmon drove his pickup truck over Anderson, causing fatal injuries. Sadly, these are not isolated incidents. The US Justice Department reported that teenagers and young adults account for a significant proportion of our country's hate crimes, both as perpetrators and as victims. "Hate-motivated behavior, whether in the form of ethnic conflict, harassment, intimidation, or graffiti, is often apparent on school grounds," the report stated. Dr. Maria Trent, from the American Academy of Pediatrics, has commented that our children are "watching our words, our behavior—they're waiting for us to teach them differently for a healthy future."

We have forgotten to take care of the most vulnerable members of our family. We claim to love our children, but our behavior demonstrates neglect. "A society which abandons children severs its roots and darkens its future," said Pope Francis. This reality makes my head spin and my heart ache.

Ignatius said, "Listen long and willingly, until they have finished what they wanted to say." Are we listening to our children? Can we hear what they are saying to us? Can we hear what the child in the Epiphany story is staying to us?

Children in Bible times were not valued. They certainly weren't normally given gifts worth what would have been millions of dollars in today's world. And yet the Epiphany story places a child at the very center of the action. We might miss the importance of that if later in his life, Jesus hadn't made a point of treating children with respect and tenderness. He publicly and lovingly embraced a child, something that normally only a woman would have done. On another occasion, he told his followers to welcome children, who were considered to be at the lowest level of his society, demonstrating that even the most marginalized are important within the Divine embrace. By honoring children, Jesus was deconstructing his society's structures of power and privilege.

Was Jesus himself traumatized by the violence that surrounded his infancy and childhood (the possibility of his own murder at Herod's hands, as well as Herod's slaughter of all the male babies)? Was this why he said as an adult:

> If anyone causes one of these little ones . . . to stumble, it would be better for them to have a large millstone hung around their neck and to be drowned in the depths of the sea. . . . Such things must come, but woe to the person through whom they come! (Matthew 18:6–7)

Jesus taught that children have inherent dignity. They understand the Reign of Heaven better than adults do (Matthew 18:2). He also said, "Whoever welcomes one such child in my name welcomes me." Are we welcoming Christ's presence in children of color? Or are we rejecting him, endangering him, just as Herod did?

The Maasai people know that protecting the young and the powerless is a priority. They understand that their well-being as a society depends on that of their children. How would our society change if we too made all children's health and safety our priority? What would our world look like if we could say, with conviction, "All the children are well"?

Journal

Imagine that you are one of the three Wise Ones who come to the home of Mary and Joseph—but this time, the Holy Family are people of color living in the twenty-first century. Picture yourself sitting and watching the young Jesus play on the floor while you talk with his parents. Describe in your journal what you see and feel.

Now imagine that you are talking with Mary. Tell her about the dangers her son will face as he grows up. What does she say to you in response? What might she ask you to do to protect her son? Include this conversation in your journal.

For Further Reflection

We know that by two years old,
children are already consuming racist ideas.
They're already discerning whom to play with
based on kids' skin color,
and so if we wait till they're ten or fifteen,
they may be a lost cause, like some of us adults....
And so we have to be ever vigilant.

—IBRAM X. KENDI

Prayer

O God of justice, you sent your Christ
to establish your realm of freedom
and peace on earth as in heaven.
Prosper every effort to challenge arrogance,
prejudice and fear, and to thwart
all forms of discrimination, degradation and oppression.
Through the one who died at the oppressor's hands,
Jesus Christ, our redeemer, who lives and reigns with you
and the Holy Spirit, one God, now and forever.

—DENNIS MICHNO

DAY 5

The Story of the Good Samaritan

People of Color Are My Neighbors

Love your neighbor as yourself.

—MATTHEW 22:39

*Love is shown more in deeds
than in words.*

—IGNATIUS OF LOYOLA

*Neighborliness is nonspatial....
[We are called to love our] neighbor directly,
clearly, permitting no barriers between.*

—HOWARD THURMAN

The world was expanding during Ignatius's lifetime. Explorers like Vasco de Gama and Christopher Columbus had proven that the Earth held unknown lands, inhabited by people far different from Europeans. While many Europeans were already viewing these lands and peoples with the eyes of acquisition and profit, Ignatius challenged his followers:

> See the various kinds of persons: first, those on the face of the earth, in all their diversity of dress and appearance, some white and some black, some in peace and others at war, some weeping and others laughing, some healthy, others sick, some being born and others dying.

As we too consider this wide range of humanity, Ignatius then asks us to "hear what the Divine Persons say, that is, 'Let us work the redemption of the human race.'" Ignatius believed we are called to participate in the work of universal redemption, for this is the work of Jesus, which he has given us to share.

The Gospel of Luke tells a story that sheds light on how Jesus viewed the work he calls us to. When a religious expert comes to Jesus and asks, "What do I have to do to obtain the life that endures forever?" Jesus responds with a question of his own: "What do you think the scriptures say?"

The man replies, "Love the Lord your God with all your heart and with all your soul and with all your strength and with all your mind, and love your neighbor as yourself" (Luke 10:27).

Jesus agrees that's the right answer, but the man is still hoping to find a loophole, so he asks, "Who is my neighbor?"

The question of how I define my neighbor is still relevant today. Is my neighbor someone who lives geographically close to me? If so, then I am exempt from caring for those who are suffering in other parts of the world. Is my neighbor someone who looks like me, who believes in God the same way I do, who comes from the same socioeconomic class as I do? If so, then I am exempt from caring for people of color, people from other faith traditions (or no faith traditions), and people who have less (or more) money than I do. These are the attitudes that permit people to show genuine kindness to people like themselves, while they are indifferent or even cruel to those who seem "strange" or "other."

These are also the same attitudes that allowed the Ku Klux Klan to choose, with no sense of irony, the motto "Not for self but for others." According to one early Klan leader, Klansmen were to "be knit together as the members of our body, each co-operating with the other; so closely and vitally connected that when one member suffers the whole body suffers." Another Klan leader wrote, "Who can look upon a multitude of white robed Klansmen without thinking of the equality and unselfishness of that throng of white robed saints in the Glory Land?" The KKK newspaper, *Night-Hawk,* declared, "Be hospitable to your fellow Klansmen, he is one of many who are many in one, devoted to a common pledge and pledged to a common cause." Racism makes use of the same loophole the religious expert thought he'd found.

But then Jesus tells a story about a man who has been beaten and left half dead beside the road. In the story, two members of the religious elite walk past without stopping. Then a Samaritan comes by. Although the Jews despised the Samaritans (almost as much as the KKK despised Black people), the Samaritan stops to help the injured man. He puts medicine on his wounds, bandages him, and brings him to an inn where he can recover. The next day, the Samaritan goes on his way, leaving money with the innkeeper for the injured man's ongoing care.

"Which one of these was a neighbor to the man by the side of the road?" asks Jesus.

"The one who showed mercy," replies the religious expert.

Jesus was being his usual tricky self when he told this story. He wasn't only saying we should be willing to be inconvenienced for the sake of compassion. By making the hero of the story a Samaritan, rather than having a Samaritan be the wounded man lying by the road, Jesus turned people's expectations upside down. It is not the insider who condescends to show mercy to the outsider, but rather the other way around: the outsider is the one who understands what it truly means to be a neighbor. He is the one who comprehends Jesus' message better than the religious experts do.

As I wonder how I can apply this story to today's racism, I find myself thinking about Dylann Storm Roof, a young white supremacist. In 2015, Roof pretended to study the Bible and pray with the Black members of Emanuel AME Church in Charleston, South Carolina—and then he opened fire on them, killing nine and injuring another. In the days, weeks, and years that followed, the Emanuel congregation surprised the world by voicing their forgiveness of Roof. "I will never be able to hold her again, but I forgive you," the daughter of one victim said. The sister of another said, "We have no room for hating, so we have to forgive. I pray God on your soul."

At first glance, it seems to me that if Roof is anyone in Jesus' story, he's whoever the attacker was—the guy who beat up the man and left him to die. But then I have to look again, and when I do,

I realize that Roof is actually the dying man. He's been mortally wounded by white supremacy, no longer able to function as part of the living Body of Christ. His hatred has separated him from the Source of life. When I read the story this way, I wonder if the religious elite who failed to help the dying man aren't much like white Christians who condemn racism from the other side of the road—but then pass on by, reluctant to get their hands dirty, unwilling to be inconvenienced. White Christianity did Roof no good, while Emanuel's Black congregation let their mercy flow out to him.

The Jews needed the Samaritan to show them their own sin and woundedness. White people need people of color in a similar way. The path to enduring life always lies through the human being who is bleeding by the side of the road—and wherever we see oppression and suffering, that is where our neighbor is. Our love of God and our love of others cannot be separated.

The story of the Good Samaritan also helps me better understand the way many whites define racism versus the way people of color define it. Whites often think that racism is confined to a person's attitude and actions; *they* didn't enslave anyone, lynch anyone, or insult anyone, so racism isn't *their* problem. They are like the two religious men who walk on by the wounded man. There's no need to get involved, they think, when the problem has nothing to do with them.

People of color, however, see the larger definition of racism, the entire system that pervades our society. In Jesus' story, he's not concerned with who caused the problem. Passersby are responsible simply because the problem exists. The pain of our neighbor—who is all humanity—demands that we take action.

I can also see how this applies to the controversy over the statement "Black lives matter." People who insist that "all lives matter" are missing the point. Of course all lives matter—but Black lives are the ones bleeding by the side of the road. To fail to respond to that call is to show the smug indifference of the religious elites in Jesus' story. As Ignatius said, "Spend whatever is necessary on the care of the sick; we who are well can easily manage with dry bread, if there is nothing else." Are you willing to let go of your privileges, Ignatius asks us, so that others can finally have what they've always needed?

Historian Jamar Tisby explains that "Black lives matter" was not only a rallying cry for protests,

> but it also acted as an assertion of the image of God in black people. In Christian anthropology, saying that black lives matter insists that all people, including those who have darker skin, have been made in the image and likeness of God. *Black lives matter* does not mean that *only* black lives matter; it means that black lives matter *too*.

In the Spiritual Exercises, Ignatius challenges us to open our eyes, both to our own interior lives and also to what is really going on around us. In our compartmentalized, polarized world, it's all too easy to stay on our own side of the road, turning our eyes away from the ugliness of oppression. Jesus calls us to get involved—to spend our time, money, and energy to make a difference in the lives of others.

Are you willing to open your eyes? Will you cross the road?

Journal

The year 2020 seemed to be a turning point that opened our eyes and hearts to the reality of racism. But how do we do more than pay lip service to this new awareness? We may speak out on social media—but are we demonstrating an active commitment to being an ally to people of color? Are we doing anything to bring about actual change? It's hard to answer questions like these. Take some time now to write your responses in your journal. Be aware that the tendency to feel uncomfortable, confused, and helpless as you think about racism can trigger a desire to "stay on your own side of the road."

Activism starts with a deeper commitment to understand. This means "crossing the road" so you can begin to see into others' experiences. One way to do this is to read. Here are a few suggestions of books that may expand your understanding:

- *The Color of Compromise: The Truth About the American Church's Complicity in Racism* by Jemar Tisby

- *I'm Still Here: Black Dignity in a World Made for Whiteness* by Austin Channing Brown

- *Between the World and Me* by Ta-Nehisi Coates

- *Kindred* by Octavia Butler

- *Beloved* by Toni Morrison

- *How to Be an Antiracist* by Ibram X. Kendi

- *The New Jim Crow: Mass Incarceration in the Age of Colorblindness* by Michelle Alexander

- *Reproductive Injustice: Racism, Pregnancy, and Premature Birth* by Dána-Ain Davis

If you'd rather listen to a podcast, the *Seeing White* series on Scene On Radio (https://www.sceneonradio.org/seeing-white/) is a good way to take a deep dive into the real-life experience of racism. And the PBS series *This Far by Faith* explores the history of African American religious belief, starting with the earliest Africans brought to America and covering the Jim Crow era, the Civil Rights era, and into the twenty-first century. (It's available from Netflix.)

As you read or listen, use your journal to keep track of your emotions and reactions. What surprises you? What makes you angry? What makes you cry? What inspires you? What other responses do you feel? Don't be afraid to be honest.

For Further Reflection

A Good Samaritan is not simply one
whose heart is touched
in an immediate act of care and charity,
but one who provides a system
of sustained care.

—JAMES A. FORBES

Prayer

When you see me closing my eyes, Jesus,
unwilling to see the pain of my neighbor,
remind me of what you said about the Good Samaritan.
Make me willing to look,
to go out of my way, to spend my resources,
to do anything I can to help.
I know I can't pretend I love you,
unless I'm willing to give myself away in love
to my neighbor, whomever she is,
whatever he looks like,
wherever they lie bleeding.

DAY 6

The Fullness of Christ

The Ignatian "Magis" as an Antidote for Racism

*I have come so that all people may have life
and have it in all its fullness.*

—JESUS (JOHN 10:10, AUTHOR'S TRANSLATION)

*We should keep the greater service of God
and the more universal good
before our eyes as the norm
to hold ourselves on the right course.*

—IGNATIUS OF LOYOLA

Our maturity will be judged
by how well we ... continue to love one another,
to care for one another, and cherish one another
and seek the greater good of the other.

—DESMOND TUTU

Better, greater, more. These are words that Ignatius of Loyola uses again and again in his writing. He is constantly challenging us to go further, climb higher, dig deeper. Ignatius never calls us to move from "bad" to "good," as though goodness was some definitive destination; instead, he challenges us to be constantly moving from "good" to "better." Pope Francis said, "For Ignatius the journey is not an aimless wandering; rather, it translates into something qualitative: it is a 'gain' or progress, a moving forward, a doing something for others."

Today, Jesuits use the Latin word *magis* (which means "more, greater") to express this aspect of Ignatian spirituality. Jesuits will also tell you that *magis* refers to "the greater good" or "the universal good." The word implies a sense of Divine abundance; it speaks of the Divine Reign that is big enough to be all-inclusive, leaving no one out. The concept of *magis* is in direct contradiction to the fear that there's never enough to go around. It leaves no room for perceiving others as a threat to my own economic safety and well-being.

I'm reminded of the Gospel accounts of Jesus feeding the multitudes. In these stories, the disciples demonstrate the scarcity attitude that is still so common in our world. "Send the people away," they tell Jesus. "It would cost too much to feed them. We just don't have enough resources to go around."

Jesus of course turns their expectations upside down, as he so often does. Using what is clearly too small an amount of food, the disciples are somehow able to feed everyone who is there. The exact methodology Jesus uses to achieve that feat really doesn't matter. What does matter is the point that these stories make: as we interact with others, God calls us to use a theology of abundance as our starting point. Scarcity, competition, hoarding, and greed have no place in the Reign of Heaven.

Nor is there any space for being generous only to our own group of people, for Divine generosity reaches past all barriers. All the benefits of white privilege cannot compare with the "fullness of life" that Christ offers us. In fact, to insist on remaining within the tight confines of privilege is to cut yourself off from the universal abundance of God's Reign.

The Ignatian concept of *magis* challenges us to work for conditions that allow all people and communities to experience the fullness of life. It asks us to dedicate ourselves to the common good of all by defending the dignity and human rights of everyone, including people of color. *Magis* sees past the concept of *us and them*, for in reality, there is only *us*. The "greater good" means everyone, with no one excluded or pushed to the edges.

Ignatius's mystical experience on the riverbank outside Manresa showed him a reality constantly flowing with God's creative generosity. It gave him an optimistic confidence in God's ability to supply whatever was needed, which in turn encouraged him to set no limits on what the Divine Spirit might do through him. He worked to make himself constantly and actively available to the Spirit, always alert and ready. In a letter he sent to some students, he said, "We should never postpone a good work, no matter how small it may be, with the thought of later doing something greater."

As we consider the struggle against racism, we can be both encouraged and challenged by Ignatius's life and teaching. From him, we learn that the work of antiracism must be balanced with constant prayer and discernment, so that we do not act on impulse or out of ego. Our dependency on prayer is Christ's way of meeting us in the midst of life's complications and confusion. Ignatius calls us to also live our lives in cooperation with God's ever-flowing and generous action. As always, he perceived the intersection between the spiritual world and the physical in very real and practical terms. We can see this reality lived out in his life.

At one point in the early years of the Society of Jesus, he sent Father Andrea Galvanello to a parish in the village of Morbegno for a temporary placement. After six months, the villagers had become so fond of Father Galvanello that they wrote to Ignatius, asking that he be allowed to stay as their permanent pastor. Ignatius refused, which made a lot of people very upset with him. He resisted their pressure, however, saying that Father Galvenello was needed in other places. To confine him to one village would mean "the greater good would be lost for the sake of the lesser." Ignatius knew that God's openhanded bounty cannot be limited by human territory or division. It doesn't belong to just one group of people but to all people.

Having the wisdom to live that out in the real work can be tricky, though. Once again, it takes prayerful discernment. Ignatius wasn't saying that the good of the many outweighs the needs of the few (a philosophy that has historically led to elitism and marginalization). Instead, his perspective means we don't settle for simplistic answers. We take the time to seek out the root causes behind oppressive systems, and we tackle the roots rather than the symptoms. Although wounds may need bandaging now, what we are really working for is a world where no wounds are inflicted. This isn't easy. We will need to work with others who know more than we do. And yet again, we will need to undergird all our actions with prayer.

Magis also does not mean to simply do more and more things until we become exhausted workaholics. Author Marcus Mescher cautions that "*magis* isn't about the best, the most, or the greatest. It's not an exhortation to give more generously, raise our standards for excellence, or add more items to our to-do list." In the Spiritual Exercises, Ignatius warns us against the overcommitment that can lead to burnout, and we need to keep this in mind as we commit to the work of antiracism. Engagement with antiracism cannot be treated as a social-justice–themed extravaganza, a frantic display of ever-increasing commitments. To prevent this from happening, again and again we need to undergird our anti-oppression work with prayer. Always, Ignatius reminds us that we need both contemplative and active engagement with the work of God. That is the only way we will have the energy to work unceasingly against racism.

And we must always be aware of the temptation to allow our egos to become inflated, even when we are working hard for others. We want to do great things for God and for the world—but doing so can be an opportunity for pride and ambition. In the work of antiracism, this can lead, ironically, to whites perceiving themselves as superior to the people they are trying to help. It can contribute to the "white savior" tendency, where white people seek to "help" and "empower" people of color, rather than affirming and respecting the richness and potential already within these communities. With this attitude, antiracist work can be all about white people, rather than people of color, and white people may arrogantly seek to impose what works for them into settings they don't truly understand. 'To seek to bring all people to salvation by one road is very dangerous," Ignatius wrote. "The one who does so fails to understand how many and various are the gifts of the Holy Spirit."

"*Magis* is less about doing *for* others," Mescher explained, ". . . than it is about being *with* others." He goes on to say:

> This is how we come to better understand who people are, what they most deeply desire, and how we can partner with them to work toward that end. Not to be the voice of the voiceless (which may be well-intended but can nonetheless be paternalistic), but to be advocates, allies, and accomplices in the work for justice and peace.

Ignatius himself understood the temptation to mingle ego with even our most generous impulses. "Up to his twenty-sixth year he was a man given to worldly vanities," he said in his autobiography, "and having a vain and overpowering desire to gain renown, he found special delight in the exercise of arms." After his conversion, he laid down his arms, but his essential nature was not changed; he still dreamed of achieving fame, though now his dreams focused on spiritual escapades rather than worldly ones. In his autobiography, he spoke of "vainglory"— pride in our own achievements—and said that the "remedy" is to "refer all my affairs to God, to aim at offering Him all the good that I find in myself, to acknowledge that these are all His gifts, and to thank Him for them." Ignatius described a method for doing this:

> The persons who make the Exercises will benefit greatly by entering upon them with great spirit and generosity toward their Creator and Lord, and by offering all their desires and freedom to him so His Divine Majesty can make use of their persons and of all they possess in whatsoever way is in accord with His most holy will.

Jesuit author William A. McCormick wrote that Ignatius directs us to "an open-handed disposition to give and share of what one has, with the assumption that one has a great deal to share," thanks to God's abundant generosity. "We may be quite sure that God is always ready to be liberal," wrote Ignatius, "provided he find in us a deep and true humility. . . . The closer you bind yourself to God and the more wholeheartedly you give yourself up to his supreme majesty, the more liberal he will be to you." *Magis* requires that we be "magnanimous," said McCormick, which "is a readiness to 'think big,' to embrace projects of grand scope." Magnanimity, he said,

> is not something one does ultimately out of sheer, exuberant voluntarism, but in cooperation with God. . . . [It] will not always mean doing things that make us feel good or important, nor will it always immediately satisfy our desires. Rather, one should be magnanimous in a way that can be sustained in the long-term through difficult ministries and because one discerns a call from God to be so—not just because one so desires. Mag-

nanimity is a fundamentally hopeful attitude, trusting in God's control of history. The magnanimous person knows that his work will bear fruit despite human foibles, for God ultimately directs the work.

"God would readily give us much greater graces," wrote Ignatius, "if our perverse wills did not stand in the way of his bounty.

For Ignatius, our work is always the work of Jesus: achieving salvation—the state of spiritual and physical well-being—at both the individual and communal levels. "The purpose of this Society," he wrote, "is not directed merely at the salvation and perfection of the souls of its members by divine grace, but rather by the same grace to work assiduously for the salvation and perfection of the souls of our neighbors." Ignatius sometimes got angry if he heard that someone was seeking to join the Society of Jesus in order to find help and healing for himself. Instead, Ignatius wanted people who understood their individual well-being depended on the well-being of others. As Martin Luther King Jr. wrote, "We are caught in an inescapable network of mutuality, tied in a single garment of destiny. Whatever affects one directly, affects all indirectly."

Within the living, breathing, interwoven community that is Christ's Body on earth, the "greater good" is always expressed through our interdependent solidarity with one another. A live-and-let-live attitude has no room in this reality, for our existence is tied up with one another. "The earth, its inhabitants, and the environment," wrote Pope Francis, "are all part of a common good, belonging to all and meant for all." This is the reality of the Reign of God. "Love," wrote Ignatius, "consists in the mutual sharing of goods."

As we learn from Ignatius of Loyola, we will soon recognize that the word *progress* is fundamental to his spirituality. In our own individual lives, we have been learning and growing ever since we were born—and we don't graduate from the school of life until we die. The same holds true in anti-oppression movements. Antiracism work is not a sprint but a marathon. We aren't done with this work until we are dead.

Ibram X. Kendi has a bestselling book titled *How to Be an Antiracist*. Although I have used his book in numerous talks and writings, the title is a bit troubling to me. In Ignatian spirituality, "salvation" means constant growth; it is a way to see God's movement in human lives. In antiracism work, this constant growth can be understood best by conjugating the verb in the active form: as antiracism *working*. Perhaps a better title for Kendi's book would be *Becoming an Antiracist*, because this work will take a lifetime of intentional engagement. It is not enough to sit in a book club for two weeks discussing Kendi's book and then say, "I am now antiracist." Instead, antiracism work requires our constant and continued work, just like our faith requires constant and continual work with Christ to bring about the Reign of Heaven.

In his spiritual exercises, Ignatius asks you and me to make room for grace, to allow ourselves to enter into a new culture of growth, where we constantly continue to improve—as the community around us also improves. "Praise and thanksgiving to God our Creator," wrote Ignatius, "from whose infinite liberality and bounty overflows the fullness and fruit of all good things."

Antiracism work is a lifelong commitment, a new declaration of personhood, a new identity, and a sacramental way to continuity. Meeting Christ in others in the daily now will help us progress together toward the Divine Reign. "The *magis* is the fire," said Pope Francis, "the fervour of action that rouses us from slumber," so that all of us can move forward to become better, greater, stronger.

Are you ready to begin?

Journal

Consider the following questions, and then write your answers in your journal:

- Do I live my life from the assumption that I have access to God's abundance? Or do I operate from an assumption of scarcity, afraid I will not have enough to meet my needs?

- Whichever my answer was to the previous question, how does that affect the way I live my life? What impact does it have on my attitudes toward others, especially people of color?

- In what areas of my life might God be calling me to put into practice the concept of *magis*?

- Can I name specific actions I can take in the next week that will express my belief that God is calling me to grow bigger, better, stronger? How will those actions be connected to the well-being of my larger community?

For Further Reflection

You have been called by God ...,
not with a mere general intent,
but with an investment therein
of your whole life and all its activities,
you are to make yourselves a continual sacrifice
to the glory of God and the salvation of your neighbor....
From this you can realize what a noble
and royal way of life you have taken up:
for not only among human beings
but even among angels, there is no nobler activity
than that of glorifying their Creator
and bringing God's creatures back to the Divine Spirit....
Offer yourself to God on your neighbors' behalf every day:
... may God also graciously continue
and increase his gifts in you all,
so that you will steadily persevere and grow.

—IGNATIUS OF LOYOLA

Prayer

Help me, Spirit of Love,
to grow ever stronger, ever deeper,
ever better at serving you.
Use all the talents and abilities you have given me
to bless your Body here on earth.
Show me how to work for communities of color
so that each of their members may experience
the fullness of your life.

DAY 7

Christ as Reconciler

Building Bridges of Justice

All this is from God,
who reconciled us to himself through Christ,
and has given us the ministry of reconciliation.

—2 CORINTHIANS 5:18

God ... values love's works
more than its words.

—IGNATIUS OF LOYOLA

Bridges are built
not with passivity or avoidance

*but with the deep, hard work
of seeking to understand.*

—LATASHA MORRISON

n the beginning, Ignatius's conversion was focused only on himself. Aware that his way of life had separated him from God, his first impulse was to go on pilgrimage to Jerusalem. He intended to live where Jesus had walked, and thus align himself more completely with Jesus. His plan fell through, however, when he was denied permission to remain in the Holy Land, and he was forced to return to Europe. Then, as he progressed along his spiritual path, he came to realize that the best way to align himself with Jesus was by reaching out to others.

Jesus' work on earth focused on building bridges between human beings and God, welcoming all those who were suffering and oppressed into a new harmony in the Reign of Heaven. The Apostle Paul wrote that "God was pleased to have all his fullness dwell in Jesus, and through him to reconcile to himself all things, whether things on earth or things in heaven, by making peace through his blood, shed on the cross" (Colossian 1:19–20). Ignatius now made this Divine work of reconciliation his own.

During Ignatius's lifetime, the world had expanded in ways that had been unimaginable even a generation earlier. Explorers were crossing the Atlantic, and the Protestant Reformation was introducing new ideas. Ignatius recognized that these changes offered both huge challenges and immense opportunities. Even in the early years of his Society, he began sending Jesuits to India, Japan, Ethiopia, and South America. He was working to build bridges to God all around the world.

Education had played an important role in his own spiritual growth, and he became convinced that education was also essential to the work of Jesus. Through his efforts, the Society of Jesus established a network of colleges around the world. As the general superior of the new order, he never forgot the mission God had given him. He continued to build bridges that would reach out to the marginalized, even setting up a house for women who had once been prostitutes. Constantly, he reminded his followers that their other work should never prevent them from visiting the sick and reaching out to children. Ignatius also allowed Christ to use him as a bridge between divisions in specific and practical ways: he acted as mediator between Pope Paul III and the King of Portugal when they were at odds; he brought a resolution to a mortal feud between two villages; and he was able to reconcile an estranged married couple, the Duke Asconcio Colonna and Jane of Aragon.

Like Ignatius, we too are called to the work of reconciliation. As we finish the Second Week of the Spiritual Exercises, he continues to challenge us to not only identify with Jesus during his time on earth but to also commit ourselves to Jesus' ongoing work of salvation. "He has committed to us the message of reconciliation," wrote the Apostle Paul. "We are therefore Christ's ambassadors as though God were making his appeal through us" (2 Corinthians 5:19–20). Jesuit father Pedro Arrupe defined reconciliation as "breaking down the barriers that separate humans from God and from each other." Father Arrupe also noted that as part of the "ministry of reconciliation," we are called to "break down the barriers of prejudice between classes and peoples and races."

Racial reconciliation does not come easy. The divisions in our society are old and ingrained. It will take hard work on everyone's part to build the bridges we so desperately need. As Ignatius understood, building the Reign of Heaven requires active engagement. Prayer is good—but it is not enough if we are not following it up with action. Ignatian author Vinita Hampton Wright pointed out that while "forgiveness is an interior discipline, reconciliation is an outward process."

The word *reconciliation* comes from Latin roots that meant "to bring together again, to restore union." Note that reconciliation does not mean "homogenization"—making everyone the same. It is not assimilation. It does not erase the identity of one group so that it becomes immersed and overwhelmed by a dominant group. Reconciliation is not what happens in a "melting pot."

But historically, America has had a sense of a selective culture. If a person brings a nonwhite culture, such as Mexican or African, we don't say, "Work with us to build bridges between us so that we can better understand you. Help us to learn from you because we recognize that you bring new ideas and cultural wealth." No, instead we say, "You must assimilate to our culture because you are too different." This is what America's so-called melting pot really is—a crucible that tries to melt everyone down to one uniform flavor, the flavor of being white. If you can't manage to lose everything that makes your flavor distinct and unique, then you are not welcome in the pot. This is contrary to the spirit of reconciliation that Jesus modeled.

The United States prides itself on being diverse and open to all cultures, but the inherent racism that drives American laws and policies says the complete opposite. The Constitution and the Bill of Rights guarantee us certain "inalienable rights," and yet we receive these freedoms only so long as we align ourselves with white American values and ideals. Progress is being made; the US Congress has more members who are people of color than ever before. Still, if a Black Muslim woman wants to become a CEO, she has to work a thousand times harder than a white man would to get there.

The problem with defining America as a "melting pot" is that it implies, "If you come to America, you have to lose all sense of your cultural identity." That's a very different statement from the call Jesus gives us to build bridges of reconciliation. Helen Neville, who researches racial identity at the University of Illinois, has stated, "Mentally healthy African Americans possess a positive African American identity grounded in African cultural values." The same holds true for other communities of color. The pressure to be assimilated into white America is psychologically wounding.

The bridges that reconciliation builds allow communication and mutual enrichment to cross back and forth. But that does not mean that differences are erased. In fact, reconciliation affirms that differences are real. If I were exactly the same as you, we would have no need to have a bridge of understanding span the difference between us. But because we are different from one another, we need to find ways to create harmony, harmony that is based on respecting each other's unique qualities rather than eradicating them. The Book of Revelation describes the people of God as coming from every "nation, tribe, people, and language" (7:9). Clearly, God sees and celebrates our differences. We are not expected to assimilate into a homogeneous mass. The melting-pot perspective has no place in the Reign of Heaven.

Nor can the Reign of Heaven be achieved by wishes and make-believe. We must be willing to see the reality of people of color.

"White people used to call me an Oreo," a woman once told me. "Black on the outside, but white on the inside. They meant it as a compliment. They were saying I was just like them on the inside, even though I have black skin. I never told them I was offended. But now those same people tell me they don't even see that I'm Black, 'cause they say they 'don't see color'—and that's even worse. It's like my identity has become invisible. It's like they're crossing me out."

And yet many white people believe that "colorblindness" is a virtue. James Baldwin had this to say about the attitude that underlies comments like "I don't see color": "American white men still nourish the illusion that there is some means of recovering the European innocence, of returning to a state in which black men do not exist. This is one of the greatest errors Americans can make." Although race is a societal reality (not a biological one), it is nevertheless very present in our world, causing real-life suffering. To pretend otherwise is a luxury that only white people can claim.

Colorblindness prevents us from seeing the world as it really is, with all its problems. Although it can be scary to see suffering and injustice, to refuse to do so is to deny the experience of our fellow humans. To love our neighbors, as Jesus explained in the story about the Good Samaritan, we must be willing to see their pain. We must listen to their stories and honor their experiences. In doing so, we will be forced to acknowledge our differences—and that's a good thing.

Genuine listening asks that we let go of our presuppositions and assumptions. Pastor Rich Villodas made the point that "the ones who need to listen first and more often are the ones who have enjoyed the privileges of power." He went on to say:

> racial justice and reconciliation require a self-emptying. . . . Those without power are already empty. The onus is on those with power to listen deeply, relinquishing their social power for the greater good of reconciliation. In this country, our White brothers and sisters need to lead the way in listening deeply to the stories and experiences of people of color.

Reconciliation starts between individuals, but it must extend throughout the structure of society. It must work to undo centuries of injustice. To that end, every year since 1989, Representatives John Conyers and Shelia Jackson have presented to Congress a bill that's known as H.R. 40, which, if passed, would create a commission to examine the possible payment of reparations to African Americans descended from enslaved persons. The name of the bill recalls the Reconstruction Era, when the government promised newly emancipated people "forty acres and a mule," a guarantee that was never actualized. If it had been, it would have been the first government attempt at reparations after slavery.

President Andrew Johnson, however, overturned the order, and Reconstruction failed. The Union troops withdrew from the South, and the Black Codes—laws designed to limit the freedom of African Americans and ensure their availability as a cheap labor force—replaced slavery. Then came Jim Crow segregation and federal redlining (the practice of marking minorities' neighborhoods as having high credit risk, and then denying loans to anyone who lived in that area). These in turn fed into inequities in the justice system, causing mass incarceration of people of color; underfunded schools for children of color; and the dangerous racial bias of police officers.

Slavery remains as one of the ugliest roots of inequality and exclusion. Historically, much of our nation's wealth was built on the backs of Black Americans: corporations, universities, and elite families made and maintained their fortunes through the institution of slavery. Economic disenfranchisement is at the core of our nation's history. Representative Sheila Jackson has said that "though remote in time from the period of enslavement, these racial disparities in access to education, health care, housing, insurance, employment, and other social goods are directly attributable to the damaging legacy of slavery and racial discrimination."

H.R. 40's goal is not to make white people feel guilty, and it's not asking for some form of official apology. Instead, it seeks to build a society where Blacks are truly equal to whites. Many people, however, see that goal as being either unrealistic or uncalled for. One Republican Senator stated, "I don't think that reparation for something that happened one hundred and fifty years ago, for whom none of us currently living are responsible, is a good idea."

Senator Jackson, however, has said she will not give up on H.R. 40. By passing this bill, she stated, "Congress can start a movement toward the national reckoning we need to bridge racial divides. Reparations are ultimately about respect and reconciliation—and the hope that one day, all Americans can walk together toward a more just future."

The trauma of the Black community (and other communities of color as well) requires the hard work of reconciliation. It is time to put into everyday practice the spiritual reality that the Apostle Paul described in his letter to the Ephesians:

> But now in Christ Jesus . . . he himself is our peace, who has made the two groups one and has destroyed the barrier, the dividing wall of hostility. . . . His purpose was to create in himself one new humanity out of the two, thus making peace, and in one body to reconcile both of them to God through the cross, by which he put to death their hostility. He came and preached peace to you who were far away and peace to those who were near. For through him we both have access to the Father by one Spirit. Consequently, you are no longer foreigners and strangers, but fellow citizens with God's people and also members of his household. (2:13–19)

Another way to envision reconciliation is to acknowledge that trauma causes wounds—and wounds need to be healed. Racism is an ongoing and ancient trauma that is still wounding all of us today. Reconciliation seeks practical, real-life healing, at the community level as well as the interpersonal. True reconciliation starts with restored relationships and then moves to restore what racism has taken from the oppressed. As author and theologian Chanequa Walker-Barnes wrote, "Racial reconciliation must be invested in the healing, bodily, mental, socio-emotional, spiritual and financial wounds inflicted by White Supremacy."

The process will be complicated, requiring immense coordination of all our skills and resources. Building bridges across racial division is not for the faint of heart. As human beings, we all tend to defend our identities and shore up our power, rather than emptying ourselves to make room for justice and understanding. But that is no excuse for avoiding the work. As Ignatius would remind us, "The more desperate things seem, the more must we hope in God."

The late Catholic priest and author Henri Nouwen wrote in his book *The Wounded Healer* that all human beings suffer—"and that a sharing of suffering can make us move forward." We need to be aware of our own wounds, the ones we carry as well as the ones we inflict, and how they shape the way we perceive the world.

Our world has been wounded for hundreds of years. It's time to heal. Are you willing to join in the hard work of reconciliation?

Journal

Have you ever said (or thought), "I don't see color"? If so, what did you mean by that? What did you perceive as the positive value of that statement? Can you understand now why that statement is counterproductive to the work of reconciliation? Write your answers to these questions in your journal.

Now imagine you are sitting with Jesus, talking with him about the meaning of reconciliation. Describe in your journal what Jesus might have to say about the work of reconciliation. Finally, consider how you can put his words into action within your life.

For Further Reflection

Repairing what's broken is a distinctly biblical concept,
which is why as people of faith
we should be leading the way
into redemption, restoration, and reconciliation.

–LATASHA MORRISON

Prayer

Most merciful God,
we confess that we have sinned against you
in thought, word, and deed,
by what we have done,
and by what we have left undone.
We have not loved you with our whole heart;
we have not loved our neighbors as ourselves.
We are truly sorry and we humbly repent.
For the sake of your Son Jesus Christ,
have mercy on us and forgive us;
that we may delight in your will,
and walk in your ways,
to the glory of your Name.

The Grace I Keep

I ask for the grace of unlimited commitment
to the work of Jesus in the world around me.
*May I see and make use of opportunities
to fight racism each and every day.*

WEEK THREE

The Crucifixion and the Suffering of People of Color

In the Third Week of the Spiritual Exercises, Ignatius calls us to focus on the suffering and death of Jesus. We walk with Jesus on his journey toward Calvary, and then we stand beside the cross as he dies. Ignatius instructs us "to ask for sorrow, compassion, and shame because the Lord is going to His suffering for my sins." Jesuit author Michael Ivens wrote that this is "the key to the contemplative union-in-action by which through his apostles Christ continues to labor and suffer in the mission of the Church in the world." We participate in Jesus' solidarity with human pain and weakness.

The suffering of Jesus continues today, for he is present in all who are oppressed and wounded by injustice—and we are called to join also with this pain. As well as Jesus' physical agony, during the Third Week we share with him the experience of abandonment, rejection, and hopelessness, for this too continues to take place in our world. People of color have been failed by the social, economic, and political systems on which we all depend. They have been thrust into dead-end situations they cannot escape; they have suffered the endless cost of racism in our world.

As Jesus' companions through this Week, we cannot hold ourselves separate from this. We must allow ourselves to viscerally feel the agony of racism's violence and inequity. In the words of Jesuit author Gerald M. Fagin, "To enter into the dying of Jesus, we must give up attachments that divide our hearts. We must let go of egoism and individualism, of prejudices and biases, and of insensitivity to the suffering of the world around us."

What does this mean for us as we read about immigrant children separated from their parents on our borders? Or when we watch videos that show Philando Castile being shot by a police officer in his own car, while a four-year-old sobs in the backseat? Do we care when we read this statement released from the director of the US Centers for Disease Control and Prevention: "What we know is this: racism is a serious public health threat that directly affects the well-being of millions of Americans. As a result, it affects the health of our entire nation"? Are we outraged when we hear about the growing practice of disrupting students' virtual classes with messages such as "Burn like a Jew" and "Kill all Jews, Gas them all"? Do we shed tears when we read stories of elderly Asians assaulted in the street because of the suspicion that they brought COVID-19 to American?

In Week Three, Ignatius challenges us to no longer hold ourselves separate and indifferent from stories like these. Instead, we are to allow our own hearts to be broken—and in doing so, join ourselves at an even deeper level with Jesus.

The very reality and meaning of the Crucifixion
calls us to see the exclusion and violence,
recognizing in the racist patterns of our society
the false condemnation of Pilate, the insults of the crowd,
the sense of desolation that Jesus experienced
as he hung on the cross.
And we, as individuals, must in shame
recognize those moments when we have contributed
to the terrible legacy of racism in our world
by joining the crowd shouting insults,
by remaining silent in the face of racial injustice,
and by nailing Christ to the cross
in the form of his sisters and brothers.
… Jesus' sacrifice on the cross shows us a pathway
of radical love and sacrifice
that is the only lasting antidote to the racism
that lurks within the human heart.

—ROBERT W. MCELROY

DAY 1

Christ's Choice

The Power of Love vs. the Power of Hate

Who shall separate us from the love of Christ
Shall trouble or hardship or persecution
or famine or nakedness or danger or sword?
… No, in all these things we are more than conquerors
through him who loved us.

—ROMANS 8:35, 37

Attend as much as you can to this,
that you regard one another kindly,
so that there may be natural love between you.

—IGNATIUS OF LOYOLA

*Jesus rejected hatred
because he saw that hatred meant death to the mind,
death to the spirit,
and death to communion with his Father.
He affirmed life; and hatred was the great denial.*

—HOWARD THURMAN

The goal of the Third Week, writes Ignatius, "will be to ask for an intimate knowledge of our Lord, who has become human for me, that I may love him more and follow him more closely." In the First Week, we considered our complicity with systemic sin. Now, as we follow Jesus to his death, we see the real-life pain and suffering that sin causes.

Throughout the Gospel accounts of these days of Jesus' life, we hear him assuring his followers of his steadfast love. Even as his own friends deny and betray him, he never sinks into anger or hatred. Like any human being, he is afraid as he realizes his death is fast approaching. "My soul is overwhelmed with sorrow," he tells his disciples (Matthew 26:38). And still he consistently affirms love in the face of hatred and continues to commit himself to a path of self-surrender. "Yet not what I will," he prays to his Father, "but what you will." Neither Jesus' unique relationship with God nor his own Divine powers shield him from suffering and death. The death he will endure will not be pretty or antiseptic; it will be violent, cruel, and bloody. It will demonstrate Jesus' absolute solidarity with all who are oppressed and hurting in our world.

Many Christians repeat the formula, "Jesus died for my sins." Some Christians go so far as to say, "If I was the only person in the world, Jesus would have still died for me." While I believe there is truth in both these statements, they focus on an equation that includes only Jesus and me. I lay claim on Jesus' suffering as something that benefits me spiritually—and then I look no farther. More and more, however, Black theologians are affirming an alternative way to look at Jesus' confrontation with sin and evil: they see it as a demonstration of solidarity with the oppressed and suffering throughout history.

The authorities could not tolerate Jesus' embodiment of justice; they perceived his radical message of love as a threat to their own power. Like many societies throughout history, those who enjoy power want to protect their privilege, and they do so by oppressing the vulnerable. This is what happened in Jesus' day, and it has happened again and again around the world, including in the United States, where the new nation expanded across land stolen from its original inhabitants, while it prospered and grew strong from the labor of Africans, Asians, and other immigrant groups.

We'd like to think that the terror and brutality of racism is something that lies only in the past, that we live in more enlightened times. The reality of recent events denies us that comfort. In 2017, a man at a gas station in Washington State began shouting at three brothers who had stopped for gas. "Go back to your country! I'll shoot you!" He then got in his car and threatened to drive directly into the brothers, swerving at the last minute. Later, he told police that he hated "those people," and added, "They shouldn't be in our country."

This story is just one of thousands. Sometimes the victims are Muslim; other times they are Jewish. They could be Asian,

Latinx, or Black. In 2020 in Iowa, a white woman intentionally ran over a fourteen-year-old Latina girl who was on her way to her high school; the driver admitted to trying to kill the girl because "she looked Mexican." In 2021 in New York City, a man, woman, and their one-year-old child were slashed with a knife; the violence was apparently triggered by the fact that the family was dressed in traditional Hasidic garb. Also in New York City, a white man knocked a sixty-five-year-old Asian woman to the ground and then punched and kicked her, shouting, "You don't belong here, you Asian!" The same year, a Michigan man confronted a group of Black teenagers at a state park, shouting at them that they had no right to use the public beach; he then hit one of them in the face with a bike lock, knocking out the boy's teeth. Since 2010, the FBI has had reports of about six thousand hate-crime incidents every year. Government studies show the real number is as high as 260,000 per year, since many victims are afraid to report the crimes—and nearly 90 percent of the nation's law enforcement agencies fail to submit hate crimes to the FBI.

What do we do in the face of hate? Ignatius of Loyola challenges us to follow the example of Jesus, who countered hate with love. "In your relationships with one another," wrote the Apostle Paul, "have the same mindset as Christ Jesus" (Philippians 2:5). Jesus' commitment to love exposed him to the powers of hate—but the God of love refused to let violence and death have the last word. The God of love is also present every time a person of color suffers a hate crime. Now it is up to us to make sure that hatred isn't allowed to have the last word in our world today.

As always, Ignatius teaches us that love must be put into action. Action starts with a changed heart and mind—but good thoughts and strong emotions alone are not enough. If we use Jesus as the pattern for the way we live our lives, then we will actively seek ways to protect people of color from the forces of hate.

The Southern Poverty Law Center (SPLC) says that hate must be countered with acts of goodness. "Sitting home with your virtue does no good. In the face of hate, silence is deadly. Apathy will be interpreted as acceptance—by the perpetrators, the public, and—worse—the victims. If left unchallenged, hate persists and grows."

The SPLC offers some practical suggestions. "Hate must be exposed and denounced," it counsels. "Do not debate hate group members in conflict-driven forums. Instead, speak up in ways that draw attention away from hate, toward unity. . . . You can spread tolerance through social media and websites, church bulletins, door-to-door fliers, letters to the editor, and print advertisements. Hate shrivels under strong light."

Psychologists often talk about the human fight-or-flight response to danger. Jesus demonstrated another option, the option that Martin Luther King Jr. made his own when he fought racism with nonviolence. In King's words, Jesus "knew that the old eye-for-eye philosophy would leave everyone blind. He did not seek to overcome evil with evil. He overcame evil with good. Although crucified by hate, he responded with aggressive love."

King pointed out that loving our enemies, as Jesus challenged us to do, does not mean we like our enemies. It does not mean we accept their hate-driven actions. Instead, King said, we join with God in bringing love into the world.

Civil rights leader and theologian Howard Thurman said that because we carry the Image of God, we have the responsibility to love in ways that make us immune to our world's fear, hatred, and deception. As we identify with Jesus rather than our own egos, we find in God a sense of security and deep well-being that empowers us to take action. "The person who is going forth to labor in the Lord's vineyard," wrote Ignatius, "should walk humbly toward that which is difficult and hard; for the rest of the building will be safely fixed if it is based on humility for its foundation." Summarizing what Jesus says to us, Thurman wrote:

> You must abandon your fear of each other and fear only God. You must not indulge in any deception and dishonesty, even to save your lives. … Hatred is destructive to hated and hater alike. Love your enemy, that you may be children of your Father who is in heaven.

Jesus made himself an ally for the poor and oppressed. He countered hatred with love. He chose love.

What do you choose?

Journal

The hate in the world can be overwhelming. We may respond by wanting to hide, by feeling helpless, by becoming numb, or by refusing to acknowledge how dangerous hatred truly is. Write in your journal about your reaction to this Day's reading.

Be honest about your feelings. Then read your journal entry to Jesus as a prayer, and ask him to help you find his presence in the midst of your feelings.

It can be hard to know how to take loving action, but many organizations offer helpful resources. Check out these websites, and then write in your journal ideas you could put into practice in your life.

- The Southern Poverty Law Center, "Ten Ways to Fight Hate: A Community Response Guide"
  https://www.splcenter.org/20170814/ten-ways-fight-hate-community-response-guide

- The Anti-Defamation League, "Join Us in Fighting Hate for Good"
  https://www.adl.org/take-action

- The Leadership Conference on Civil and Human Rights, "Resources to Hold White Nationalists Accountable and Combat White Supremacy"
  https://civilrights.org/heres-10-things-you-can-do-to-stop-white-supremacy/

- The United States Department of Justice, "Preventing Hate Crimes in Your Community"
  https://www.justice.gov/hatecrimes/preventing-hate-crimes-your-community

For Further Reflection

The story of the Christian tradition
might be conceived as a love story:
a narrative that identifies love at the heart of reality
but recognizes the deep challenges
that love is for human beings.
The history of modern Christianity, however,
has been an epic failure to love,
where the stories of Christian tradition
were mobilized for the self-love of White supremacy
and the destruction of non-White, non-Christian others.

—JEANNINE HILL FLETCHER

Prayer

Jesus, I want to follow you.
I want to be like you.
Teach me to love as you loved.
Teach me to stand up for love,
to push back against hatred.
Give me courage to identify with those who suffer.

DAY 2

Christ Accused and Found Guilty

People of Color as Innocent Victims

Pilate came out and said . . . ,
"I find no basis for a charge against Jesus."

—JOHN 19:4

I ask for what I desire.
Here is it what is proper for the Passion:
sorrow with Christ in sorrow;
a broken spirit with Christ so broken;
tears; and interior suffering
because of the great suffering
which Christ endured for me.

—IGNATIUS OF LOYOLA

*Theology must work out the relation
between the murderous crucifixion of Jesus of Nazareth
and the murderous crucifixion
of countless poor, excluded, and despised
children, women, and men.*

—M. SHAWN COPELAND

I n the Third Week, Ignatius asks us to think about the questions we asked ourselves during the Second Week. Are we ready to confirm our commitment to follow Jesus? Are we willing to follow him all the way? We pray for the strength to say yes to those questions as we enter into the experience of Jesus in the days and hours leading up to his death. As we walk with him through his last days, we are challenged to identify with people of color who were also innocent of any crime and yet were forced to suffer, just as Jesus did.

Jesus had a last meal with his friends, and then they went to the Garden of Gethsemane. Jesus wanted to pray, but he also needed the support of his friends during this time of fear and anguish. Instead, his friends fell asleep, leaving him alone with his anxiety. And then a crowd of people brandishing weapons interrupted his prayers. The religious authorities arrested him and put him through a mock trial. They blindfolded and hit him. "Who hit you?" they shouted each time they struck him. "Can't you use your powers to tell? Prophesy!" Witnesses were called who told lies about Jesus.

Jesus had threatened the authority of the religious leaders, revealing their hypocrisy, and now they declared him guilty of blasphemy. After the death sentence was handed down, the crowd continued to beat him, spitting in his face. As dawn broke, they dragged him to the Roman authorities to be killed.

In his book *The Cross and the Lynching Tree,* James Cone makes the case that the mob violence that drove Jesus to his death parallels the lynching mentality in the United States during the late nineteenth century and into the second half of the twentieth century. "In the 'lynching era,'" Cone wrote, ". . . white Christians lynched nearly five thousand black men and women in a manner with obvious echoes of the Roman crucifixion of Jesus. Yet these 'Christians' did not see the irony or contradiction in their actions." (Although Cone refers to five thousand lynching victims, most historians agree that this number only reflects known lynchings, and that the actual number is most likely much higher.)

Lynching denied those who had been accused of a crime their right to a legal trial. In most cases, their crime, like Jesus' offense, did not exist. The reasons given for condemning a Black person to death include a range of acts, from voting to teaching children to read, from starting a chapter of the NAACP to mailing a Christmas card to a white person, and from driving or walking through a white neighborhood to having a consensual relationship with a white woman. Many times the only reason given for a lynching was that the person was Black. At Jesus' so-called trial, the crowd shouted, "Crucify him! Crucify him!"—and in a similar way, lynchings were often cheered on by angry mobs.

Cone gives this horrific but historically accurate description of lynchings:

> Burning the black victim slowly for hours was the chief method of torture. Lynching became a white media spectacle, in which prominent newspapers, like the *Atlanta Constitution,* announced to the public the place, date, and time of the expected hanging and burning of black victims. Often as many as ten to twenty thousand men, women, and children attended the event. It was a family affair, a ritual celebration of white supremacy, where women and children were often given the first opportunity to torture black victims—burning black flesh and cutting off genitals, fingers, toes, and ears as souvenirs. Postcards were made from the photographs taken of black victims with white lynchers and onlookers smiling as they struck a pose for the camera. They were sold for ten to twenty-five cents to members of the crowd, who then mailed them to relatives and friends, often with a note saying something like this: "This is the barbeque we had last night."

This account makes us cringe. It should. It's not exaggerated. It really happened, to real human beings, people innocent of any crime except for having black skin. Like Jesus, they were blameless—and like Jesus, they were condemned unjustly to an excruciating death.

One of the last reported lynchings in America took place in 1981, when Ku Klux Klan members killed nineteen-year-old Michael Donald, a technical college student who had never committed a crime in his life. The Klan, however, was angry about a court case involving a Black man accused of killing a white police officer. One Klansman said, "If a Black man can get away with killing a white man, we ought to be able to get away with killing a Black man"—so he and another Klansman went for a ride through Mobile's mostly Black neighborhoods until they spotted Michael Donald.

Donald was walking home after buying a pack of cigarettes for his sister from a convenience store. The two men pulled up beside him and asked for directions to a local club; then they forced him into the car at gunpoint. They took him into the woods, and when Donald managed to briefly escape, they chased after him, caught him, and beat him with the branch of a tree. While one man continued to beat Donald, the other wrapped a rope around his neck and pulled it tight. Then he slit his throat. Finally, the two men left Donald's body hanging from a tree.

Like Jesus, Michael Donald was an innocent victim who had committed no crime. Thankfully, lynchings are no longer commonplace in America—but innocent Black men continue to be accused of crimes they did not commit. Termaine Hicks is just one example.

In 2001, in Philadelphia, Hicks, a twenty-six-year-old father of one, was walking home when he heard a woman screaming. He used his cell phone to call 911—but when the police arrived on the scene, they mistook Hicks for the woman's attacker and shot him three times in the back. When they realized they'd shot an unarmed man who did not match the description of the attacker, the officers conspired to cover it up. They testified at trial that Hicks had lunged at them with a gun. Based on this lie, Mr. Hicks was convicted of rape, aggravated assault, possessing an instrument of crime, and terrorist threats. He was sentenced to up to twenty-five years in prison. When he came up for parole, he was denied because he still refused to admit his guilt.

Then, years later, thanks to the Innocence Project, both the chief medical examiner for the City of Philadelphia and an independent medical examiner concluded that Hicks was shot from behind—which meant he couldn't have been lunging at the police at the time. The gun the officers said they had found in Hick's pocket turned out to be the off-duty weapon of another Philadelphia police officer. In 2020, Termaine Hicks was released from prison.

But not every wrongly accused Black man is so lucky. In 2011, the State of Georgia ended Troy Anthony Davis's life with a lethal injection. Davis had been convicted of murdering a police officer, but he always maintained his innocence. He was denied his request to take a polygraph test, and there was no forensic evidence to convict him. Seven of the nine witnesses who had testified against him recanted their testimony, and DNA evidence did not support his conviction. Politicians from both sides of the aisle called for a stay of execution, as did the NAACP, the Innocence Project, and Amnesty International—but the State of Georgia refused to listen. On the morning of his death, Troy Davis shared this message with the world: "The struggle for justice doesn't end with me. The struggle is for all the Troy Davises who came before me and all the ones who will come after me."

Today, the struggle for justice continues. According to data from the National Registry of Exonerations, in the last decade dozens of imprisoned people—most of them Black men—have been exonerated of their crime. The Registry reported that Black people are seven times more likely to be wrongfully convicted of murder than white people are. In 2020, 52 percent of the people on death row were Black, even though Blacks make up only 13.4 percent of America's total population. This is not because Blacks commit more murders than white people; they don't. The skin color of the victim also plays a role in whether the death penalty is used. A 2019 study found that people accused of killing white people are found guilty and executed at seventeen times the rate of those convicted of killing Black people. Since 1976, when the death penalty was reinstated after a four-year suspension, nearly three hundred Black people accused of murdering white people have been executed, compared to only twenty-one white people accused of murdering Black people. Robert Dunham, executive director of the Death Penalty Information Center, has stated that "the modern death penalty is the direct descendent of slavery, lynching, and Jim-Crow segregation."

In Jesus' last moments, he prayed, "Father, forgive them, for they do not know what they are doing" (Luke 23:34). Moments before Troy Davis died, he made this statement: "I ask to my family and friends that you all continue to pray, that you all continue to forgive. Continue to fight this fight. For those about to take my life, may God have mercy on all of your souls. God bless you all."

Are you willing to pray for innocent people like Troy Davis? Will you allow your prayers to lead you to action? Will you take up the fight?

Journal

As you imagine Jesus being condemned to death on the cross, how do you feel? Picture yourself watching while he faces his crowd of accusers. Write about your reactions in your journal.

Now imagine the death of Michael Donald at the hands of the Ku Klux Klan. How do you feel this time? Are your reactions similar to those you felt as you pictured Jesus being condemned to die? Why or why not?

It's not pleasant to read stories like those included in this chapter—but however uncomfortable you feel after this Day's reading, sit with the discomfort; lean into it and allow it to challenge you. Write down things you want to learn more about. If you had the power to do absolutely anything in reaction to the feelings this Day's reading aroused, what would you do? What stands in the way of you taking this action? What could you begin to do to protect the lives of innocent people of color?

For Further Reflection

Suffering naturally gives rise to doubt.
How can one believe in God
in the face of such horrendous suffering
as slavery, segregation, and the lynching tree?
Under these circumstances, doubt is not a denial
but an integral part of faith.
It keeps faith from being sure of itself.
But doubt does not have the final word.
The final word is faith giving rise to hope.

–JAMES H. CONE

Prayer

Lord, Jesus Christ,
who reached across the ethnic boundaries
between Samaritan, Roman and Jew,
who offered fresh sight to the blind and freedom to captives,
help us to break down the barriers in our community,
enable us to see the reality of racism and bigotry,
and free us to challenge and uproot it
from ourselves, our society and our world.

—JOHN BUCKI, S.J.

DAY 3

Taking Up the Cross

The Work of Justice

*Whoever wants to be my disciple
must deny themselves and take up their cross
and follow me.*

—JESUS (MATTHEW 16:24)

*Let us go forth eagerly,
sure that whatever cross we have to bear
will not be without Christ, and that his aid
… will always be with us.*

—IGNATIUS OF LOYOLA

*Every man and woman is born into the world
to do something unique and something distinctive
and if he or she does not do it, it will never be done.*

—BENJAMIN E. MAYS

As the years went by and Ignatius grew in spiritual maturity, he continued to actively seek God's will for his life. The common thread was always this: he wanted to follow Jesus. Identifying with Jesus was what united Ignatius and his companions even in the years before the Society of Jesus formally came into being.

In 1537, on his way to Rome, Ignatius took time out from his journey to seek a greater understanding of how God wanted him to express his devotion to Jesus. According to his first biographer, Pedro Ribadeneira (who was one of Ignatius's companions), Ignatius "went into a deserted and solitary church some miles from the city to pray. There amidst the greatest fervor of his prayers, he felt his heart changed, and God the Father appeared to him, together with his most Blessed Son, who carried the Cross upon his shoulders." During this vision (known as the Vision at La Storta), Ignatius saw God the Father, "with exceedingly great love," give Ignatius and his companions into Jesus' hands. Ignatius came away from this experience with a renewed sense of optimism and commitment. He encouraged his companions to take heart, knowing that whatever "crosses" they were called to carry, Jesus would be with them. "The most sacred name of

JESUS was imprinted in his soul," wrote Ribadeneira, "with an earnest desire to take our Savior for his Captain, carrying his Cross after him."

This vision was not only vital to Ignatius's sense of his personal mission in life; it also shaped the entire focus of the Society of Jesus when it came into being. Everything Ignatius's followers did was an expression of their identification with the cross of Jesus. For the early Jesuits, this meant that they saw themselves as being called to actively participate in Jesus' "ministry of reconciliation" (which we discussed during Week Two on Day 7).

We have sometimes limited our understanding of the cross to each person's individual relationship with God. But scripture makes clear that the cross was not only for our individual healing and spiritual salvation. It also had another goal: the bringing together of people who had been separated by ethnic divisions. Jesus sought to "reconcile both groups to God in one body through the cross" (Ephesians 2:16). This is not secondary or incidental to our personal salvation; it is part and parcel of the healing work of the crucifixion. In Jesus' supreme act of self-giving on the cross, he demolished the barriers that separated people.

In three of the Gospel accounts of the crucifixion, a Black man named Simon the Cyrene helps Jesus when he stumbles beneath the weight of the cross. Ignatius believed that all of us are like Simon; we are all called to help Jesus carry his cross. We do this by becoming actively involved in bringing healing to our world. As author Adam Borneman wrote, "Taking up our cross and following Jesus means entering into the lives of 'the other'. . . . To the degree that we neglect this calling, we risk rebuilding the very walls that Jesus dismantled at Calvary."

Ignatius and his followers heard Christ's call to the work of reconciliation, and they worked hard to bring harmony wherever they encountered division, discord, and even outright warfare. Three years after Ignatius's vision at the chapel of La Storta, he was able to convince the people in a nearby village to give up the feuds that had been festering there for years. This was just one of many similar incidents. Warring factions had divided many Italian communities (remember Romeo and Juliet?), and the ongoing vendettas made violence and murder a part of everyday life. Ignatius and his followers worked hard to reconcile these war-torn communities. The early Jesuits brought the leaders of opposing factions together and acted as moderators for peace discussions. Many times they were successful.

Ignatius's understanding of the work of the cross also inspired him to do whatever he could to help society's outcasts—the sick, the imprisoned, the poor. He and his followers worked to get prisoners' sentences suspended, and they also concerned themselves with the injustice of unfair loan practices. Always, Ignatius sought to be part of the ongoing work of the cross, a spiritual work inseparably linked with the world's practical realities.

The trauma associated with the experience of racism is a part of our current world's realities. It is a trauma that calls for more than "thoughts and prayers." It demands the same active hard work that Ignatius and his followers devoted to the problems of their day as they sought to carry the cross of Jesus.

I too have experienced this trauma. I was fortunate, however, in that I was not born into it. Growing up in a household where my mom, dad, siblings, and everyone in our church were all Black, I never felt I needed to justify my identity or my presence in the world. I always believed in myself. As a boy, I thought

I had a superpower—the ability to excel at whatever I did—and my ego stretched out way past the end of my nose. But then, as an adult, I came to the United States, and for the first time, I questioned my own value. The near-daily assault of racist behaviors, both big and small, exhausted me. I began to feel numb, dissociated from a sense of my true identity.

I do not want to make this discussion about me. I only say this because I believe my experience is a taste of what every person of color experiences in this country. And I wonder: What would Ignatius do if he were alive today? What action would the cross of Jesus compel him to take?

People of color need to be able to reconcile the difference between the racist messages they receive and their reality as Divine image-bearers. All of us have a God-given right to a positive and strong sense of who we are. The humility that Ignatius called for never denied that reality but instead, always affirmed it. The cross of Jesus works to disrupt racist ideologies and institutions that negate the Divine identity of all people. This too is a work of reconciliation.

When I was a freshman in high school, I had the opportunity to travel to Moscow, Russia, for a week of cultural immersion. It was a rude awakening for me. I did not understand the language, I did not like the food, and I felt frustrated that people did things so differently from what I was accustomed to. The people I met did not seem very friendly or interested in getting to know me. Again and again, I had to remind myself of the lessons the nuns had taught me before my departure. Their script went something like this: "Patrick, expect to feel out of place when you are in a new country. Do not expect everyone around the world to be just like you or the culture from which you come. Be open to learning new ways of thinking and living. This is the way we build bridges. This is the way we become a larger community."

Since coming to the United States, I have often had a similar feeling as I had during my time in Moscow. I try to remember what the nuns told me. But I also can't help but wish that white America could hear the same lesson. If we could construct bridges between our differences—as Ignatius helped to build between the feuding communities of Italy—couldn't we begin to learn from one another? Instead of insisting that white culture is the norm to which all Americans must comply, couldn't we find a new and deeper way of being community?

Adam Borneman wrote that through the work of the cross, "we begin to see the world through the eyes of those previously estranged to us." He went on to say:

> We come to more deeply understand Jesus' constant reiteration that the issue is not whether we will extend the kingdom of God *to* the "other," but whether we will recognize that the kingdom of God is emerging *through* the other, that it is ushered in through the margins, through the forgotten, through what is foreign and alien to us.

Ultimately, Borneman concluded, "reconciliation is not something that we do, but something that God does through us by the power of the Holy Spirit."

The vision Ignatius had at La Storta of Jesus bearing his cross was something that stayed with him throughout his life. It became for him not only a source of encouragement and inspiration but also a frame of reference that shaped the way he engaged with the world. In the *Constitutions* he drew up for the Society of Jesus, he wrote, "It is likewise highly important to . . . accept and desire with all possible energy whatever Christ our Lord has loved and embraced. . . . For He gave us an example that in all things possible to us we might seek, through the aid of His grace, to imitate and follow Him, since He is the way that leads us all to life."

Jesus loved and embraced the stranger. Even as he prepared himself for his own death, he reached out in love to those around him. He gave everything he had, including his life, to the work of reconciliation and healing.

The work of the cross still continues in our world today. It calls us to join in Christ's work of justice and reconciliation for all the world. It asks that we love as Jesus loved—actively, practically, with the willingness to work hard and give of ourselves, so that we help to heal the trauma of racism.

Are you willing to make this work your own? Will you take up your cross and follow Jesus?

Journal

Carrying the cross of Jesus means making antiracism a way of life. Your commitment to the cross will shape in practical ways how you invest your resources, whether those be your time, your skills, your money, or something else. Theologian and activist Jemar Tisby suggests these possible ways to take direct action:

- Vote in your local elections. Identify your local prosecutor and ask about their perspectives on racial justice and the policies they advocate to address injustice and inequality.

- Support the take-down of Confederate monuments and flags in your area.

- Choose to read books by authors of color.

- When you witness acts of microaggressions or overt racism, call them out. Don't remain silent.

- Participate in local marches or protests. Raise awareness for them and widen the net of exposure. Invite friends to come with you. Post about them and start conversations on social media.

- Celebrate Juneteenth, the holiday that commemorates the end of slavery in the United States in 1865. Support instituting Juneteenth as a national holiday.

- Attend a Black church or another minority congregation. Stay after the service to get to know people. Talk with the pastor and explore opportunities to build relationships or partner in the community.

- Create something that speaks to racial justice. Write

a blog. Create a piece of artwork. Write a research paper. Write a song. Write a sermon. Host a forum.

- Donate money to organizations that advocate for racial and social justice. A few trustworthy organizations that actively fight against systemic racism include Be the Bridge (BTB), Equal Justice Initiative (EJI), Innocence Project, The Marshall Project, Southern Poverty Law Center (SPLC), Vera Institute of Justice, Prison Fellowship, and Black Lives Matter.

Does anything else occur to you? Write in your journal about practical ways you can carry the cross of Jesus as someone working to bring racial reconciliation and healing. Make a plan in writing for how, when, and where you will begin.

For Further Reflection

*Every day you are given opportunities
to make the world better,
by making yourself a little uncomfortable and asking,
"who doesn't have this same freedom or opportunity
that I'm enjoying now?"
These daily interactions are how systems of oppression
are maintained, but with awareness,
they can be how we tear those systems down.*

–IJEOMA OLUO

Prayer

Jesus, I want to follow you,
all the way to the cross.
I want to be like Simon the Cyrene,
who did not let you carry your cross alone.
Show me how I can bring the power of the cross
into every situation of
injustice and oppression I encounter.
I know I may stumble,
just as you did on your way to Calvary,
but I know you are by my side,
your hand outstretched to help me
get to my feet and continue on.
When the weight of racism overwhelms me, strengthen me.
When I'm tempted to despair, encourage me.
When I can no longer see the way, be my Light.
Jesus, I want to follow you.

DAY 4

Beneath the Cross

Where Do You Stand?

Near the cross of Jesus stood his mother,
his mother's sister, Mary the wife of Clopas,
and Mary Magdalene.

—JOHN 19:25

I shall make no attempt to evoke joyful thoughts,
not even good and holy ones about subjects like
resurrection and final glory,
but rather bring myself to grieve.

—IGNATIUS OF LOYOLA

Every human being is called to solidarity
in a world battling between life and death.

—IGNACIO ELLACURIA, S.J.

During this Week of the Exercises, Ignatius invites us to imagine ourselves standing at the foot of the cross as Jesus is dying. We know the familiar story of the crucifixion, but now Ignatius asks us to *experience* it. Bring the scene alive, he says, with all our senses. Hear the noise of the crowd, the groans of the men on the crosses, the weeping of the women who have gathered there. See the blood on Jesus' forehead, on his hands and feet, the sorrow on the face of his mother as she looks up at him, the color of the sky above your head, the rough wood of the beams that make the cross. Smell the odor of the dust beneath your feet, the stench of sweat and blood, the scent of moisture in the air. Let yourself stand there with Mary, looking up at her son.

As we enter into the experience of Jesus' Passion, Ignatius tells us, we should "begin with great effort to strive to grieve, be sad, and weep." Ignatius is not suggesting we manufacture these feelings. Instead, he is acknowledging that humans don't like to immerse themselves in negative emotions. We'd rather be numb. We'd rather avoid unpleasant things—like the sight of a man bleeding on a cross—so that we don't have to encounter our own emotions of disgust, sorrow, guilt, and fear. Allowing ourselves to enter this experience is hard work, as Ignatius knew. Author Charlotte C. Prather, in her book on the Spiritual Exercises, wrote:

When making the Exercises of the third week, I often had to pray for the grace even to want to experience them. Although on a conscious level I felt committed to this process and did in fact desire a closer union with Christ, what went on at other levels amounted at times to mutiny. My body would either refuse to sit still or else it would fall soundly asleep. My mind wandered freely. At times my brain felt like a badly tuned radio which was receiving at least three channels at once.

In the Middle Ages, followers of Christ often dwelt on the horrors of the cross, and artists portrayed the crucifixion in gory detail. Today, we'd prefer to sanitize the reality. Churches sometimes have images of the risen Christ floating in front of the cross, as though he was able to skip over the death-and-dying piece and go straight to resurrection. No matter how pretty we might try to make the crucifixion, though, Jesus' death was not joyful. He was not filled with jubilant triumph as he hung there dying. Instead, alongside his physical agony, he experienced the rejection of his friends, the humiliation of being stripped of his clothes, the loneliness and hopelessness of physical pain, and the abandonment of his Father. Perhaps for the first time in his life, Divinity was hidden from him. "My God, my God," he cried, "why did you forsake me?" (Mark 15:34). It is not easy to watch Jesus suffer in this way.

Experiencing another's pain is never fun. Even when we truly love the other person, we may be tempted to walk away. We find excuses to soothe our conscience: "I have other responsibilities that demand my attention," we say—or, "I can't do any real good anyway, so there's no point in staying." Even if we physically remain, we may find ourselves emotionally distanced, unable to be truly present to our loved one's suffering. "It's just too painful," we may tell ourselves, as though that excuses us, as though no one should expect us to expose ourselves to emotions that hurt.

Jesus' friends and followers had similar feelings. Wanting to protect themselves, most of them kept their distance from the cross. Judas had actively betrayed his friend, while the others had not, but still, most of them did not stay with him as he endured the cross. Out of the twelve disciples, only John was there with Mary and the other women.

Mary must have been in anguish as she watched her son die, but she could not leave him to suffer alone. She would rather go through the pain with him than abandon him. If she could have, she would have born the agony in her own body, so that he wouldn't have had to. She knew she was helpless to protect him, but still she chose to stay with him on his terrible journey through suffering.

Other women stood with her. Like the women of Argentina who in 1977 confronted the dictatorship that had stolen their children; like the Mothers of the Movement who are spreading the awareness of police brutality and racial injustice; and like Monifa Bandele, Jasmine Johnson, and Rosa Aka-James, mothers who are each fighting against the effects of institutionalized racism, the women at the cross courageously took their stand with the suffering.

Meanwhile, the others—all the people Jesus had healed and helped—stood their distance. They hung back where they wouldn't have to be confronted with the true agony Jesus was going through.

The tendency for whites to distance themselves from racism has a similar dynamic. Racism is painful to watch. It makes people feel guilty, uncomfortable, scared, angry, defensive. Rather than enduring these emotions, many people, usually unconsciously, don't let themselves experience the full horror of injustice and oppression. Despite the rise of hate crimes and white supremacist movements, recent research indicates that in the twenty-first century, apathy is what racism usually looks like.

As we've talked about racism so far in this book, we've mostly focused on acts of horrendous cruelty. Often, that's where our thoughts go when we think about racism. We remember the laughter of the Nazi guards at the death camps; we see the snarling face of a white man attacking an elderly Asian woman; we think of the jeers of the Ku Klux Klan as they watched a Black man burn to death. And those scenes do reveal racism's true ugliness.

But in the twenty-first century, racism also has another face. Think of Officer Chauvin's expression as George Floyd died beneath his knee, that look of bored disinterest. The video shows the officer's hands resting in his pockets, his sunglasses pushed back on his head. Annoyance briefly flickers across his face in response to the crowd that has gathered to plead for Floyd's life, but for the most part, he seems as unconcerned as if he were stepping on an insect on the ground. Meanwhile, the other officers watching seem equally unconcerned. They play with stones; they comment on the smelliness of Mr. Floyd's feet. They are indifferent to his agony.

Holocaust survivor and author Elie Wiesel once said, "The opposite of love is not hate, it's indifference." For the indifferent person, he went on to stay, the feelings of others are of "no consequence. . . . Their hidden or even visible anguish is of no interest." In Paul L. Wachtel's book, *Race in the Mind of America,* he wrote, "Perhaps no other feature of White attitudes . . . is as cumulatively responsible for the pain and privation experienced by our nation's Black minority at this point in our history as is indifference." Research psychologist Janet Helms estimates that about one-half of all white people are simply indifferent about the issues that impact people of color. It's not that they wish them ill; they simply don't care one way or another.

Various things make it easy for white people not to care. In many American communities, whites have little contact with people who are racially different from themselves. They only see living, breathing people of color on the news and in the media. Having never sat down at a table with a person of color, never talked with one, never seen firsthand the suffering of a person of color, it's easy to rely on stereotypes and misinformation. It's also more comfortable.

Janet Helms has said that when whites come face to face with the visceral reality of oppression and injustice, they are often thrown into guilt, confusion, uncertainty, and fear. These may have been the same emotions that Jesus' friends and followers were avoiding when they kept their distance from the cross. Like them, when we avoid the real-life pain of racism, we cut ourselves off from all our feelings. In this anesthetized state, we may be protected from fear and shame and sorrow—but it's impossible to feel connection or compassion.

Ironically, the "woke" white person—the person who has allowed herself to feel the reality of racism—often manufacturers still other defense mechanisms. Desperate to find a way to feel good about herself again, she tries to redefine herself as a "good white person," an antiracist, a righteous defender of evil.

We can see this narrative fleshed out in countless movies. Take *Freedom Writers* and *Dangerous Minds,* where a white teacher is able to transform teenagers of color into exemplary students. Or *Amistad,* where the white lawyer defends the rights of enslaved Africans. And then there's *Dances with Wolves,* where a white man helps a Native tribe escape the federal army. And *Remember the Titans,* where a white football coach helps a Black team in a game rigged by the white referees. These are all "feel-good" movies that most white people would never consider were racist in any way.

But take another look. The protagonist in each of these movies is a white person. We feel good about his heroism and courage. We identify with him, rather than the people of color he "saves." We want to be him, so that we too can feel good about ourselves. As we watch these movies, we associate ourselves with the hero's struggles—not with the situation endured by the people of color.

Racism is an immense problem with no fast, easy, or simple solutions. In the face of that immensity, it's uncomfortable to accept our own responsibility for the problem. White people didn't choose to be born white, after all—and now, they may think, there's not much they can do about it except try to be really good white people. But this kind of thinking puts them at the center of the story, just as all those white-savior movies do. Racism isn't about white people, and antiracism isn't about white people finding ways to be comfortable with their guilt. The work of antiracism isn't about redeeming ourselves; it's about real and practical solidarity with innocent people who have experienced centuries of injustice. It's about being willing to stand with Mary at the foot of the cross.

Ignatius believed that paying attention to our emotions is essential to our spiritual journey. In the Spiritual Exercises, he teaches that the "movements" in our souls—our emotions—are one way that God communicates with us. If we aren't willing to feel those emotions, we might as well be plugging our spiritual ears, refusing to hear what the Divine Voice has to say.

Guilt and sorrow are two of the emotions we may feel when faced with the reality of racism, but another emotion is anger. Anger can shake us out of our indifference and apathy. Peace activist William Sloan Coffin wrote, "Tolerance is a wonderful thing but joined by passivity, it is lethal. If we are not angry with the structure of power we have little sympathy with the victims of power." And as Thomas of Aquinas wrote, "Anger is the passion that moves the will to justice."

Ignatius too knew the positive power of anger. He wrote, "I would not have the emotions, particularly anger, to be entirely extinguished and dead"—but then he added the warning that all emotions, including anger, need to "kept in proper control." Sometimes we need to get angry in order to fuel our drive to change, but our anger should fuel our love, not our hate. William Sloan Coffin said that anger can be "a measurement of our love."

Recently, I had the experience of spending several days with a friend while she kept vigil at her dying brother's bedside. All her attention was on him, her love for him flowing out to him through her hands, her voice, the expression on her face. She was angry about a situation that had contributed to his death, an injustice that had been done to him by a medical institution as well as a so-called friend, but she did not let her anger deter her from the expression of her love. Instead, it gave her the energy to sit beside his bed day after day, keeping him company as he journeyed ever closer to death.

Was Mary angry at the authorities who killed her son? As she listened to the jeers from the crowd, was she sick with fury? Maybe. But her focus on her son held steady.

In the First Week of the Spiritual Exercises, when we considered our sin, we were the focus of our thoughts. We were contemplating our own guilt and shame, as well as the love that God gives us. In the Third Week, Ignatius asks that we shift our attention. We are no longer dwelling on our own sorrow; now we are sorrowing with Jesus. He and all who suffer are at the center of our meditation.

Jesuit author George Aschenbrenner describes the challenge of this Week:

> The focus is not on your suffering but on that of your beloved. A great emptiness of self and ego is required if this grace is to be effective. Such a grace is never easy, especially in our twenty-first-century American culture of self-absorption. As you prepare to ask for the grace suggested, you should appreciate, as much as you can, what it is you are asking of God. The consolation you seek comes from entering the suffering of Jesus. This ability to get out of your own suffering and to enter his teaches a very important lesson: to enter the suffering of other people you must get free of the all-absorbing clutches of your own.

Ignatius described his lifelong work as being "under the cross." To take our stand with Ignatius and with Mary beneath the cross of Jesus means we enter into the work of antiracism not as a way to feel good about ourselves or to inflate our egos. Instead, we empty ourselves of our own pride and self-centered identity. We open ourselves to the experience of others. We seek to serve them in humility, in whatever way we can be useful.

Ignatius had definite ideas about humility. He taught that we can experience it at different levels: at the first level we realize that we can never be "the lord of all creation"; at the second level, we let go of our attachments to privilege, material possessions, and reputation; and finally, at the third level, we want to be "more like Christ our Lord," with our goal being to "desire and choose poverty with Christ poor, rather than riches; insults with Christ loaded with them, rather than honors; . . . to be accounted as worthless and a fool for Christ, rather than to be esteemed as wise and prudent in this world." In other words, we let go of our ego-centered identity and identify ourselves totally with Christ.

This depth of humility is driven by love that, wrote Ignatius, inspires us "to imitate Jesus in bearing all wrongs and all abuse and all poverty, both actual and spiritual." This is both an "earnest desire" and a "deliberate choice." The humility Ignatius described does not dwell on guilt or self-hate, because it is not concerned with self at all. Totally occupied with the reality of the other, it no longer needs to self-justify. It is open to learning, to new understanding. It stands as near to Jesus as it can get.

Where do you stand in relation to the cross? At a distance? Or close to Jesus, ready to share in his suffering?

Now ask yourself the same question about people of color. Do you take your stand alongside them—or at a safe distance? Are you ready to feel their pain as if it were your own?

Journal

Here are some questions for you to consider and write about in your journal:

- Has my desire for emotional comfort kept me from entering into the experience of people of color? If so, what effect has this had on my life? How has it shaped my attitudes toward people of color?

- How do I feel when I receive criticism or feedback from people of color? Am I able to take the feedback and use it to grow—or do I feel defensive and resistant? How can I begin to grow in this area?

- I like to be perceived as competent and worthy of respect and admiration—but the work of antiracism asks that I realize my own ignorance and lack of authority. How can I cultivate a spirit of teachability and humility? How can I walk in love and openness, so that I can learn without becoming defensive?

For Further Reflection

ways remember that there is no conversion to God
if there is no conversion to the oppressed....
It is not us who are going to save the poor,
it is the poor who will save us.

—IGNACIO ELLACURIA, S.J.

[handwritten: SAYING THE NAMES SO THEY MAY LIVE IN OUR]

Prayer

Jesus, make real to me the sorrow of your death.
May I stand with Mary your mother
and cry for the loss of your life.
And may I also stand
with the mothers of Michael Donald and Troy Davis,
George Floyd and Brionna Taylor,
Daunte Wright and Trayvon Martin,
and all the others who have lost their lives to injustice.
May I know their names.
May I honor their memory
by working for a safer world for all people of color.

DAY 5

The Power of Compassion

Active Participation in the Sorrow of Oppression

Jesus had compassion on them.

—MATTHEW 14:14

*No one should call himself a friend of Christ
unless he cherishes those souls
that Christ redeemed by the shedding of his Blood.*

—IGNATIUS OF LOYOLA

*Compassion is not a relationship
between the healer and the wounded.*

It's a relationship between equals.
… Compassion becomes real
when we recognize our shared humanity.

—PEMA CHODRON

"**P**assion of Christ, strengthen me," Ignatian wrote in the Third Week of the Spiritual Exercises. "Within thy wounds hide me." With these words, he challenges us to encounter the crucifixion not so much as a spiritual event but as the flesh-and-blood experience of Jesus. He calls us to join in that experience as if it were our own.

In his life and writings, Ignatius always emphasized "effective love" (love shown in action) over "affective love" (love based on feelings or sentiment). Throughout the Third Week, compassion is a consistent theme. It is the grace we ask God to give us as we pray and examine our hearts during these days. Ignatius often closed his letters with "I implore God to grant us all the grace to know His holy will and to accomplish it perfectly"; this phrase again indicates the importance he placed on action. It is not enough to have spiritual thoughts and feelings; we must put them into practice.

The Hebrew word that has been translated as "compassion" in most English Bibles comes from the word for *womb*; it implies that compassion is like the love a mother feels for her unborn child. A pregnant mother physically and often emotionally prioritizes the needs of the baby. She sees the child as both a part of her (in that she feels the baby's needs as if they were her own) and also as separate from her (in that she is willing to sacrifice her own needs and resources to actively nourish and protect the vulnerability of the child).

In a similar way, the word *compassion* indicates how we are to participate in Jesus' suffering; we are not to hold ourselves separate as spectators, but instead, we open ourselves up to his pain, feeling it in our own hearts and flesh. At the same time that we connect to Jesus in this embodied way, we detach from our own selfish needs. This allows us to move past our own concerns and take practical action on behalf of the Christ who is present in all who suffer.

Following Ignatius's example, a group of Jesuits working in the Philippines in the seventeenth century set aside time to educate those in the community who were old or sick. At the first class, however, the fathers realized that several people were absent because they were too sick or weak to come alone and no one was willing to bring them. One of these was an old woman, a slave, whose "masters" refused to take her anywhere because they found her so loathsome. Another was a man who kept his face covered because of an ulcerated wound that had eaten away his mouth and nose. The Jesuit fathers insisted that all these people be gathered together alongside the "cream of the townspeople"—and then one of the fathers knelt before the old woman. He picked up her feet, which were putrid and abscessed, and gently kissed each of them, his lips touching the fetid wounds. Then the father went to the man with the damaged face, removed the covering, stroked his cheek, and talked with him face to face without flinching. These actions by the Jesuit fathers were not condescending or patronizing. They were done in humility, inspired by the self-giving "womb-love" a mother would feel for her hurting child.

As a Black man in America, I often wonder where this womb-love is in our world today. It seems I have barely had time to recover emotionally from the tragedy of a Black person's death when yet another one occurs. When I talk with my white brothers and friends, they seem perplexed by my sorrow, my frustration, my fear. "After all," they say, "the police brutality didn't happen to *you*, Patrick." They don't seem to understand that it could have been me. Nor do they understand that I cannot hold myself separate from my Black brothers' and sisters' deaths. My reaction to these conversations reminds me of the old African-American spiritual, "Sometimes I Feel Like a Motherless Child." I do not feel womb-love.

I wonder: When it comes to people of color, does America *ever* feel womb-love? When we think of police brutality, does womb-love move us to action? When we consider the inequities in our health-care system, does womb-love drive us to work for change? When we read about injustice in our courts and laws, does womb-love inspire us to seek a fairer system? Does the lack of opportunities for people of color in our educational system fire us with a womb-love that's ready to take on the world?

"But I do feel sorry for all those things," a white friend said to me when I asked her these questions. "I feel so bad that that's the way things are." She "felt sorry"—but she didn't feel the compassion that would impel her to change "the way things are."

I didn't tell my friend that experts in the field of emotions insist that compassion is not at all the same thing as pity. Pity exists alongside a sense of superiority: "I'm sorry you are hurting, but thank goodness I'm not in your situation." In contrast, compassion arises from a deep experience of shared humanity and solidarity. Researchers in the fields of psychology and neuroscience have found that compassion has three elements: an intellectual understanding that another's suffering is real, an emotional sense of pain in response to the suffering, and a commitment to take action and do something to alleviate the suffering. For compassion to exist, all three elements must be present. This means that compassion can be a powerful force when it comes to social justice.

However, compassion is also not the same thing as kindness. Although kindness does imply action, it is more generic, less focused. If I am a kind person, I am friendly and considerate to everyone I encounter. But kindness alone won't move me to look past the immediate boundaries of my personal world. This means that many white people can choose to never confront the reality of systemic racism because, for whatever reason, it is invisible to them. These people would never kick a Mexican child or steal medicine from a Black woman—but at the same time, they refuse to look at the actual, if unseen suffering, of immigrant children separated from their parents and Black women denied adequate medical care.

Kindness won't dismantle our nation's racist structures. Kindness won't change the fact that the United States currently imprisons a larger percentage of its Black population than South Africa did during apartheid. It won't protect the thousands of missing and murdered indigenous women. It won't solve the problem of "food deserts" in inner cities, where the lack of adequate transportation and grocery stores forces people to rely on fast food. And it won't do anything to change the reality that the average Latina woman earns just barely more than one-half what the average white man earns.

Political scientist Terri E. Givens, in her book *Radical Empathy: Finding a Path to Bridging Racial Divides,* agrees that social justice doesn't happen because we are kind or nice people. She equates compassion with what she calls "radical empathy," which she says is a "practice, not a state of being." She connects this to several steps, which include: the willingness to be vulnerable, opening yourself to the experiences of others, taking action, creating change, and building trust.

Resmaa Menakem, author of *My Grandmother's Hands: Racialized Trauma and the Pathway to Mending Our Hearts and Bodies,* said in an interview that when he thinks about compassion, "I think about doing. I think about purpose. I think about practice. I think about moving." The Dalai Lama said something similar, that for him compassion "is not an idle wish to see sentient beings free from suffering, but an immediate need to intervene, to engage, to try to help."

You may be nodding along with all this; nothing I've said about the meaning of compassion should have triggered any controversy in most of your brains. But there's a problem with compassion: it's not something that most of us experience easily or naturally, not when it comes to people our brains perceive as being outside our own "tribe." Neuroscientists have found that when people witness or imagine the pain of another person, the same neuro-networks light up on an MRI that would if the people were actually experiencing firsthand pain themselves—but they've found that white people have far less neurological arousal when they witness a Black person's pain than when they are exposed to another white person's pain. From an evolutionary standpoint, scientists hypothesize, empathy was useful only so far as in it enabled to people to cooperate with their own community. To feel empathy for an "enemy"—someone outside the tribal group—would have been counterproductive to the safety of the tribe.

Researchers have found that this difference in empathetic response doesn't only happen in people who make no bones about their racist beliefs; it also occurs in people who think of themselves as "liberal, progressive antiracists." Their reactions are not conscious—but they are real. This unconscious physiological response (or lack of one) will unavoidably shape many aspects of our world, including how much physical force police use and the amount of pain a doctor can recognize in her patients.

Decades before this research was conducted, back in the 1960s, psychologist Kenneth B. Clark challenged white liberals to step past "parochial empathy" (feeling the pain of those who are like us) and engage in open and honest conversation with people of color, He asked whites to "transcend the barriers of their own minds" in order to listen with their hearts and "reconcile [their] affirmation of racial justice with [their] visceral racism." Clark believed that heartfelt conversations were the path to dislodging the mechanisms of institutional racism. The empathy that he called for was more than a feeling; it required active political intervention. He challenged America to undergo a "therapeutic crisis of truth."

Ignatius of Loyola understood that compassion does not always come easily to us. To help us enter into the suffering of Jesus, he outlined a form of contemplation he called "application of the senses." As we explained earlier, this prayer technique asks us to enter into Jesus' experiences in the Gospels with all our senses. We don't just read the stories; we also picture the scene as though we were there. We feel it with our flesh. We can use this same form of prayer to enter compassionately into the experiences of those who are different from ourselves. As we read or hear their stories, we can imagine they are happening to us. Ignatius invites us to be joined with Christ in each suffering person, despite the discomfort we may feel as we start to feel their pain.

We can also use the prayer of Examen that Ignatius recommended in order to become more aware of what lurks within our unconscious. Psychologists and neuroscientists confirm the effectiveness of a similar technique, what they refer to as "mindfulness meditation"—a state of mind that anchors our awareness in our emotions, thoughts, and bodily sensations. In mindfulness practice, we look into both ourselves and the reality of the world while letting go of our usual judgments and preconceptions. This state of awareness is based on what Aldous Huxley called an "impartial response to the present situation as a whole," which Huxley said, "opens the way to understanding," as it also frees us from "over-simplification, over-generalization, and over-abstraction." The Ignatian Examen is a tool that can facilitates the mindful awareness that allows us to step free from old, habitual ways of thinking and reacting.

Hard-science research indicates that a regular practice of this can reduce inner prejudice. Mindfulness does this in several ways: by reducing our negativity bias (our tendency to respond with negative emotions to certain triggers); by diminishing anxiety about encounters with people who are different from ourselves; and by helping us to see others as equals. Attorneys and doctors have begun recommending these practices to reduce their unconscious biases toward clients and patients.

Ignatius told his followers to practice the Examen twice a day. If we were to begin a similar practice, compassion—the active identification with those who suffer—would form deeper pathways in both our hearts and our brains. It would lead to both internal personal healing and external societal healing. Justice worker Susan Raffo has commented that healing "is about taking the time to notice what gets in the way of feeling connected to your life, your community, and your sense of possibility. Healing, at its core, is about slowing down so that we can better listen, to ourselves and each other." This internal and external listening is essential to the Examen. Ignatius knew that the effects of this practice are seen not only within our interior worlds but eventually they impact our entire world.

The Task Force for Global Health has said that compassion and justice are two sides of the same coin. Recent events during 2020 and 2021 have been a wake-up call to us all, challenging us to deepen our compassion as we find ways to work for justice. The task force stated: "To realize a compassionate society in which justice prevails, compassion and justice must be built upon millions of individual actions that are fueled by informed awareness and deep empathy. It will take intentional, concerted efforts by all of us to bring about the change that we want to see."
Mahatma Gandhi is credited with saying, "Be the change you want to see in the world." Are you willing to change yourself in order to change the world? Are you willing to begin to truly listen, both to your own heart and to the voices of people of color? Will you take Ignatius's counsel—and enter into the wounds of a broken world, so that healing can begin?

Journal

In the Civil Rights era, psychologist Kenneth Clark advised white people to talk with Blacks, with the goal being to listen rather than to impart whites' own point of view. This involves letting go of our own sense that we already know what we need to know—and instead being genuinely curious about another's experience. Psychologist Erich Fromm described some of the steps necessary for the listening that leads to compassion:

1. The basic rule for practicing this art is the complete concentration of the listener.

2. Nothing of importance must be on the mind; the mind needs to be free from anxiety as well as from selfish motivations.

3. The listener must exercise the imagination.

4. The listener must have a capacity for empathy with another person that's strong enough to feel the experience of the other as if it were her own.

Fromm concludes that "understanding and loving are inseparable." In other words, when we truly listen to someone, we can begin to understand that person—and as we understand, we come to love.

Write in your journal about your reaction to Fromm's ideas about listening. How have you experienced them in your life? How might you make room to have this experience more often?

Conversations that lead to understanding are not easy. We may encounter anger and resentment. If that happens, don't try to deny the other person's right to their feelings, but also don't say, "I understand how you feel," and then try to relate an experience of your own you feel is parallel. Instead, say something along the lines of, "Please tell me more." Ask questions. Don't assume you can know what it feels like to be a person of color. This may require that you ask God to grant you the grace of humility, as well as the grace of inner compassion that inspires you to actively work for change.

How might you find more opportunities to talk with people of color? How do you feel about doing this? Beginning a conversation may seem awkward. Be willing to feel awkward. Don't let that be an excuse for not engaging in an open conversation with a Black friend, an Asian colleague, or an Arab neighbor.

Use your journal to commit in writing to doing this. Then find an opportunity to ask if the person would be willing to talk to you about some of the things that have been in the news lately. If they don't want to, don't push it. If they are willing to talk, be open to their hurt and anger. Don't get defensive. Remember, it's not about you. Ask if there is anything you can do to help. If there is, make notes in your journal and follow through. And then don't let this conversation be an isolated incident. Build on this conversation to create ongoing communication.

For Further Reflection

When our hearts are small,
our understanding and compassion are limited. . . .
We can't accept or tolerate others and their shortcomings,
and we demand that they change.
But when our hearts expand, . . .
we have a lot of understanding and compassion
and can embrace others.

—THICH NHAT HANH

Prayer

O God of Mercy,
we pray that we may be open
to your movement in our hearts,
so that we may hear the stories of others, and be inspired;
so that we may see the suffering of others,
and be compassionate;
so that we may understand others, and walk with them;
and so that, with the help of Christ
who taught us how to love,
we may do our part to make real your Reign.

DAY 6

Dying to Self

Inner Attitudes That Contribute to Justice

*Unless a kernel of wheat falls to the ground and dies,
it remains only a single seed.
But if it dies, it produces many seeds.*

—JOHN 12:23

*So order the inner person
that its order overflows into the outer.*

—IGNATIUS OF LOYOLA

*The beauty of anti-racism is
that you don't have to pretend to be free of racism
to be an anti-racist.*

*Anti-racism is the commitment
to fight racism wherever you find it,
including in yourself.
And it's the only way forward.*

—IJEOMA OLUO

A s we've already mentioned, after Ignatius's conversion, his original plan to follow Jesus brought him to the Holy Land, where he soon learned this was not where God was leading him after all. He realized then that as a follower of Jesus, his calling was to help other human beings. The priesthood seemed a likely way for him to meet this goal—but he lacked the educational background needed to study for the priesthood. So the once-proud soldier, now thirty-three years old, enrolled in a Latin grammar school. His classmates were boys eight to fourteen years old. Imagine what he must have looked like, a grown man bearing the scars of battle, sitting there among a crowd of schoolboys!

For the next two years, Ignatius studied hard, but he was often distracted. As he was trying to memorize Latin grammar rules, he would find himself instead thinking about spiritual matters. "Not even in my prayer nor at Mass do I receive such vivid understandings," he said to himself (according to his autobiography). Ignatius might have easily taken pride in his own insights and considered them to be far more worthy of his attention than the lessons of a schoolboy. But by this point, he had progressed a good deal farther along his spiritual journey.

This was no longer the same man who had craved the attention and approval of the nobility, especially the ladies. It was also not the same man who had so needed to prove he was right that he had considered killing another man over a theological argument. Ignatius had begun to die to his old self in order to become something new. Gradually, he now realized that his wandering mind was not proof of his own spiritual maturity but was rather the "Devil" who was trying to "call his soul away from his studies by delightful but irrelevant insights."

He went to his teacher, a man named Jeronimo Ardevol, and asked to talk with him. The two men sat down side by side in a church, and Ignatius confessed how little progress he was making in his studies. "I promise," he told his teacher, "never again to neglect to follow your lessons." He went on to insist that Ardevol treat him as he would the youngest boy in the class, chastising him if he ever noticed him being negligent or inattentive. "He who goes about to reform the world must begin with himself," Ignatius wrote later, "or he loses his labor." He had learned this wisdom the hard way, while sitting in a classroom of young boys.

I can relate to Ignatius's experience. When I was twenty-four, I did an internship in the Congo during my graduate studies. I did not speak any Swahili, but I have always been good at languages, so I was confident I could learn quickly. My advisor placed me in a classroom with children, where I would be immersed in the language. So there I was, learning alongside little boys who were twenty years younger than me. They laughed at my pronunciation of words. They teased me when I tried to put sentences together. They never missed an opportunity to correct me when I said something wrong or out of context. My presence in their classroom was a source of great delight to them—and a lesson in humility for me. I had to let go of my picture of myself as an expert, a fast-learner always at the top of my class, and instead be willing to learn from little boys.

In the *Constitutions* Ignatius wrote for the Society of Jesus, he called for the humility that expresses itself in what he referred to as "greater abnegation." This was one way Christ's followers could more fully identify with the crucifixion. By now, however, Ignatius understood that human beings are perfectly capable of using even their acts of charity and kindness to fatten their sense of themselves and their own importance. The self-denial Ignatius was advocating begins within our own hearts, with a sincere attitude of "dying to self," and only then is it expressed in external actions.

Jesuit author Joseph Veale wrote an article where he imagined what Ignatius might have to say to us today. "For those setting out on a life of serious faith and wishing to give themselves to . . . a life in which service and prayer compenetrate," Veale's modern-day Ignatius says, "the precondition of authenticity and growth is self-abnegation. But if that is not experienced as the other side of love, it were better forgotten." He continued:

> True prayer leads people out of themselves, outward towards God and towards others. It makes for a humility that is wholly unconscious of itself. It is gentle and supple. It makes the spirit more open to God, more selfless in service, more unpretentious. It is the enemy of falseness and unreality. Just as the same devices of self-seeking contaminate both prayer and service, so the same graced dispositions of self-stripping open up either prayer or service to the action of God.

During this Third Week of the Spiritual Exercises, the challenge is to identify with Christ's total self-giving on the cross. Not only do we enter into his suffering—and the suffering of all people—but we also work to experience a "death" of our own. The Christian scriptures speak of it often: our old self is crucified with Jesus (Romans 6:6); we no longer live but Christ lives in us (Galatians 2:20); we die daily (1 Corinthians 5:31); and we take up our cross and follow Jesus (Luke 9:23). This is what Ignatius learned as he sat in Master Ardevol's classroom, and it is what he believed was the necessary foundation to a life of active service to others. "There is no better fuel for the fire of God's love," he wrote, "than the wood of the cross." In other words, it is our willingness to die to self, as Jesus did on the cross, that enables us to truly love.

But the concept of dying to self can seem at odds with what we know today about healthy self-actualization and identity. It looks much like a self-destructive urge to belittle ourselves, a claim to be "nothing" when actually we are most definitely "something." The humility that Ignatius advocated in the Spiritual Exercises—"to imitate and be in reality more like Christ our Lord," choosing "poverty with Christ poor, rather than riches; insults with Christ loaded with them, rather than honors," and "to be accounted as worthless and a fool for Christ, rather than to be esteemed as wise and prudent in this world"—is not very attractive to us in the twenty-first century. What healthy person longs for poverty, insults, and worthlessness?

However, although Ignatius may have been writing with the vocabulary of another age, he understood that true humility does not deny the reality of our own gifts—the qualities and skills God can use to bring healing to our broken world. The word *humility* comes from the same ancient root as does *human*: having to do with the earth. Humility implies a groundedness, as well as a true expression of our humanity. Genuine humility releases us from our need to be constantly proving our own worth, allowing us to enter into a larger sense of self, a self that finds expression in connection to God and others. Humility negates insecurity and empowers us for the work of antiracism. It allows us to use our true abilities far more effectively in service of others.

But many white people seem to be caught in a narrative of insecurity, where they perceive many things to be a threat. If their ancestors—the "forefathers" of our nation—are acknowledged as the racists they were, whites may feel this as an assault on their own identity. They may also look at people of color and see them as being dangerous to their economic security, as well as to a familiar and valued way of life. Their egos may be personally affronted by the claims of antiracism.

The *ego* is a term with various meanings in our world today. Psychologically speaking, it generally refers to our sense of our self. From that perspective, the ego has a necessary and healthy function, but we may also forget that our ego—the "set of clothes" we wear to interact with the world—is not our full reality. Alan Watts wrote, "Our normal sensation of self is a hoax, or, at best, a temporary role that we are playing, or have been conned into playing."

The ego, the persona we may think of as our "self," is not the same as our internal, spiritual being. The psychotherapist Carl Jung referred to this deeper part of us as the Self (with a capital S), that which unifies all the "pieces" of ourselves, both conscious and unconscious, into a single whole. Ignatius might have used the word *soul* to refer to a similar reality; in the Middle Ages, the soul was thought to be the "immortal substance" that brings together the dichotomies of body and mind into a single being. It was that which bore the "image and likeness of God." Along similar lines, Jung defined the Self as "God within us." It is our truest identity—and true humility is grounded here rather than in an external sense of inferiority or pride, self-affirmation or negation.

The ego, however, has a tendency to define itself in relation to others. "I am this," it says, "because they are that." Racism, even if unconsciously, can be a powerful affirmation of the white person's ego. It says, "You are better than most of the world, simply because you are white."

Most of my white friends, people I love and respect, would be unwilling to accept that this attitude forms any part of their sense of themselves. The reality doesn't mean they're hypocrites; it certainly doesn't mean they're "bad people." But growing up within systemic racism means that white people have inevitably absorbed the belief that they are superior.

To admit this, however, is a threat to the ego. In her book *White Fragility,* Robin DiAngelo wrote that white people hate to admit to their own racism because it is dangerous to their self-identity. Comedians Keegan-Michael Key and Jordan Peele have said that *racist* is the only "racial slur" that hurts white people the way the n-word hurts Blacks; nothing is more insulting, especially to white people who consider themselves to be "good people," then the implication that they are enjoying privileges as white people or that they have internalized racist attitudes. DiAngelo wrote:

To suggest that I am racist is to deliver a deep moral blow—a kind of character flaw assassination. Having received this blow, I must defend my character and that is where all my energy will go—to deflecting the charge, rather than reflecting on my behavior. In this way, the good/bad binary makes it nearly impossible to talk to white people about racism, what it is, how it shapes all of us, and the inevitable ways that we are conditioned to participate in it.

"If you want to be of use to others," Ignatius wrote, "begin by taking pains with yourself: the fire that is to enkindle others should be lighted at home." Along the same lines, the great activist Howard Thurman wrote, "You can't stand in the midst of the world and struggle for fundamental change, unless you are standing in your own space and looking for change within." We cannot join together in the work of antiracism until we have looked inside ourselves and addressed whatever we find lurking there deep in our unconscious. And if our egos are wrapped up in our antiracism, we will not be effective activists for justice. We have to let go of our need to be "good people," and instead open ourselves to our full reality, with all its brokenness, as we come into the presence of God. This letting go of the ego's demands is the "dying to self" the Bible was talking about.

But the emphasis on our internal reality can be confusing. In other chapters, we've talked a great deal about the need for intentional action, and we've focused on the external effects of racism. Ignatius himself said that love must be active to be real. But he also taught that action must be fueled from within. The knowledge that we are imperfect, that we bear within ourselves the inherited lies of white supremacy, will help keep us humble. It keeps us from thinking that we've "arrived," that we can claim the identity of "woke" as our permanent label. Ignatius's call for constant, daily self-examination keeps us grounded in our true humanity. It works against the ego's claim to any form of superiority.

"Anti-racism work is not self-improvement work for white people," wrote activist Rachel Cargle. "It doesn't end when white people feel better about what they've done. It ends when Black people are staying alive and they have their liberation." I implore you: don't forget the real work that antiracism calls us to. Be willing to dig deeper into your own hidden assumptions. I don't think less of you because I know they're there. You did not create white supremacy, and you are not to blame for the fact that you've been steeped in it your whole life. But you *are* responsible now for examining yourself. True antiracist work is rooted in this total self-honesty. As Ibram Kendi reminded us in his book *How to Be an Antiracist*, the word *racist* "is not the worst word in the English language; it is not the equivalent of a slur. It is descriptive, and the only way to undo racism is to constantly identify and describe it—and then dismantle it." Can all of us—whites and people of color together—become more alive to the Presence that is the deepest identity of ourselves and every other living being?

Humility lets go of the lies we've told ourselves about our own selves. It holds us accountable to deeper standards than the ego's surface need to look good. When we work for justice, humility reminds us that our work is not about *us.* We are grateful for honest feedback that helps us see ourselves more clearly. As Robin DiAngelo wrote:

If I believe that only bad people are racist, I will feel hurt, offended, and shamed when an unaware racist assumption of mine is pointed out. If I instead believe that having racist assumptions is inevitable (but possible to change), I will feel gratitude when an unaware racist assumption is pointed out; now I am aware of and can change that assumption."

In the *Constitutions*, Ignatius calls us to have "pure intention" as we work in service to God and others. He asks that we have "sincere zeal" that is not based on any selfish benefit to ourselves. "The person who loves perfection," he said, "must be filled with humility like a lamp with oil: for lamps are full within and give light without, and their influence makes itself felt in whatever direction they are turned."

One of the few books that Ignatius had in his room at the time of his death was *The Imitation of Christ* by Thomas à Kempis. Over the years, he must have pondered these words many times:

Anyone who is not totally dead to self will soon find that he is tempted and overcome by piddling and frivolous things. Whoever is weak in spirit, given to the flesh, and inclined to sensual things can, but only with great difficulty, drag himself away from his earthly desires. Therefore, he is often gloomy and sad when he is trying to pull himself away from them, and easily gives into anger should someone attempt to oppose him.

[INVITATION TO CONVERSION

With this understanding firmly rooted in his mind, Ignatius wrote, "You may be sure that the progress you make in spiritual things, will be in proportion to the degree of your withdrawal from self-love and concern for your own welfare." The man who was willing to humble himself by learning alongside boys twenty years younger than himself knew it was only through the humility of "dying to self" that he would be able to "help souls." Without this, he would have been of little real use to others. "He who seeks to scale the heights," Ignatius wrote, "must go far down into the depths."

Jesus spoke about seeds that fall into the ground to die. The ego is much like the outer shell of those seeds. As human beings, we hate to have our sense of who we are hidden in the earth, much less allow it to break. That "dying" is uncomfortable, even agonizing sometimes—but death always is. Jesus went to his own physical death not because he had a masochistic urge to suffer, but because he was resolved, despite the pain, to give everything for the sake of love.

Jesus also knew that when the outer seed dies, possibilities come into the world that never existed before. Something new is released. A larger identity grows from the broken shell—one that is able to be fruitful and productive in the work of justice.

Are you willing to die to white supremacy? Will you let the hard shell of your ego crack open, so that you can be born into a new reality of love and justice for all?

Journal

Movies are another way to gain more understanding of the experience of racism as more than an intellectual concept. Here are three suggestions:

- *13th* (a documentary that reveals the history of racial inequality in the United States, focusing on the fact that the nation's prisons are disproportionately filled with Black Americans)

- *I Am Not Your Negro* (based on the book by James Baldwin, which explores racism through the stories of Medgar Evers, Malcolm X, and Martin Luther King Jr.)

- *The Hate U Give* (about the shooting of an unarmed Black man)

- *Just Mercy* (based on a true story about racial bias in the criminal justice system)

As you watch any of these movies, you may be uncomfortable—but consider this quote from Robin DiAngelo:

> The key to moving forward is what we do with our discomfort. We can use it as a door out—blame the messenger and disregard the message. Or we can use it as a door in by asking, Why does this unsettle me? What would it mean for me if this were true?

Write in your journal about any discomfort you experienced while watching the movie. Can you pinpoint the source of your uneasiness? Can find any area where your ego is feeling threatened? Invite the Divine Spirit to reveal to you any hidden prejudices that are operating within you. Don't be afraid of the discomfort and pain of new insights, for your true identity is safe in Christ.

For Further Reflection

You have to get over the fear
of facing the worst in yourself.
You should instead fear unexamined racism.
Fear the thought that right now,
you could be contributing to the oppression of others
and you don't know it.
But do not fear those who bring that oppression to light.
Do not fear the opportunity to do better.

–IJEOMA OLUO

Prayer

How can I discern my own inner racism, Lord?
Cleanse me, I pray, from my hidden errors in thinking.
Also, I ask that you restrain in me
any intentional acts of racism.
Let not the habits of systemic racism rule my life.
Point out anything in me that is harmful to people of color,
and lead me into a new and better future.

—BASED ON PSALM 19:13,14 AND 139:24

DAY 7

The Ongoing Crucifixion

Seeing Christ in the Dying Faces of People of Color

*They are crucifying the Son of God
all over again and subjecting him to public disgrace.*

—HEBREWS 6:6

*I will try to foster an attitude of sorrow,
suffering and heartbreak
by calling often to memory the labors,
fatigue and suffering which Christ our Lord suffered.*

—IGNATIUS OF LOYOLA

But all our phrasing—race relations, racial chasm,
racial justice, racial profiling, white privilege,
even white supremacy—serves to obscure
that racism is a visceral experience,
that it dislodges brains, blocks airways,
rips muscle, extracts organs, cracks bones, breaks teeth.
You must never look away from this.
You must always remember that the sociology,
the history, the economics, the graphs, the charts,
the regressions all land, with great violence, upon the body.

–TA-NEHISI COATES

I n 1922, the poet Countee Cullen wrote, "The South is crucifying Christ again," and then concludes, "Christ's awful wrong is that he's dark of hue / The sin for which no blameless-ness atones." Cullen was describing the lynchings we discussed in an earlier reading, which took the lives of thousands of people of color. Theologian James Cone points out that the sequence of events in a lynching exactly echo what Jesus endured: trumped-up charges, a sham trial, the terror of those around the victim, the valiant women who sorrow at the loss of their beloved son or friend, the beating and hanging on a tree while the mob shouts insults, and finally the agonizing death.

Over the past years, as I have listened to story after story of police officers killing Blacks, I have been reminded that this modern-day expression of racism also parallels the experience of Jesus Christ. In 2021, during the season of Lent, I watched the trial of

Officer Derek Chauvin, who, in 2020, squeezed the life out of George Floyd, a forty-six-year-old Black man, and I found myself making parallels between Mr. Floyd's death and that other story that was playing out in my head during Holy Week—the Passion of Jesus Christ on the cross.

Like millions of others around the nation, during Chauvin's trial, I heard several testimonies, listened to different narratives, and considered countless interpretations from the media and other "experts." I was reminded that justice for the Black community lies in the hands of white men who have had their knees on the necks of Black people for more than four hundred years. As I watched the trial, I was struck by the comfort the white police had applying force to a Black body without ever thinking of any retribution, let alone the demands of simple humanity.

The facts of Floyd's death are well-known at this point. At 8:09 p.m. on May 25, 2020, police stopped Floyd on the corner of 38th Street and Chicago Avenue in Minneapolis, after a store cashier reported that Floyd had used a counterfeit bill to buy cigarettes. Officer Chauvin pinned Floyd to the ground with his knee. Onlookers heard Floyd shout, "I can't breathe"—a phrase that soon took root in the Black Lives Matter movement. We know that Chauvin kept his knee on Floyd's neck for more than nine minutes. The prosecuting lawyer at Chauvin's trial said that the nine minutes can be broken down into three sections: four minutes and forty-five seconds as Floyd cried out that he couldn't breathe; fifty-three seconds as Floyd had seizures due to low oxygen; and three minutes and fifty-one seconds as Floyd was nonresponsive. At some point during that time, someone called for emergency medical assistance, which arrived at 8:20 p.m. An ambulance followed at 8:27, and an hour later, Floyd was pronounced dead in the hospital. This, in my mind, was the Passion of George Floyd.

Although the word "passion" has taken on additional meanings in common parlance, in biblical terms, the Passion of Christ relates to the mistreatment and suffering of Jesus Christ. That story, as we all know, concluded with Christ's unjust crucifixion. In a similar way, George Floyd's story ended in death by suffocation, for a presumed twenty-dollar crime. Across America, we are witnessing in real-time a wider story we could call the Passion of Black Americans, unfolding on city streets, in prisons, and in courtrooms.

We all know what happened in Jerusalem two thousand years ago. We have eye-witness accounts, thanks to the Gospels, that tell us that during the celebration of Passover, Jesus was arrested and condemned to crucifixion. We know from the Jewish historian Josephus that the government had been colluding with the religious authorities to plan Jesus' execution. At the time, no one challenged the death sentence they handed down—and as today, silence equals death.

Jesus was arrested by officers of the law, just as George Floyd was. Jesus' crime was having the audacity to speak out in spaces the authorities of the day wanted to control. George Floyd's primary crime was being a Black body in a white space. The consequence of that trespass is something that every member of the Black community fears every single day. As a frequent victim of police profiling, I too can empathize with the threat that women and men who look like Floyd, who have similar skin tones, have experienced for hundreds of years.

Jesus was powerless on the cross, yet the soldier still pierced his side with a spear, and "immediately, there came out blood and water" (John 19:34). In the case of George Floyd as he lay under the knee of

Officer Chauvin, handcuffed and unresponsive, he was still seen as a threat to the police. Like Jesus on the cross, Floyd was subdued, dying, and yet the police officers, like the soldier who thrust his sword into Jesus' body, still needed to demonstrate their control, their power and dominance. Then, when the paramedic arrived and Chauvin continued to press on Mr. Floyd, almost immediately, according to the newspaper accounts, "his breath was gone." A different time, a different land, and different authorities—but the story is the same.

Like so many communities of color, Jesus' people had been colonized and oppressed. Generation after generation, they had endured systemic political and economic injustice. Then Jesus came along with a new message—good news for the poor, the imprisoned, the marginalized. But not so good news for the privileged and powerful. He challenged the status quo. He said that everyone matters. He inspired people to reclaim their dignity.

Jesus was condemned because of the jealousy of both the government and the religious authorities; they saw him as a threat to their power. As I thought about this, I found myself wondering: Are some white males jealous of Blacks' strength? Do they see them as threats to their own sense of power and authority? I remembered that Officer Chauvin said, "We had to control this guy because he's a sizable guy." Once again, I could see the parallels to Jesus' death.

As I watched Officer Chauvin's trial, which by association was also George Floyd's, I once more experienced a sense of powerlessness. I watched again that tragic video, shot by a quick-thinking young girl, just seventeen when she filmed the scene, who had stopped at the store for a single purchase. I see the brutal violence toward a man who reminds me of my Black father, who reminds me of my Black brother, who reminds me of my Black cousins and friends—who reminds me of myself. I see my brother gasp for air and beg for breath, while the tormented bystanders are forced to watch, incapable of interceding—just as John and Mary standing at the foot of the cross were unable to save their friend and son. I hear George Floyd call for his mother, as Jesus too called out to Mary from the cross.

The teenager who filmed the video of Mr. Floyd's death testified at the trial, "It's been nights I stayed up apologizing and apologizing to George Floyd for not doing more and not physically interacting and not saving his life," she said. She feels guilt for not intervening to protect Floyd, despite the armed officers at the scene. Did Simon of Cyrene, the African man who helped Jesus carry the cross, feel similar guilt and shame whenever he remembered the day Jesus died?

And yet like the witnesses who recorded Christ's death, this teenage girl has had an essential role in the Passion; her videotape helped bring Floyd's assailant to justice. The video proves that in broad daylight, a white man showed his disrespect for Black life. Thanks to the account the teenage girl's camera captured, we know that Officer Chauvin murdered George Floyd.

As Christians, we would often prefer to focus on Easter rather than Good Friday. We'd rather sing about Jesus' triumphant victory over death than spend time gazing at his bloody flesh hanging on the cross. But Jesus insists that we remember his murdered body. "Look at my scars," he told Thomas (John 20:27). "See the proof of my suffering. Don't forget that this was what I experienced."

The resurrection of Jesus does not mean we have a free pass to ignore those who continue to experience the reality of crucifixion. Easter Day does not erase the violence and injustice of Good Friday. That same violence and injustice are all too alive today, which we can see as the Passion of George Floyd that unfolded yet again in the trial of Officer Chauvin. In the words of Pope Francis, "The Easter message does not offer us a mirage or reveal a magic formula. It does not point to an escape from . . . the difficult situation we are experiencing. . . . That is today's scandal."

All suffering people share in Christ's Passion. This means not only that Jesus is with them in their oppression and pain—though he is—but also that all humanity is challenged to see Jesus in the suffering of those who face racial injustice. It is a call to align ourselves with Christ's presence in people of color, to take action on behalf of liberation and equity.

I know some people are offended when I compare George Floyd to Jesus Christ. Let me be clear: I'm not saying Floyd was flawless or that he's the Savior of all humanity. He wasn't *the* Son of God—but he was *a* son of God. When we gaze upon his murdered body, we can see the presence of the crucified Christ.

The Gospels repeatedly say that Jesus was deeply moved when he looked at people who were in pain. He didn't hold himself separate. He gave not only his heart but his flesh in solidarity with those who felt the agony of injustice. This stands in shocking contrast to the lack of emotion Officer Chauvin displayed as he pressed the life out of George Floyd. In the video, we see Floyd's desperation and agony, while Chauvin wears a disinterested and unconcerned expression. The girl who took the video said that Chauvin's blank stare was "cold" and "heartless." From what we can see in the video of the other officers, they too look unmoved by Floyd's anguish. Their lack of empathy is the exact opposite of Jesus' attitude toward suffering.

So what about us? As we watched the murder of George Floyd, did we suffer with him? Did we feel the even deeper pain underlying his death, the centuries of injustice and brutality toward people of color? If so, we cannot sit waiting for justice. The Passion of Christ—and the Passion of George Floyd—demands that as followers of Christ, we stand up, speak out, and act.

What about you? What will you do?

Journal

When you first learned the details surrounding George Floyd's death, what was your initial reaction? How have your thoughts and feelings evolved since then?

What do you feel about being asked to compare George Floyd's murder with Jesus' death on the cross? Does the comparison shock you? Make you uncomfortable? If so, where do those feelings come from? Take time to write about them in your journal for as long as it takes for you to get to the bottom of your reactions.

Now describe in your journal an imaginary scene where you are sitting with both George Floyd and Jesus. Both have endured their deaths, and are now able to reflect on what happened. What do you think they would say? What would you like to say to each of them?

For Further Reflection

Christ's followers who remember him repeat Christ's solidarity with the victims of deception and violence.

—JOHANN BAPTIST METZ

Prayer

Come Holy Spirit, we need your presence
to confront the horror that has infected our human spirit.
We are sick with racist actions, with cruelty to one another
with ideologies of superiority
and other kinds of self-centered motivations.
We need your help. We need your wisdom,
your courage and your love to create a world
where every man, woman, and child
can breathe freely the air of equality
without fear or prejudice.
Forgive us. Help us to continue to untangle
the threads of oppression in the systems of our society
and the arrogance of our hearts,
to realize freedom and justice for everyone.
Bless us with the vision to bring true renewal
and commitment to effect justice.
We are one; created in your love.
We are your people; all of us.
Heal our wounds and make us a healthy.

—SUSAN RUDOLPH, O.S.B.

The Grace I Keep

I ask for the grace of spiritual strength,
that I might daily help Jesus to carry his cross.
May my inner determination be expressed in outward acts
that help to build a world of justice and racial reconciliation.

WEEK FOUR

Resurrection and
the Power of Possibility

In Week Four, the final week of the Spiritual Exercises, Ignatius challenges us to share in the joy and fulfillment of the risen Christ. Although this might seem like an easier "movement" within our hearts, this too is a grace we must receive from God. In a world where systemic racism causes inequities and injustice, it is often hard to feel joyful.

The world is a hard place, full of pain and oppression, but the joy of the Resurrection does not ignore that pain. Instead, it holds it within the Divine embrace—and then transforms it. In each of the incidents when the risen Jesus appears to his friends and followers, he meets them in their sorrow and fear, and then he leads them from there into a new understanding of hope and peace.

The Resurrection is about the Divine power to make all things new. It is the reality of the ongoing creation at work in our world, constantly turning death into life. The Resurrection reveals to us the living God who is dynamic and active, not dead, passive, or static. This is the God who brings hope and life to even the darkest places of death and division.

After Easter, Jesus himself is transformed. As Jesuit author Louis M. Savary wrote:

> The body of Jesus becomes a universal body that incorporates all of us within it. It is no longer a finite, limited body; it is cosmic-sized. It is present everywhere in the universe. . . . You and I no longer simply observe Jesus from the outside, as the disciples did. You and I live in Christ. We experience Christ from inside him, which is where we live (Col. 1:18–20). . . . Despite our many disappointments and failures, joy and hope are always available when we recognize that we are living, moving, and enjoying life with the great Christ Body.

In the Third Week, we identified with the suffering Jesus present in all who suffer and are oppressed, and we committed to sharing in the ongoing work of the cross to bring healing to our world. Now, however, we focus on hope. We open our eyes to the ways God can and will raise our world out of tyranny and persecution, into the light of justice and freedom.

Some of the early church fathers taught that the Divine likeness—the Image of God—requires that all humanity be united into a single community. Until that happens, the Divine Image is incomplete, for we need each other to truly represent all that God calls us to be. In the Resurrection, according to this teaching, all divisions within the human community will be healed. Every barrier of sin that separates human beings from each other will be eradicated. In the words of the fourth-century bishop, Gregory of Nyssa, "Then a universal feast will be kept around the Deity by those who have participated in the Resurrection; and one and the same banquet will be spread for all, with no differences cutting off any creature from an equal participation in it."

This is the Resurrection reality we are called to experience during this Week of the Spiritual Exercises, a reality that is both "now" and "not yet," a reality that calls us to do all that we can to participate in it and make it visible. "The Divinity, which seemed to hide Itself in the Passion," wrote Ignatius in the Spiritual Exercises, "now appears and shows Itself so marvellously in the most holy Resurrection by Its true and most holy effects."

When Ignatius speaks of "effects," he is saying that the resurrected Christ is not merely spiritually present in the world. Instead, Christ is active, busy; he is on a mission, a mission he invites us to share. While we are called to share in his sufferings on the cross—the experience of Divinity being hidden beneath injustice and oppression—during this Week, Ignatius also challenges us to see past the suffering, so that we can recognize the living Christ at work in our world.

For Ignatius, God's love is always blossoming into new life as we participate in the Divine mission of justice. When we commit to the struggle to demolish racism, we can lay claim to the power and hope of the Resurrection. We make room for new possibilities in our broken world.

DAY 1

Flesh and Blood

Seeing Black Bodies

Put your finger here; see my hands.
Reach out your hand and put it into my side.
Stop doubting and believe.

—JESUS (JOHN 20:27)

He appeared to His Blessed Mother
in Body and in Soul.

—IGNATIUS OF LOYOLA

Between me and the other world
there is ever an unasked question: . . .
How does it feel to be a problem?

*To have your very body and the bodies of your children
to be assume to be criminal, violent, malignant.*

—W.E.B. DUBOIS

gnatius of Loyola believed in the Incarnation—the literal "enfleshment" of Divinity in the body of Jesus. His meditation on the Incarnation did not end with the Nativity, when Jesus was first born as a baby in Bethlehem. Instead, the Spiritual Exercises remind us that Incarnation is expressed throughout the life of Jesus. It is vital to our understanding of the crucifixion. And, for Ignatius, the Incarnation was also an essential aspect of the Resurrection. As we begin Week Four of the Spiritual Exercises, Ignatius wants us to remember that the crucified Jesus and the risen Christ are one and the same.

In the Gospels, Jesus makes clear that the body—flesh and blood and bone—is important to the Reign of Heaven. He touches bodies, heals bodies. And his own body is real and present: it eats, breathes, spits, sleeps, cries. His body contains Divinity, but it is also fully human; it is a body like yours or mine. And after the Resurrection, his body, though transformed, is still real and solid. The risen Jesus is not an ephemeral ghost; he can be seen and touched. He can join his friends in a meal.

Christianity has sometimes glossed over this. After all, the Resurrection is a tall claim; it strains our credulity. It's easier by far to skip over the scarred hands, the naked belly that still bears the sword wound, and the breakfast on the beach—and focus on a more mystical reality we can all agree on.

The church has held up the Mystical Body of Christ as an inspiring and comforting concept. Jesuit author Emile Mersch wrote that within this spiritual body, "there is no longer any separation." He insisted that the Mystical Body makes it impossible for Christians to hide "under their egoisms of class, of race, or of persons, under theories of massacre and of hostilities, of reprisals and of parties." Pope Pius XII, in 1942, issued a papal encyclical (a letter sent to all the Catholic bishops) on the doctrine of the Mystical Body, pointing to it as an example of interracial communion.

However, the concept of the Mystical Body has often been so "spiritual" that it is invisible. It's divorced from the everyday realities of flesh and blood. It's sanitized, scrubbed clean of sweat and blood. Technically, its flesh has no color whatsoever—and yet even in its insistence that it unites all people into one, it creates a concept of "good whiteness" that swallows up and dissolves any tinge of brown or black. It becomes a spiritual melting pot.

A "raceless" spirituality creates a Christianity that supports the status quo. For white people, it can provide a blank space where they can draw an image of Christ who looks like them, who represents their own interests. A Mystical Christ who is disconnected from the living, breathing Jesus of Nazareth allows room for racism.

Theologian and activist Howard Thurman insisted that the actual gospel is at odds with any concept of a bodiless, mystical Christ. Jesus' message, he said, was never about spiritual salvation in a hazy, golden afterlife. To sever the spiritual from the physical is to miss Jesus' real message. It allows us to overlook the fact that the historical Jesus was a disinherited person who came with a message of hope for people like him, a message that challenged the authority of all oppressors. Author and theologian James Cone also emphasizes that Jesus' message about the Reign of Heaven always focuses on justice for the poor; it cannot be reduced to "escape to a transcendent reality, nor. . . an inward serenity which eases unbearable suffering."

You may have noticed recently that antiracist language frequently speaks of "bodies," especially "Black bodies." The Black Lives Matter website refers to "a world that harms and dehumanizes Black bodies." Why the emphasis on bodies? Because, said Elizabeth Barnes, it's a reminder that "racism isn't just about the ideas that you have in your head." We can make the concept of social oppression, Barnes said, sound almost disembodied; "we talk about prejudice like it's just a matter of ideas." By forcing our society to hear the term "Black bodies," we emphasize the reality that racism—in the form of slavery, lynching, police brutality, and inequities in the legal and medical systems—does physical harm to flesh and bones. People bleed and die because of racism. They suffer malnutrition and they live in unsafe conditions. They are beaten, choked, and shot.

Author Ta-Nehisi Coates also explores the theme of Black bodies. In his articles and books, he has shown how racism began with the control and exploitation of Black bodies when human beings from Africa were turned into commodities, objects with monetary value but no other merit. "They transfigured our bodies into sugar, tobacco, cotton, and gold," he wrote; by the time of the Civil War, the collective value of Blacks' "stolen bodies" was worth four billion dollars. And yet individually, each of these bodies was disposable. The racism that is rooted in slavery, wrote Coates, "dislodges brains, blocks airways, rips muscle, extracts organs, cracks bones, breaks teeth." These are not pretty images.

Racism is not pretty.

Racism does violence to human bodies.

But if the Resurrection is only a spiritual reality, not a physical one, then we can refuse to see what is in front of us. With our heads in the disembodied clouds of "spirituality," we can close our eyes to the images of our brothers and sisters who are bleeding and dying. "To be a Negro in this country," wrote James Baldwin, "is really never to be *looked* at. What white people see when they look at you is not visible." And writer and scholar Ralph Ellison said, "I am an invisible man . . . I am invisible, understand, simply because people refuse to see me." This is why when I first came to the United States, I was never called on in the classroom; my raised black hand was simply not seen. I too was invisible.

And yet I have friends who insist that they do see me—they just don't see me as a Black person. They think they are looking with the eyes of the unbodied, mystical Christ, from a place of such superior spirituality that race no longer matters. But only a white person can say that race doesn't matter. We who are people of color know how much it truly does matter. Like the resurrected body of Jesus, our bodies too bear scars.

In his book *Racism without Racists,* sociologist Eduardo Bonilla-Silva wrote that when white people insist they "don't see color," they are also refusing to see the actual identities and concerns of people of color. They are insisting that racism is no longer a reality, that it no longer damages bodies. Being "colorblind" allows whites to continue to live within a white world they assume is the norm; it allows them to be truly blind to what is real.

As we meditate on the Resurrection during this Week of the Spiritual Exercises, Ignatius reminds us to perceive the risen Jesus with all our senses. After the Resurrection, Jesus did not turn into some hazy, generic white man; he was still the unique, one-of-a-kind person who was born in Bethlehem—a human being with brown skin, a member of a colonized people. As James Cone has said, Jesus "was not a 'universal' man, but a particular Jew who came to fulfill God's will to liberate the oppressed."

"Now you are the body of Christ," wrote Paul in his first letter to the Corinthians, "and each of you is a part of it" (12:27). This Body that Paul wrote about does have spiritual reality—but the Incarnation means that spiritual and physical reality has been forever merged into an indivisible whole. We can't separate our faith in Christ from the human flesh of the historical Jesus.

The particularity of Jesus must also be expressed within the Mystical Body of Christ. Each of us, with our individual grace and brokenness, is called to participate in it. It cannot be complete if each member is not visible and seen. We must see each other fully, in three dimensions and in living color—and we cannot ignore the pain racism inflicts upon our fellow members. "God has put the body together," wrote Paul, "so that there should be no division in the body, but that its parts should have equal concern for each other. If one part suffers, every part suffers with it; if one part is honored, every part rejoices with it" (1 Corinthians 12:24–26).

When Thomas could not believe that Jesus had actually risen from the dead, Jesus said to him, "Touch me. See me. Put your hand on me." With these words, Jesus made clear that the Resurrection is not the doorway into an airy, disembodied realm of existence. Instead, he invited his followers to find a new and transformed way of interacting with flesh and blood. Theologian M. Shawn Copeland wrote, "If my sister or brother is not at the table, we are not the flesh of Christ. If my sister's mark of sexuality must be obscured, if my brother's mark of race must be disguised, if my sister's mark of culture must be repressed, then we are not the flesh of Christ." When we finally understand what Jesus was saying to us, she said, then we can "as *his body* . . . embrace with love and hope those who, in their bodies, are despised and marginalized."

Ignatius teaches us that we find the risen Christ present in the physical world around us. Our faith does not find its expression in the invisible, intangible realms of some imaginary spirit world. "Do not look upon what you spend on natural needs as lost to religion," Ignatius wrote. In our day, he might have said, "Don't consider the work of antiracism to be separate from your spiritual life."

The Resurrection calls us to the work of antiracism. It insists that people of color are visible. Their physical suffering is real. Their bodies matter.

Can you see the risen Christ in Black bodies, in brown bodies? Do you see his scars? Will you reach out with your hands and touch the Body of Christ?

Journal

Imagine that you were alive at the time of Jesus' death, and now it is the week after the crucifixion. As you sit alone in an outdoor place, you look up and see Jesus coming toward you. Use your journal to record a colloquy—a conversation—with the risen Jesus. How do you feel in his presence? What does he look like? Ask him any questions you have about what it means for you to now be a part of his Body on earth.

Now bring today's reading into your conversations. Discuss with him any questions that the reading brought to your mind. Be open with him about your feelings. Does anything in you resist or feel defensive about the ideas we've discussed today? What does Jesus say to you in response? Finally, ask Jesus to explain to you how you can personally participate in the work of antiracism in order to be a more healthy member of his living, breathing Body. Write all this in your journal.

For Further Reflection

We were all given the one Spirit to drink.
Even so the body is not made up of one part but of many.
Now if the foot should say,
"Because I am not a hand, I do not belong to the body,"
it would not for that reason stop being part of the body.
And if the ear should say, "Because I am not an eye,
I do not belong to the body,"
it would not for that reason stop being part of the body.
If the whole body were an eye,
where would the sense of hearing be?
If the whole body were an ear,
where would the sense of smell be? ...
The eye cannot say to the hand,
"I don't need you!"
And the head cannot say to the feet,
"I don't need you!"
On the contrary, those parts of the body
that seem to be weaker are indispensable,
and the parts that we think are less honorable
we treat with special honor. ...
God has put the body together,
giving greater honor to the parts that lacked it,
so that there should be no division in the body,
but that its parts should have equal concern for each other.

—1 CORINTHIANS 12:13–17,21–23,25

Prayer

Jesus,
you are the resurrection and the life.
You are alive in our world, present in flesh and blood.
May I work to protect your living Body,
present in all who suffer and are oppressed.
Give me eyes to truly see
and hands that are willing to touch.
Let no one be invisible to me.
Remind me, Jesus, that I need your entire Body,
not just the pieces that look like me.

DAY 2

Radical Healing

Building Solidarity with People of Color

*If the Spirit of him who raised Jesus from the dead
is living in you, he who raised Christ from the dead
will also give life to your mortal bodies
because of his Spirit who lives in you.*

—ROMANS 8:11

*We should not break
this divinely constituted oneness and fellowship,
but rather strengthen and consolidate it ever more,
forming ourselves into one body.*

—IGNATIUS OF LOYOLA

> *Today our prime ... objective must be*
> *to form men-and-women-for-others;*
> *men and women who will live not for themselves*
> *but for God and his Christ—for the God-human*
> *who lived and died for all the world;*
> *men and women who cannot even conceive of love of God*
> *which does not include love for the least of their neighbors;*
> *men and women completely convinced that love of God*
> *which does not issue in justice for others is a farce.*

—PEDRO ARRUPE, S.J.

The risen Jesus was solid and substantial, but his body was not the same as it had been before his death. Now it could walk through walls (John 20:19). It could appear and disappear suddenly (Luke 24:31). Something altogether new had happened to the cells of his body. He was not merely resuscitated, as Lazarus had been when Jesus raised him from the dead. Instead, the resurrected Jesus had been radically healed, in a way that transformed his body into something altogether different. Empowered by this new energy, he stepped out of a more localized frame of reference and into a cosmic reality.

He makes this clear in his interactions with his old friends. The friendship between them is still there, but as he told Mary Magdalene when he encountered her in the garden, his friends can no longer cling to him, claiming him as their own and no one else's. Instead, they must release him, so that they too can participate in a new message of ever-spreading solidarity. "Go tell the others," he told Mary. "Spread the word. This is a reality that's meant to be shared—and in doing so, my body will grow ever stronger, ever larger."

The gifts of new life and healing that the resurrected Jesus brings to his friends are not meant to stop with them. These gifts are like the yeast Jesus described in his parable about the Reign of Heaven, which works its way throughout the bread dough, giving the entire mass new life (Matthew 12:33). As Jesus forgave his friends for leaving him to die alone, he encouraged them to forgive others too. "Doubting Thomas" was convinced of the reality of Resurrection—and then, according to tradition, carried the gospel to India. Jesus and Peter were reconciled after Peter's denial, and Peter went on to lead the church. The Resurrection cannot be contained within a single moment of time. It continues to grow, to spread, to bring people together into a new and living solidarity.

The generative profusion of the Resurrection rises above all human attempts to squelch it. Even as white colonizers sought to use Christianity to endorse slavery and oppression, enslaved Africans saw through the lie to the truth. As Juan Williams wrote in *This Far by Faith,* "Africans did not simply adopt the religion of the European Colonist; they used the power, principles, and practices of Christianity to blaze a path to freedom and deliverance." Over the years since slavery, not only has Black Christianity inspired and empowered African Americans in their fight for justice, but, Williams concluded, "it reformed Christian theology," as well as Christianity itself. "Individual black people took on a cloak of faith, an unshakable belief that God would carry them through slavery and lift them up to freedom."

They marched "for an end to segregation and for the promise of equality as God's children," and "then they transformed the church." This is the transformative and effervescent healing of the Resurrection.

Our world today needs Resurrection healing. We need the "yeast" of Jesus to unite our divided parts into an organism of thriving solidarity, where the wounds of marginalization and oppression are healed, and justice spreads out to touch the lives of more and more people.

Resurrection solidarity does not eliminate our unique individuality, and neither does it equate unity with uniformity. Instead, this form of solidarity celebrates and affirms differences; it makes room for multiplicity to bear fruit. Theologian Ada María Isasi-Díaz wrote that "solidarity is not a matter of agreeing with, of being supportive of, of liking, or of being inspired by, the cause of . . . people." Instead, as Ignatius knew, solidarity must be expressed in action, in experience.

Nor does solidarity look like paternalistic or condescending charity to the "less fortunate." Father Greg Boyle, the Jesuit priest who works with inner-gangs, wrote that solidarity:

> lies less in our service of those on the margins, and more in our willingness to see ourselves in kinship with them. It speaks of a kinship so mutually rich that even the dividing line of service provider/service recipient is erased. We are sent to the margins NOT to make a difference but so that the folks on the margins will make *us* different.

Will white Christians join with people of color in this work of solidarity? Many are, but many others with whom I'm spoken are uncomfortable with what they see as the "divisiveness" of today's protest movements. They point to those who take to the streets to fight injustice, and they lump them together as "rioters" and "looters." Words like these have power. They allow us to hold ourselves separate—and feel justified and righteous in doing so.

Our world has been sliced and diced by polarizing words that have turned us into factions: pro-life versus pro-choice, gun restrictions versus pro-gun, Democrat versus Republican, CNN versus Fox News. Christianity in particular has been partitioned into discrete sections by words like these. As followers of Christ, we are not united in a living and inclusive Body. Instead, the implication is that Christ takes sides.

We all carry the image of our Creator. Each and every one of us is called to be God's agent on earth. In this most essential and shared identity, we are all equal. Not one of us should be diminished, marginalized, or rendered invisible. And yet as Christians, our gaze so often falls short of this reality. Instead, we look at other elements of our culture—all the things that make us different from each other—and we turn those differences into tribal identities. As we prioritize those smaller identities over the Divine Image that unites us, we may also use our "faith" to affirm them. When that happens, Christianity can act as a means of preserving our divisions rather than affirming our common humanity.

As a follower of Christ, how am I to define myself? Do I claim my identity with the Jesuits, an order that in the United States consists primarily of white men? Do I think of myself as an American Catholic, when, out of the three million African American Catholics in the United States, only eight are active

HONESTY - VULNERABILITY

bishops and just two hundred and fifty are priests (according to the U.S. Conference of Catholic Bishops)? Or do I find my solidarity with my Black brothers and sisters as we take to the streets, insisting that Black lives matter?

I believe another option is still possible. Resurrection healing offers us the possibility of being *one* in Christ in a way that affirms each of our separate identities. The ongoing regenerative power of the Resurrection extends an opportunity for conversion, healing, and reconciliation. Black, brown, white . . . indigenous, Asian, Latinx . . . we can find a shared identity in the risen Christ.

Pope Francis called on Christ's followers to work for unity through prayer. In 2021, he said in a sermon: "We today can ask ourselves: Are we protecting our unity with prayer, our unity of the Church? Are we praying for one another?" If we were, he went on to say, "Now, as then, so many closed doors would be open, so many chains that bind would be broken, and we would be amazed."

Prayer is essential to our lives as spiritual beings, but in the Spiritual Exercises, Ignatius insisted over and over that our primary vocation is to *labor with Christ.* We are called to actively and intentionally work to heal the wounds of division and injustice. This shared vocation is a unifying force for solidarity. "If you want peace, work for justice," Pope Paul VI said in 1972. Today, perhaps we might say, *If you want justice, work for unity.*

The first step toward active solidarity must be overcoming our fear of each other. Like many other Black men, I can easily be driven by fear of whites, especially white police. Conversely, many white people are afraid of Black people, especially Black men. "Fear," said Bertrand Russell, "is one of the main sources of cruelty." William Shakespeare had another piece of timeless wisdom: "In time, we hate that which we often fear." Martin Luther King Jr. offered us the hope of a cure when he said that human beings "often hate each other because they fear each other; they fear each other because they don't know each other; they don't know each other because they cannot communicate; they cannot communicate because they are separated."

Communication helps us to step out of our fear and take a step closer to solidarity. Silence, on the other hand, which is the opposite of communication, allows us to participate implicitly in an unjust system that sustains personal interests, upholds privilege, and deepens lies and divisions Inspired by Dr. King, let me say that division anywhere serves as a threat to solidarity everywhere.

The resurrection of Jesus signals the end of all division, but in the meantime, we suffer from an unhealed wound. We have never fully cured the systemic ailment that harms us all. Many of us are exhausted, sometimes to the point of numbness or indifference, by the constant barrage of Facebook posts, magazine articles, news stories, television shows, and face-to-face discussions of racism. Some of us would like to ignore the issue, others claim it's an ailment that was cured long ago, and still others want to get out the first-aid kit and slap on a Band-aid. Meanwhile, people of color continue to feel the pain of this ancient and ongoing wound.

And yet the power and reality of the resurrected Christ inspired Martin Luther King Jr. to say: "I refuse to accept the view that [humanity] is so tragically bound to the starless midnight of racism and war that the bright daybreak of peace and [kinship] can never become a reality. . . . I believe that unarmed truth and unconditional love will have the final word." The same Energy that raised Jesus from the dead now lives in us (Romans

8:11). This fertile power insists that racism will not have the final word.

As Divine image-bearers, we are called into mutual love and respect. Willie James Jennings wrote in *The Christian Imagination* that Jesus created a new space between all divisions, and "in that space a common life must ensue that allows the formation of a new identity," an identity that comes from our solidarity with the risen Body of Christ.

The Spirit that raised Jesus is still busy and productive. It constantly inspires people to exercise their unique gifts in ways that enrich and expand the entire Body. It amplifies the voices of those who have been voiceless; it shines its light on all who were once invisible. Racism, on the other hand, is similar to what Ignatius called the Devil, the enemy of human life, for instead of empowering people, it intimidates them; instead of inspiring their gifts, it suppresses them; instead of giving them a voice, it silences them.

Solidarity is the grace from God that interrupts the Devil of racism. It heals the wound of white supremacy. It pushes us to discomfort with whatever dishonors the Divine Image in another human being. Resurrection solidarity leads us toward the transformation of our world. It calls us to a new life that never stops growing and spreading, sending its life out in ever-wider circles of compassion and justice. Without that solidarity, we will continue to collude with the dehumanization of Christ's Body on earth.

The Resurrection empowers us to become one with the excluded and dominated, the exploited and ignored. It opens up endless possibilities for justice. The radical new life in Christ's body topples every "dividing wall of hostility" (Ephesians 2:14).

Are you ready for Resurrection power? Will you let it unite you with Christ's ongoing work of love?

Journal

Today, use an Ignatian Examen to structure your journal time.

First, *be present with God.* Simply sit in silence, opening yourself to the Divine Spirit who is also your own deepest identity.

Then, *express your gratitude.* Write in your journal a thank-you letter to God, listing all the things for which you are grateful today.

Next, *look back over the past day.* Ask yourself: Where did I have opportunities for solidarity with the resurrected Body of Christ? Write your answer in your journal.

Now, *reflect on your actions.* Ask yourself: Did I take advantage of these opportunities? Or did I ignore them? Write your answers in your journal.

Finally, *look forward.* Write your plan for how you will act in the future, collaborating more fully with Christ's call to solidarity within his risen Body. Be specific.

For Further Reflection

*Solidarity is not a feeling of vague compassion
or shallow distress at the misfortunes
of so many people, both near and far.
On the contrary, it is a firm and persevering determination
to commit oneself to the common good;
that is to say to the good of all and of each individual,
because we are all really responsible for all.*

—POPE JOHN PAUL II

Prayer

*Lord, grant me the grace to always receive you
as the ONE who lives within me.
Lord, open my eyes to see you as ONE
in me and in everyone.
Lord, thank you for coming to meet me where I am,
and now bring me back where you want me to be.
Open my eyes to seeing you in my community as ONE.
Lord, give me courage to recognize the times
when I resist being ONE with you.
Lord, help me to see the shortcomings
that take me away from seeing you in everyone as ONE.*

DAY 3

Resurrection Power

Overcoming a Culture of Death

The mind governed by societal systems leads to death,
but the mind governed by the Spirit brings life and peace.
The mind governed by societal systems
is hostile to God's law of love;
it does not submit to God's justice....
But if Christ is in you,
then even though you live within systemic injustice,
the Spirit gives life....
And if the Spirit who raised Jesus
from the dead is living in you,
that Spirit will also give life to you,
even in the midst of a culture of death.

—ROMANS 8:6,7,10,11 (AUTHOR'S PARAPHRASE)

Nothing resists the truth for long:
it may be assailed, but never overcome.

—IGNATIUS OF LOYOLA

Living in a climate of deep insecurity,
Jesus, faced with so narrow a margin of civil guarantees,
had to find some other basis
upon which to establish a sense of well-being.
He knew that the goals of religion as he understood them
could never be worked out within the then-established order.
Deep from within that order he projected a dream,
the logic of which would give to all the needful security.
There would be room for all,
and no [one] would be a threat to [others].

–HOWARD THURMAN

I n his Spiritual Diary, Ignatius wrote about his struggles to discern how God wanted him and his followers to live. In 1544, he devoted six entire weeks to seeking what God desired. He emerged from this time with a clearer sense of how he and his Society would serve God through a life of solidarity with the poor. They would not do this passively, cloistered away from the dirt and turmoil of the ordinary world. Instead, their prayer would flow out in action. They would seek to actively be God's hands and feet on earth, allowing the Energy of the Resurrection to flow through them, transforming the world around them in specific and practical ways.

As someone who has chosen to follow in Ignatius's footsteps, I too seek to live my life in this way. I try to be a man of the Resurrection, letting Christ rise to new life in me daily. But this year, it was difficult for me to feel the joy of Easter. Instead, I was in pain. I was sad.

During the Easter season of 2021, I was once again traumatized by the deaths of people of color, senseless deaths that took place during that holiest of seasons. On March 29, in Chicago, police shot Adam Toledo, a thirteen-year-old Latino boy who had his hands in the air in surrender. A few days later, on April 3, Gabriel Cassos, a twenty-one-year-old Latino man, was coming home from prayer at a Bronx mosque when someone began shooting; as Cassos ran from the gunman, toward the police, the officers shot and killed him. On April 7, in Maryland, two Black men, Dominique Williams and James Lionel Johnson, were shot in the back and killed, when an off-duty police officer falsely assumed they were stealing a car. The same day in California, another Black man, Roger Allen, was shot and killed after a routine check of an occupied parked vehicle; the officers saw what they thought was a gun in his lap (it turned out to be a toy). And then, on April 11 in Minnesota, a police officer killed twenty-year-old Daunte Wright after he was stopped for having expired registration tags; the white officer who shot him said she'd meant to taser him but pulled her gun instead.

The Easter season is usually one of my favorite times of the year. I'm a very social creature, who loves to get together with friends to eat and celebrate. I enjoy the services that commemorate Jesus' love and sacrifice, followed by his triumphant resurrection. But this year, for me and for many others in the Black community, the sin of racism eclipsed Easter joy.

Then, during the week after Daunte Wright's death, I Face-Timed with a friend from Minneapolis. She was distraught, crying so hard she was unable to get words out of her mouth. Finally, when she was able to verbalize her distress, she broke my heart. She insisted that I personally knew Daunte Wright.

I said I did not. I was so vehement about it that, looking back, I remind myself of Peter when he denied over and over that he knew Jesus. "No," I repeated again and again, even as my friend tried to convince me otherwise. "I did not know the man."

But then, after we said goodbye, I was forced to admit the truth to myself: I do have a connection to Wright. Not so long ago, his sister was in an AP Spanish class of mine in Minneapolis. I remember her well; she was a smart and attentive student.

Upon reflection, I recognized that my denial of knowing Daunte Wright could not be blamed simply on a faulty memory. I didn't want to claim knowledge of Wright, because that would bring his death too close to me. It would make it too real. I realized then that racism is like the coronavirus: sooner or later, it will affect either you or someone you know. Both are viruses that have invisibly infiltrated every region of the world. Pope Francis got it right when he said, "Racism is a virus that quickly mutates and, instead of disappearing, goes into hiding, and lurks in waiting."

My friend in Minneapolis is a white woman, married with two white children. She is upper-middle class and volunteers in the Catholic high school where I once taught. I am a Black man, a religious who has taken vows of poverty, chastity, and obedience. I teach the psychology of race and racism at a university in Omaha and also work as a psychotherapist. My friend and I live hundreds of miles apart, and we have not seen each other for over two years. Our lives look very different—and yet on that day in April, we were both suffering the same pain: the loss of a former student's brother. Racism casts a wide net that sooner or later catches us all.

While you are reading this chapter, someone you know or someone who knows someone you know is suffering some kind of racial injustice in America. It is not a matter of *if* but *when* you will hear that someone who is in some way connected to you has died because of the systemic racism that is deeply ingrained in America's DNA. Today, none of us can avoid the ravages of racism, none of us can pretend or protest that it doesn't exist in the United States. We are all victims of it, whether it affects us directly or indirectly. Whether we are Black, brown, or white, we will all pay the price for our systemic sin. None of us is immune to the consequences of it. The next victim might be someone you love. It is not a matter of who or if; it is a matter of where and when.

Given the many incidences of police violence against Blacks, I have begun to suspect that some white officers are afraid of Black skin. These officers identify Black skin as a danger they must protect themselves from: They stand ready to shoot suspects proactively, instead of reactively, when their lives are actually threatened. Thus, to be Black in America means living with a constant fear of being killed, even by those who are theoretically tasked with the job of protecting us.

My black skin not only dictates my racial identity but also defines and embodies my sense of "home." If you are Black, your color travels with you wherever you go; it is not simply a trait you possess, like having green eyes or big feet. *Black* is something I engage with every day; it gives me direction and orients me, just as my belief in Jesus directs and orients me. Now, *Black* had become the place that buried me alive, even during Easter, when I should have been filled with hope. I could not pretend to be happy while my brothers and sisters were dying.

I sat with my pain a long time, waiting to see what would happen next. I prayed for a way to deal with my discomfort in a Christ-like way, but all I could feel was rage. I couldn't stop thinking about the many people of color who are victims of systemic racism. I remembered the *Washington Post* database of police shootings in the United States, which shows that although Blacks make up only 13 percent of America's population, they are killed by police at double the rate of whites—and 40 percent of them are unarmed at the time they are killed. Why is simply being Black a good enough reason for some police to shoot to kill?

But perhaps what most of all had me trapped in Good Friday, unable to move on to Easter, was the lack of response from my fellow Christians. Where were their voices of outrage? Why weren't they standing up to call for justice? James Baldwin once wrote, "From my point of view, no label, no slogan, no party, no skin color, and indeed no religion is more important than the human being." Jesus would have agreed. So why don't his followers today understand that?

More than a thousand years ago, the prophet Isaiah expressed my own feelings now in the twenty-first century:

> Their deeds are evil deeds,
> and acts of violence are in their hands.
> Their feet rush into sin;

they are swift to shed innocent blood.
They pursue evil schemes;
acts of violence mark their ways.
The way of peace they do not know;
there is no justice in their paths.
They have turned them into crooked roads;
no one who walks along them will know peace.
So justice is far from us,
and righteousness does not reach us.
We look for light, but all is darkness;
for brightness, but we walk in deep shadows. . . .
We look for justice, but find none;
for deliverance, but it is far away.
So justice is driven back,
and righteousness stands at a distance. (59:6–9,11,14)

And then, in the midst of my dark despair, the Spirit lit a spark of light. I felt compelled to know Christ more intimately through the pain of my fellow Black Americans. I was inspired to love Christ more dearly through the trauma of racism. I became motivated to follow Christ more closely as a Black-skinned man bearing within me the power and witness of Divine love and justice.

Easter, I realized, never erases the crucifixion. We look around us and see evidence everywhere that we are still far from the Reign of Heaven. We see violence and injustice. We see power that walks all over the vulnerable ones in our society. We see entire communities being scapegoated. And we see apathy and indifference. The world was no better in Ignatius's day. Humanity has always lived in a world where we must see the ever-present reality of suffering and sin

And yet Ignatius heard the Divine call to disrupt the culture of death that surrounded him. He understood that Jesus' victory over death is *through* death.

Like Daunte Wright and so many others, Jesus was a victim of the state. He was one of the vulnerable ones who suffered under the crushing foot of unjust power. He struggled to breathe on the cross, and then he gasped, "It is finished."

God knows my rage at injustice. God-the-Parent must have wept while God-in-Jesus was put to death. Today, God is offended when some people try to deny others the life-giving breath that is the Divine gift to us all. God gasps for breath every time another Black person is killed. God is with us, screaming for justice.

But Jesus rose again. When he came in his transformed body to the disciples, the Gospel account says he *breathed* on them, demonstrating that human power could not rob him of the life-giving Energy we call the Spirit. Through the Divine Breath, our humanity is restored. Even though we live in the sorrow and darkness of Good Friday, the Breath of Life is still moving. Resurrection Energy is at work in our world. Ultimately, the culture of death will not triumph.

"I don't believe in death without resurrection." Archbishop Oscar Romero said shortly before he was murdered. "If they kill me, I will rise again in the Salvadorian people." As Romero fought against the unjust regime that was crushing his people, he understood that the power of the Resurrection is relentless; it works not only in spite of death but *through* death.

In 1966, another force for Resurrection, Martin Luther King Jr. preached in Atlanta about the ongoing interplay between death and resurrection. "Good Friday is as much a fact of life as Easter," he said; "failure is as much a fact of life as success; disappointment is as much a fact of life as fulfillment." Then he added that God didn't promise us we would avoid "trials and tribulations" but that "God has the power to give you a kind of inner equilibrium through your pain." It is that equilibrium that allows us to continue the endless work of Resurrection.

The real meaning of Easter is not about hunting for pastel-colored eggs, wearing new clothes, or tables groaning beneath the weight of baked ham and leg of lamb. The Resurrection is far more than that. Jesus' empty tomb is the evidence that death will never have the last word, not only in the eternal sense but also in the arc of justice that bends over our world.

When my ancestors found the strength to sing, to dance, and to rebel against their so-called masters, that was Resurrection. They looked at the stories in the Bible, and they saw that God had brought justice out of many impossible situations. That knowledge inspired people like Harriet Tubman, who not only escaped from slavery herself but also led another seventy people safely through the Underground Railroad to freedom. "The resurrection," wrote M. Shawn Copeland, "confirmed their expectation of freedom as the end of enslavement."

And then, when slavery finally came to an end, that was the bursting forth of Resurrection. When the Civil Rights movement was born out of the Jim Crow era, that too was Resurrection. Today, our world needs us to again make space for Resurrection power.

My hope, even amid the death that's all around, comes from the risen Christ. I know that my human imagination is often limited by the culture of death within which I live. I see the rich exploiting the poor; I see the vulnerable suffering the consequences of corrupted power. But I know that Resurrection

Energy is unstoppable. It tells me that God has no limits when it comes to transforming our world.

Our job, as Ignatius of Loyola came to understand, is to actively, intentionally cooperate with that energy. Apathy is not a safe stance to take, for the more we deny the existence of racism among us, the more we will die from it. If Ignatius were alive today, I believe he would invite us to pray and engage in uncomfortable conversations about race, recognizing that racism is a sin that is everywhere. He would insist that we expose the privileges and disadvantages of skin color. And then he would challenge us to discern what action God would have us take.

Today, God wants *you* to be a channel for Resurrection Energy. Will you allow yourself to be a Divine force that changes the world?

Journal

List in your journal all the situations where you have encountered the culture of death in the past week. These might include incidents of racism and violence in the news, but they might also be racist comments you overheard, attitudes you observed, or even movements within your own heart and mind.

Now, offer each of these situations to God. Imagine that you can see the power of the Resurrection reaching into them, in the form of light. Now describe in your journal how you see these situations being transformed.

Finally, imagine that Resurrection Energy is flowing through your own muscles and brain. Will you open yourself to it? What might hold you back? Write about your feelings—and then describe the images that come to you when you imagine this Energy using you to change the world. Remember, Ignatius was willing to spend six weeks waiting to discern what God wanted him to do. Have the same persistence and patience as you ask God to show you where and how you should take action.

For Further Reflection

Jesus's resurrection is the beginning of God's new project
not to snatch people away from earth to heaven
but to colonize earth with the life of heaven.

—N. T. WRIGHT

Prayer

God, you say to me,
"Speak up for those who cannot speak for themselves,
for the rights of all who are destitute.
Speak up and judge fairly;
defend the rights of the poor and needy" (Proverbs 31:8–9).
Give me Resurrection power to hear your word,
to live your word, to change the world.

DAY 4

The Resurrection and the Imagination

Empowered to Envision a Better World

Be made new in the attitude of your minds;
and put on the new self,
created to be like God in true righteousness and holiness.

—EPHESIAN 4:23–24

We cannot expect too much from God.

—IGNATIUS OF LOYOLA

The desire of God's heart
is immeasurably larger
than our imaginations can conjure.

—GREG BOYLE, S.J.

Ignatius of Loyola was blessed with a powerful imagination. During his convalescence after his battle injury, he at first passed his time daydreaming about all the marvelous things he might do in pursuit of the woman of his dreams. He imagined ways he might earn glory and honor when he returned to the battlefield. He pictured himself being lauded and admired at court.

But as the days went slowly by, Ignatius realized these fantasies were a form of "vainglory"—an empty, fruitless stroking of his ego. But he did not make the mistake of thinking that his imagination itself was sinful. He recognized that the imagination can be a powerful vehicle for growth, both internally, within our own hearts and minds, and externally, in the physical world.

Now, as Ignatius read about Jesus and the lives of saints, his autobiography says "he would stop to think, reasoning with himself: 'How should it be, if I did this which St. Francis did, and this which St. Dominic did?' And thus he used to think over many things which he was finding good, always proposing to himself difficult and laborious things. And as he was proposing these, it seemed to him he was finding in himself an ease as regards putting them into practice." Ignatius had discovered something that today psychologists, sports coaches, and business leaders know to be true: the imagination is a potent tool for creating a better future.

Psychologists define imagination as the ability to form a mental image of something that is not currently perceived through the five senses. This image is not limited to a visual "picture" in the mind; the imagination, as Ignatius, knew is even more powerful when it incorporates all five senses as well as emotions. Coaches teach athletes that the imagination is a robust way to enhance their performance; in fact, they've learned that peak performance depends as much on mental "practice" as it does on physical preparation. Bill Gates and Steve Jobs used their imaginations to envision how personal computers could change the way we work, how we educate our children, and how we entertain ourselves; the power of their imagination changed our world.

Today, our world has been shaken by pandemic and social crises, but the destruction of these events also creates opportunity for something new to emerge. Imagination—the capacity to create mental models of things that don't yet exist—allows us to seize these opportunities and find new ways forward. Imagination enables us to not merely adapt to a new reality but to thrive by shaping it with justice and love.

When Ignatius surrendered his pride and passion to Jesus, he didn't abandon his ability to have big dreams. His fantasies no longer focused on himself, however. Instead, God used them to create pictures and possibilities that were huge and far-reaching. The Resurrection proved to Ignatius that Divine Imagination has no limits, and he saw no reason to place ceilings on his own capacity for possibility.

Ignatius also understood that the imagination is a powerful devotional tool. He wrote:

> When we contemplate Christ our Lord, the representation will consist in seeing in imagination the material place where the object is that we wish to contemplate. I said the material place, for example, the temple, or the mountain where Jesus or His Mother is, according to the

subject matter of the contemplation. Imagine Christ our
Lord present before you upon the cross.

This practice not only allows us to deepen our connection to
Jesus; it also stretches our minds, making room for the limitless
inspiration of the Divine Spirit.

This is what my ancestors instinctively did, and their spirituals gave a mighty voice to their dreams. In fact, they did
exactly what Ignatius had recommended: "The makers and sing-
ers of the spirituals insert themselves and us in the action," wrote
M. Shawn Copeland; "they take up the position of first-person
witnesses and narrators of key actions or events. They allow us
to hear Joseph beg, Mary weep, the sound of the trumpet, the
heavy silence of the angels, and the voice of Jesus."

My community has always been good at imagining. But I
wonder how many of us allow our capacity to dream become
the fuel that inspires us to work for justice. Or do we relegate
the imagination to childhood? Do we doubt our own ability to
imagine the Reign of Heaven?

Jesuit author Dean Brackley wrote about our tendency to
mistake the genuine surrender of our selfish pride for the "false
humility that leads us to bury our talents in a napkin. The times
call for imagination, creativity, and bold action." He went on to
say: "When the idea of a worthwhile project comes to us, we
feel it would be arrogant to attribute [it] to God's work in us.
. . . So we refuse to take our ideas and desires seriously." This,
Ignatius would have said, is actually "a fear with the appearance
of humility."

When we take the imagination seriously, trusting that God
can and will use it for the Divine Reign, we will be pushed past

our fear. We will come alive in new ways. We will be empowered for the fight for social justice.

But when we let ourselves sink into apathy and indifference, the fire of our imagination flickers out. We can no longer envision the possibility of a better world. Something within us is dead. Along these lines, social ethicist Sharon Welch wrote:

> We need to learn that failure to develop the strength to remain angry, in order to continually love and therefore to resist, is to die. The death we face is not as immediate as that faced by many African Americans. The Euro-American who gives up the struggle against war or against racism does not face physical death. The death that is experienced by those who turn from rage, who forego resistance is nonetheless real. It is the death of the imagination, the death of caring, the death of the ability to love. For if we cease resisting, we lose the ability to imagine a world that is any different than that of the present state; we lose the ability to imagine strategies of resistance and ways of sustaining each other in the long struggle for justice. We lose the ability to care, to love life in all its forms. We cannot numb our pain at the degradation of life without numbing our joy at its abundance.

While I was working on this book, I called a friend to catch up. My heart ached as I listened to her describe her reaction to the many acts of violent racism that had happened recently. "As a follower of Christ," she said, "and as someone who believes in the power of the Spiritual Exercises, I do not want to live with despair, but I do not see any hope soon. I do not want to be pessimistic, but honestly, I had hoped we would have had a better country after all that has happened."

I do not blame her for her discouragement. I too have shared it many times. And yet somehow I find the way to be a man of hope. I believe the Reign of Heaven is waiting to emerge from our world of oppression and injustice. Resurrection seeds are ready to sprout and burst forth with new, green possibility. Dr. King's Beloved Community—a community of healed relationships and healed social systems—may seem impossible, but as theologian Chanequa Walker-Barnes has reminded us, "As followers of the risen Christ, we are called to believe in the impossible every day."

"The Possible's slow fuse," wrote poet Emily Dickinson, "is lit by the Imagination." Jesuit author Michael Paul Gallagher said the imagination is the ability "to glimpse and grasp possibilities . . . a gradually explosive power of new perception." He went on to say, "Imagination is the location . . . of our potential healing. It is crucial for the quality of our seeing, because it can save us from superficiality and torpor and awaken us to larger hopes and possibilities."

The Resurrection is a call to *imagine.* It challenges us to broaden our perspectives and discover the full volume of what God is calling us to be and do. Imagination fuels empathy, allowing us to explore what it means to feel, see, and think as another person. It enlightens the ignorant darkness of racism. "A dream is the bearer of a new possibility," wrote Howard Thurman, "the enlarged horizon, the great hope."

The imagination not only empowers us as individuals; it also has the power to re-create our world, allowing us to be co-creators with God. We will find our way out of the sin of systemic racism when we can imagine a new way of being community together. We must imagine something beyond our current situation.

In 2016, the Jesuit Superior General, Father Arturo Sosa, called on us to "think creatively about the ways in which our service to the mission of Christ Jesus can be more effective . . . to think about ways of deeply understanding the unique moment of human history in which we are living and to contribute to the search for alternatives for overcoming poverty, inequality, and oppression." As followers of Jesus, Father Sosa said, we "seek not only the improbable, but the impossible, because nothing is impossible for God." The Resurrection shows us the impossible becoming possible.

Jesuit author William Lynch wrote that to be a Christian is "literally to imagine things with God." What is God calling you to imagine?

Journal

Have you ever experienced the power of your own imagination to change the outside world? If so, write about this time in your journal.

Now let your imagination play for a while. Ask God to inspire you with dreams for a better world. Then brainstorm in your journal ideas for ways you personally could work to end racism. Don't allow any sense of false humility—or common-sense!—hamper you. Imagine big. Imagine wild. Imagine crazy.

Finally, reread what you have written. Do you see seeds of Resurrection power in your dreams? Is there an idea you want to develop farther? Ask the Spirit to lay on your heart and mind God's dreams for you. In the days that come, allow God to live the Divine dream through you.

For Further Reflection

I used to think racism was the product of ignorance ...
today, I put racism down to a failure in imagination.
Imagination, among other things,
is our capacity to think what it might be like
living in someone else's shoes.
It is the faculty in the human brain that,
when activated by our choice and discipline,
results in us looking at the same world
but through different eyes.
... [R]acism is the result of an atrophied imagination.
It arises when either we refuse to imagine
what the lives of others feel like,
or when we abdicate the use of our imagination....
If ever there was a time in human history
when we needed to reactivate our imaginations,
to picture and feel the world

through the lenses of the mistrusted "other," it is now.
… Racism is a sign of crass cerebral indolence.

—MARK STIBBE

Prayer

Lord, we too desire to contribute
to that which today seems impossible:
a humanity reconciled in justice,
that dwells peacefully in a well-cared-for common home,
where there is a place for all,
since we recognize each other as brothers and sisters,
as sons and daughters of the same and only Father.
We confess that we have been slow to believe
and follow you into the newness of your kingdom.
We have feared and distrusted our brothers and sisters,
allowing ourselves to be ruled by the divisions
of race, gender, nation, and wealth
that belong to the old order.
Holy and gracious God, pardon our sins
and free our captive imaginations.
Renew us in the power of your love,
through Jesus Christ our Lord.

—ARTURO SOSA, S.J.

DAY 5

Let Us Never Forget

Opening Our Ears and Our Hearts to History

*Remember the former things,
those of long ago.*

—ISAIAH 46:9

*Recall to memory
the gravity and malice of sin.*

—IGNATIUS OF LOYOLA

*The past unavoidably impacts the present.
If we want to pursue racial justice today,
then we need to know what happened in the past
to create the circumstances of the present.*

*History provides the vital context
to pursue solutions that are rooted
in a firm understanding
in the causes and consequences of racism.*

–JEMAR TISBY

We Jesuits have an expression—"going to Manresa." After Ignatius's initial conversion, his months in Manresa were essential to the transformation he was undergoing. In Manresa, the seeds of everything he would do in life began to grow. And so, for us to say we are "going to Manresa" means we are making a pilgrimage to the beginning of our story as the Society of Jesus. Through the past, we are reconnecting to the future in new ways. For me, writing this entire book has been, in a sense, a form of going to Manresa. It has allowed me to rediscover the story of Ignatius of Loyola, while finding in that story the roots that will nourish my current vocation as a man working for antiracism. As Ignatius said, "To foresee what we shall have to do, and to call up for judgment what we have done, are the most trustworthy rules for right action."

After Jesus' resurrection, he did something quite similar while he was talking to the two disciples who were on the road to Emmaus. These two folks were downhearted and hopeless because of Jesus' death. They didn't realize that Jesus was right there in their presence. He talked to them about their history as Jews, going back through all the ancient Hebrew scriptures to reveal to them the connections to the present.

As he helped them remember the past, he showed th[e] new reality.

✠ Remembering is important throughout scripture, and it is a part of our practice as followers of Christ. Each time we participate in the Eucharist, we unite past and present as we actively remember Christ's death on the cross. Memory keeps us rooted. It nourishes the present.

But not all memories are pleasant. In the early days after his conversion, Ignatius was haunted by the memory of sins he had committed. As a boy, he had stolen fruit from a neighbor's trees and then allowed someone else to take the blame (and also pay the fine). A few years later, he and his brother were arrested for beating another man. Ignatius's many romantic escapades also got him into trouble; on one occasion, a cuckolded husband was so infuriated that he threatened to kill Ignatius.

Ignatius came to understand that he was a "beloved sinner," as we discussed in Week One; he knew that despite the bad memories of the past, he was secure in the embrace of Divine Love. But he never thought the past could simply be erased and forgotten. Memory remained an important part of the spirituality he taught. Through memory, we recognize where in the past we have "missed the mark" of God's love and justice, and this awareness helps us to do better in the future. Memory also shows us where we need to take action in the present; it may call on us to make restitution. (In 1535, fourteen years after his conversion, Ignatius returned to his hometown to make restitution for the sins he had committed there in his youth. He gave his last two acres of land to the man who owned the fruit trees he had robbed so many years before.)

We too must look back at the past in order to take action in the present. In 2021, Pope Francis preached that "we need to pray for healing of our negative memory." By this, he was not saying that we should ask God to give us amnesia. We are not to forget the past. But we do need to heal the past. And to do that, we must first allow ourselves to remember. We must tell the stories we have allowed ourselves to forget. "Just as the sacrament of reconciliation begins with the humble acknowledgement of our sinfulness," wrote Joseph Brown, a Jesuit professor of Africana who is also my mentor, "it is only by telling these stories with humility and openness that we begin the process of reconciliation."

America has not wanted to remember the true history of people of color. History texts used in schools usually omit or distort the experiences of people of color, while they exaggerate the accomplishments of whites. For example, were you taught that the Puritans participated in the massacre of the indigenous people whose lands the Puritans wanted for their own? Or did you grow up drawing pictures of happy white people in black hats sitting down to eat Thanksgiving dinner with Squanto, the token Native in the story? Did you ever learn that George Washington committed germ warfare by giving Natives blankets infected with smallpox—or did you only learn he was so honest that he confessed the truth after cutting down a cherry tree? Did you learn in school what happened at Wounded Knee Creek in southwestern South Dakota in 1890, when U.S. Army troops massacred as many as three hundred Lakota? Did you ever learn that while white World War II veterans benefited from the GI Bill and got financing for new homes, men of color, who had also fought for America, did not? And did you ever hear in any history class about November 2, 1920, when a mob of white people in Ocoee, Florida, were so enraged at a Black man who had tried to vote that for the next two days they burned an entire Black community to the ground, killing as many as sixty people in the process? Or what about the Tulsa Massacre? How old were you when you first heard that in 1921, white mobs in Tulsa, Oklahoma, attacked the city's Black community, killing as many as three hundred people, destroying the Black business district, and leaving thousands of people homeless? All these details have been omitted from our history books. Some people even suggest that it would be "unpatriotic" to include them.

History is not merely a class we take in school and then forget about once we are adults. And the importance of history is not so much about the past as it is the present. Just as each of us carries our own history within us, and we are unconsciously controlled by it in many ways, so our society also carries its history. Whether we realize it or not, history is present in the way we live our lives today. White supremacy is the legacy of our past.

In the Hebrew scriptures the original word that's been translated as "remember" is *zakar,* a word that implies not only thought but also speaking. When the Bible talks about remembering, it is not merely a private act of interior meditation on the past; it asks that memory be spoken aloud, thereby bringing it out into the community where everyone can participate it.

Many times people protest, "But I wasn't around four hundred years ago or two hundred years ago or a hundred years ago. I didn't kill Native Americans. I didn't own slaves. I didn't put Asian Americans in concentration camps." Leviticus chapter 26 in the Hebrew scriptures, which is all about remembering the past, speaks to this attitude. There, God tells the people to bring the sins of their ancestors out into the open. The people were not personally guilty of those sins, and yet God asked them to make amends for them. Wrong must be righted; the damage done must be repaired. And if the ancestors fail to do this, the job falls on their descendants. The fact that the perpetrators are dead does not erase the harm that's been done.

What would God say to America today, I wonder. White Americans deprived Black people of the rewards of their labor during slavery, and they robbed them of opportunities for wealth-building during the Jim Crow era. Even though slavery was abolished and Jim Crow policies are no longer in effect, the Black community continues to bear the economic burden of the past, even as many white families and white institutions continue to benefit from inheritances built on the backs of Blacks' labor. We also live on land that once belonged to North America's Native tribes; we prosper from businesses and farms built on this land, while today one out of every four Native Americans is living in poverty. "The plunder from the poor is in your houses," wrote the prophet Isaiah, and the same is true today for America.

The Bible recognizes that the sins of the past can be like a snowball that grows ever larger in size and momentum as it travels downhill. We are born into a world that's been shaped by the sins of our ancestors. There's no avoiding the influence those sins have on our lives today. Our ancestors' sinful choices and actions have now worked themselves so deeply into our lives and our minds that without some effort, we're not even aware they're there. As theologian Michael Rhodes wrote:

> Scripture, then, demands that I confess that white supremacy is a deadly sickness my ancestors carried with them as they created culture, founded institutions,

built schools, told stories, and gathered in churc' live and work in the world they helped to create, a. confess that I have been infected by their contagion.

People of color also carry the negative legacy of the past. Researchers are finding that intergenerational trauma is a reality. Black babies have significantly higher levels of stress hormones than white babies; their bodies already bear the weight of racial injustice. Epigenetic research has discovered evidence that trauma can rewrite DNA, and these changes can be passed down to future generations, with the result being higher mortality rates. Author and researcher Joy DeGruy uses the term *Post-Traumatic Slave Syndrome* (PTSS) to describe the enduring injury Black people carry in the form of generations of collective grief and trauma.

German theologian Johann Baptist Metz believed that followers of Christ are called to align themselves with the victims of history. After the Holocaust, he challenged the German church to face the reality of the genocide carried out in the concentration camps. "Articulating others' suffering is the presupposition of all claims to truth," Metz said. "Even those made by theology." He also said:

> For many, even for many Christians, Auschwitz has slowly slipped over the horizon of their memories. But nobody escapes the anonymous consequences of this catastrophe. The theological question after Auschwitz is not only "Where was God in Auschwitz?" It is also "Where was humanity in Auschwitz?"

Metz spoke of "dangerous memory," a term that theologian Shawn Copeland has also used. In her writing, Copeland points out that today's racial problems are the reflections of the past. Separating children from their families, placing them in cages, and ignoring their health needs have happened before. Native children were taken from their parents and placed in boarding schools, where they were abused physically and sometimes sexually. My ancestors' children were taken from their parents, tortured, and sold as property. Copeland calls on Christ's followers to reflect on these memories as a call to action in the present. In her book *Enfleshing Freedom,* she wrote that solidarity with the oppressed must begin in "intentional remembering of the dead, the exploited, the despised victims of history."

I am proud that my own order, the Jesuits, is taking steps to publicly recognize and make restitution for its historical acts of racism. They have identified more than ten thousand descendants of enslaved people whose sale benefited Jesuit institutions that still exist today, and we are working to give this group of people real and practical educational and economic opportunities. "As an Ignatian family," the effort has stated, "to grow in the solidarity that comes with journeying with Christ suffering in the world today is to see our own story is tied together with those of the descendants" of those whom the Society once enslaved.

Remembering the past is not always a negative experience that calls for repentance and restitution. Sometimes we need to rediscover the past to recognize the strengths we have in the present. Ignatius found this to be true at the time of his conversion, as he meditated on the lives of saints who had lived before him. Their example inspired him and gave him confidence to launch out into a new life. "Let everyone set before themselves for imitation," he wrote, "those who are noteworthy for zeal and greatness of spirit."

America today owes much of our strength to the past contributions of people of color. Long before the arrival of Europeans, the aboriginal peoples of the Americas had rich and vibrant cultures. They had successfully adapted to the continent's diverse environments, developing a wide range of plants and animals that are still important staples of our diet today. Native American governments in eastern North America, particularly the Haudenosaunee (the Iroquois Confederacy), were models of representative democracy that the United States used when it formed its own government (where power is distributed between a central authority, the federal government, and smaller political units, the states).

In a similar way, my ancestors' history does not begin with slavery, as many white people seem to think. In our history classes, however, we were seldom taught that when white slavers captured Africans, they were not a more sophisticated society taking advantage of primitive people. The human beings who were shipped as commodities to the Americas came from communities with large-scale civilizations that had tax systems, sophisticated irrigation, and universities.

European historians erased this history and instead gave all credit to the Greeks and Romans for the development of civilization. Even the undeniable contributions of ancient Egypt were attributed to whites, since somehow Egypt was thought to be populated by "dark-skinned whites," rather than Africans. Meanwhile, anthropological evidence has proven early African advances in mathematics, navigation, physics, engineering, and other scientific fields. Many inventions from Africa contributed to the birth of every technology that exists today, including the first paper, alphabet, ink, and pen. African astronomers were the first to develop a solar calendar that divided the year into three hundred and sixty-five days with twelve months of thirty days each. African mathematicians used geometry to build the pyramids, and we owe our present-day decimal system to their work.

Black Americans have also made more recent contributions, of course. Our lives would not be the same without them. George Washington Carver, who was born enslaved in 1864, became one of the most prominent scientists and inventors of his time, as well as a teacher at the Tuskegee Institute; he devised more than a hundred products using only peanuts. In the twentieth century, Percy Julian, who hadn't been allowed to attend high school because he was Black, went on to be a pioneer in the chemical synthesis of medicinal drugs such as cortisone, steroids, and birth control pills. Alice Ball, who died when she was only twenty-four, was another African American chemist who, in the early twentieth century, developed the first successful treatment for people suffering from Hansen's disease (leprosy). Katherine Johnson, a Black mathematician, performed the complicated calculations that enabled humans to successfully achieve space flight. (Her story is told in the movie *Hidden Figures*.) And these are only a few of the intelligent, talented people of color who have contributed to our lives.

America also owes a debt to the Black church. Jennifer Harvey, author of *Dear White Christians,* has pointed out that Black Christian leaders were essential to the Civil Rights movement, and yet their full message has not only been ignored but erased altogether. Harvey has said that Black Christians, "demanded power and resource redistribution, and part of the crisis we're in today is directly related to how deeply we have . . . ignored and rejected those calls for power and resource redistribution." She went on to say:

There's been this kind of amnesia from white Christians; we don't even know the sins that we've committed, and so we're stuck in our calls for equity and reconciliation and diversity. These calls are so hollow, but we don't even know that, because we haven't named and confessed the erasure that we actively committed moving out of the civil rights movement era.

Memory, as Ignatius taught, is essential to our spiritual pilgrimage. The Christian sacrament of memory—the Eucharist—calls us first of all to remember the suffering of Jesus and how that relates to our responsibility toward others. Second, as we join in this communal act, we are reminded to love our neighbors (as Jesus defined that word in his parable of the Good Samaritan). And finally, we ask God to remember us by being present in our lives today. As Michael Rhodes wrote, "Intergenerational confession . . . isn't just about naming our intergenerational sins. It's about *turning from them*. It's about offering our whole selves as 'weapons of justice.'"

Robert P. Jones, author of *White Too Long: The Legacy of White Supremacy in American Christianity,* wrote:

If we are finally going to live into the fullness of the promise of liberty and justice for all Americans, we will have to recover from our white-supremacy-induced amnesia. Confronting historical atrocities is indeed difficult, and at times overwhelming. But if we want to root out an insidious white supremacy from our institutions, our religion, and our psyches, we will have to move beyond forgetfulness and silence. Importantly, as white Americans find the courage to embark on this journey of transformation, we will discover that the beneficiaries are not only our country and our fellow nonwhite and non-Christian Americans, but also ourselves. We will understand that this project is not an altruistic one, but rather a desperate life-and-death struggle for our own future.

Jesuit John R. Sheets has said that in the Spiritual Exercises, Ignatius calls us to remember the past, not to change it or deny it but as a way to "lighten the present and future course of progress." This is an "act of Love directed toward the past," which finds its expression in the present and the future.

What about you? Will you embrace past, present, and future in this intentional act of love?

Journal

Today's reading is a call to actively bear the burden of educating yourself and those you know about the true history shared by people of color in America. This book has attempted to do that in nearly every Day's reading, but it doesn't end here. There are countless other resources available to you in the form of websites, books, movies, podcasts, and documentaries. Don't rely on communities of color to do the education: these stories from the past are often deeply personal for people of color, even traumatizing, and it's not their job to educate you.

In your journal today, make a plan for how you will continue your historical education once you have finished reading this book. Use the Internet to find lists of books or other resources that will help you. Create a "curriculum" for yourself that you can realistically commit to in the year ahead. (You might want to begin with New York University's "Racism Education Resource List," available at https://www.nyu.edu/alumni/news-publications/nyu-connect-newsletter/june-2020/antiracism-education-resource-list.html, or the Trying Together organization's "Racism Tools," at https://tryingtogether.org/community-resources/anti-racism-tools/.)

For Further Reflection

Looking back on the past four hundred years,
this nation's story of racism can seem almost inevitable.
But it didn't have to be this way.
At critical turning points throughout history,
people made deliberate choices
to construct and reinforce a racist America.
Our generation has the opportunity
to make different choices,
ones that lead to greater human dignity and justice,
but only if we pay heed to our history
and respond with the truth and courage
that confronting racism requires.

–JEMAR TISBY

Prayer

*For a spirit of forgiveness and reconciliation among peoples
who share a history of mutual
mistrust, hatred or aggression, we pray.
Lord of all nations, hear our prayer.
For those who have struggled in the past
and continue to do so today for civil rights,
economic justice and the elimination of discrimination
based on race, nationality or religion, we pray.
Lord of all nations, hear our prayer.
That we may make a personal commitment
to abolish social structures which inhibit
economic, educational and social advancement
of the poor, we pray .
Lord of all nations, hear our prayer.
That we may work for decent working conditions,
adequate income, housing, education and health care
for all people, we pray.
Lord of all nations, hear our prayer.*

— AUGUSTINIAN SECRETARIATE FOR JUSTICE AND PEACE

DAY 6

Kairos Time

Impatient for Justice and Patient for God

"In the time of my favor I heard you,
and in the day of salvation I helped you."
I tell you, now is the time of God's favor,
now is the day of salvation.

—2 CORINTHIANS 6:2

He who carries God in his heart
bears heaven with him wherever he goes.

—IGNATIUS OF LOYOLA

Now is the accepted time, not tomorrow,
not some more convenient season.

*It is today that our best work can be done
and not some future day or future year.
It is today that we fit ourselves
for the greater usefulness of tomorrow.
Today is the seed time,
now are the hours of work,
and tomorrow comes the harvest.*

—W.E.B. DUBOIS

In Jesus' last words before he left his disciples, he spoke to them about *Kairos*. He was referring to a sense of time that was different from the sequential linear sense we usually have. *Kairos* speaks to the "right time," the time of opportunity. It is a space when eternity and linear time intersect. This makes it both urgent and yet at the same time outside our human sense of a timetable.

I confess, the concept gives me trouble. I often feel impatient for things to change. I see the continual oppression that's destroying communities of color as a national health crisis that has now risen to a state of emergency. How can we be patient when people are dying?

In 1903, at the very beginning of his book *The Souls of Black Folk,* W.E.B. DuBois wrote about "the strange meaning of being black here at the dawning of the Twentieth Century." He insisted that this meaning was important for white readers to understand as well, because "the problem of the Twentieth Century is the problem of the color line." More than sixty years later, Robert F. Kennedy stated that America's number-one domestic problem was the race problem. And now, another fifty years later yet, the problem is still here. No wonder I am hungry for justice.

You cannot delay feeding your child when she is hungry—and you can't delay immediate justice to those who are in need of it. I have many friends who said during the trial of George Floyd's murderer that we should wait to protest until the investigation had run its course. Martin Luther King Jr. might respond to them with the same words he wrote in 1963: "You may well ask, 'Why direct action? Why sit-ins, marches, etc.? Isn't negotiation a better path?' You are exactly right in your call for negotiation. Indeed, this is the purpose of direct action."

Injustice hunger is more than the sense of appetite that says, "I think I'd like some ice cream for dinner." Instead, injustice is like starvation. It is urgent; it insists that action must be taken. As someone whose early childhood was spent in a developing nation, let me tell you, real hunger is different from appetite. At one point when I was a kid, my parents fell on hard times. Sometimes, the only dinner we had was a glass of sugar water and a small piece of bread. The hunger I felt then was nothing like the feeling I have after a long ride on my bicycle. Today, I may feel hungry after my exercise, but I am already planning my next meal. I am confident that the refrigerator and pantry cupboards will have plenty of food to satisfy me.

If you too have ever lacked a primary need, then you know what I'm talking about. Racism robs people of their primary needs—food, health, shelter, safety. When we are sitting at home comfortable and well-fed, it's easy to criticize rioters who are screaming for food. As Martin Luther King said, "Three hundred years of humiliation, abuse and deprivation cannot be expected to find voice in a whisper." Enjoying privilege does not give us license to criticize or judge those who are in need. In fact, having privilege without a moral conscience leads us down a perverse path. People of color who are crying in the streets for justice were never in privileged positions.

People ask why Black people cannot wait. We have been waiting in America for more than four hundred years. Anger is rising, and patience is wearing thin. As King remarked, "Perhaps it is easy for those who have never felt the stinging darts of [racism] to say wait." He continued: "When you have seen hate-filled policemen curse, kick, brutalize and even kill your black brothers and sisters with impunity . . . then you will understand why we find it difficult to wait." We are tired of waiting.

Today, I am starving for justice. I am starving for a day when I can walk with freedom in the land of the free. I am starving for the time when I can be seen as a man, not as a boy. I am starving for a day when I don't have to be afraid as I'm driving because I saw a police car behind me. I am starving for a day when my skin color will not define my zip code, the university I can attend, where I should worship, the type of job I should do, my function in the office, and how much I should get paid. I am starving for a day when I can have a voice at the table like everyone else and be heard and seen.

And yet there's another side to my impatience. I find myself recalling the words of the great and wise Teilhard de Chardin, S.J.:

> Above all, trust in the slow work of God. We are quite naturally impatient in everything to reach the end with-

out delay. We should like to skip the intermediate stages. We are impatient of being on the way to something unknown, something new. And yet the law of all progress is that it is made by passing through some stages of instability—and that it may take a very long time.

The year 2020 was very tough for me. As I watched the world come to a stop from the pandemic, while at the same time overt racial injustice became the new norm, I hated the realization that everything around me was out of my control; nothing was progressing at the speed I wanted. And yet, paradoxically, when I looked through the lens of Ignatian spirituality, these events have helped me to develop a more patient trust in God.

My membership in the Society of Jesus means I have taken a vow of obedience, but that doesn't mean I am always happy about it. The words "wait" or "not yet" often cause me internal conflict. I want tasks to be accomplished at my speed—which means "now!" In 2020, however, I was forced to learn patience. I gained confidence in God's timing, for I had no choice but to wait and trust.

During this time, this Gospel passage spoke to me: "The kingdom of heaven is like a mustard seed, which . . . though it is the smallest of all seeds, yet when it grows, it is the largest of garden plants and becomes a tree, so that the birds come and perch in its branches" (Matthew 13:31–32). Seeds start small, and they cannot be hurried. There is nothing we can do but wait for them to grow into something visible, something green and life-giving. Even in my impatience and hunger for justice, I felt called to have a "mustard-seed spirituality," one of trust and patience.

This insight brought me into deeper connection with the spirituality Ignatius taught, which articulates "trust" as a new paradigm that leads to spiritual growth. Ignatius's life was built on his faith in the power of Divine possibility—that mysterious, paradoxical Energy that has the audacity to transform nothing into something. As we too commit ourselves to this way of life, we find opportunities to create something new and transformed out of that which is broken.

Ignatius of Loyola left us lessons in discernment, courage, understanding, and action. His voice travels across cultures and centuries. It is a voice we desperately need now—because it is the voice of patience and trust. Like me, Ignatius knew the conflict between urgency and patience. After his conversion, he set out eagerly, filled with energy to change the world. When he reached Manresa, the place that would play such a large role in his life, he intended to only stay for a few days before hurrying on in his journey Instead, he remained there, living in a cave outside the village for ten months, while he prayed every day.

At first glance, we might think Ignatius was wasting time. In reality, he had stepped out of ordinary time and into *Kairos* time. During those hours of prayer in his cave, he developed the ideas that became the Spiritual Exercises. His willingness to wait on Divine time resulted in spiritual insights that continue to transform our world. (Note, however, that during this time of intense prayer, Ignatius also volunteered at a hospice, where he worked with the sick and dying. His example tells us that even as we wait for God, we can be busy in whatever service calls out to us from near at hand.)

"He has set eternity in the human heart," says the long-ago author of Ecclesiastes (3:11), "yet no one can fathom what God has done from beginning to end." God's timing is a mystery to us, and yet somehow we are called to participate in it. This means we don't tell hungry people to be patient while they starve to death. We don't make excuses when we hear the Divine Voice speaking through those who are oppressed and marginalized. We hear and respond to the challenge of *this* moment, this tiny slice of eternity that has been given to us.

In today's time of crisis, Ignatius invites us to hear the voice of the risen Christ as he calls us to participate in Kairos time. The Reign of Heaven is present in our world, always ready to emerge from the tiny seeds that are planted everywhere. Will you water the seeds? Will you tend to their growth? Will you take action when God calls you?

Journal

Martin Luther King Jr. once said, "We must accept finite disappointment, but never lose infinite hope." Write in your journal about why King might have said this. How might "infinite hope" relate to both *Kairos* and "eternity in our hearts"? How do you see this at work in our world today?

Next, answer these questions:

- Have I ever used "patience" as an excuse to avoid taking action?

- Have I ever criticized, even if only silently, people of color for being "impatient" when they were protesting recent situations and events? Do I feel differently now? Why or why not?

- Are there things I can do (habits I can build, actions I can take) that will help me live more in harmony with God's timing, so that even as I wait for God, I'm always ready to take action to build the Reign of Heaven?

Spend some time in prayer, asking God for the grace to be more aware of "moments of opportunity" as they come along—and the strength to seize the opportune moment and use it to build a world of justice and love.

For Further Reflection

Time itself is neutral;
it can be used either destructively or constructively.
… We must use time creatively,
in the knowledge that the time is always ripe to do right.

−MARTIN LUTHER KING JR.

Prayer

My prayer to you, O Lord,
is that at your time of favor,
the time you have chosen to act,
in the abundance of your love and kindness,
you will bring your deliverance and truth.
Pull our world out from the muck and the mud.
Don't let us sink.
Deliver us from the deep waters of hatred.
Do not hide from us.
We are in trouble, Lord. Hurry to help us.
I know I have failed you and your people again and again.
My guilt breaks my heart.
In humility, in pain, I ask you to heal me,
so that I can be a lens for your love,
shining your light into the world.

—BASED ON PSALM 69:13,14,17,19,20,29,30

DAY 7

The Unfinished Story
of Jesus' Ascension

The Power of Hope

"For I know the plans I have for you,"
declares the Lord,
"plans to prosper you and not to harm you,
plans to give you hope and a future."

—JEREMIAH 29:11

We may fairly hope that together with our spiritual good
our earthly good also will not fail to increase.

—IGNATIUS OF LOYOLA

Even when [people] are sure
that what they seek is a dream
that can never be realized in their lifetime
or in the lifetime of all who live at the present moment,
they dare to say, nevertheless,
that it will come to pass, sometime, somewhere.

—HOWARD THURMAN

The story of Jesus' life here on earth comes to an end with the Ascension. The account in the Book of Acts says he was taken up and hidden from his friends' sight (1:9). Before he left them, however, he made clear that the larger story was just beginning. "You will do even greater things than I did," he told his followers.

As Jesus stepped out of his identity as Jesus of Nazareth, he stepped into a large identity as the Cosmic Christ. The Divine Spirit, he promised, would now fill his new Body here on earth, a Body made up of individuals of every kind. The Ascension is much more than a departure of Jesus from the visible stage. It's an open door to human freedom, responsibility, and accountability in Christ.

Some of my earliest memories are of celebrating Ascension Sunday. In my community, this day was as much an extravaganza as Easter. We children didn't understand the theological meaning, of course, but we knew from the time we woke up that this was a day of freedom and joy.

In a family of five, we didn't often have the opportunity to have much variety in our wardrobes, but for Ascension Sunday, we each had new and beautiful clothes. We put them on and went to church. I remember the jaunty tilt of my father's hat as I walked along holding his hand.

"Welcome," a church member said with a joyful smile as we ascended into the temple. Inside, the choir was already singing—and they continued to sing for another ninety-five minutes or so (after all, they'd been practicing the songs for a month, and they wanted to make sure everyone had a chance to fully appreciate the mixture of spirituals and praise songs).

Sometimes, I played the drum for the choir, and sometimes I sang with them. I even had the opportunity to have some solo parts. During the celebration of Ascension, as I stood at the front of the church singing my heart out, I felt as though I were singing from a prime spot in the Apollo Theater in Las Vegas. I couldn't have been any prouder.

I remember one Ascension Sunday when my dad had given me a three-piece sky-blue suit with a clip-on tie. I was so proud that I chose to sit with my friends in the congregation, so that I could show how fresh and clean I was. This did not feel like pride to me, so much as a way to give glory to a Christ who had also loved his Dad so much that he had rejoiced to go back home to him.

Try to picture the scene as I sat there in the pew. See the bright red and yellow dresses caressing dark skin; see the joyful brown and black faces. Notice an older woman sitting next to me, dressed like a rainbow, her clothes so brilliant they outshine everyone else's. She's wearing an amazing and elaborate hat, the sort of headdress our church referred to as a "Holy Ghost catcher." Listen as we sing "This Little Light of Mine." Watch as the elderly woman throws back her head and goes into an ecstasy. Imagine the joy of the moment.

In fact, the woman got so excited, she began kicking up her feet. Her pointed shoe hit my leg and caught on the fabric of my brand-new pants. When I looked down, I found she'd made a hole in the cloth. My joy in the Ascension was seriously dimmed at that moment.

Looking back at this memory, I find myself pondering how the disciples must have felt when Jesus disappeared from their sight. On the one hand, he had already told them his leaving would be the beginning of something entirely new in their lives. He'd even indicated he would always be present with them in some sort of mysterious and empowering way. And yet, at the same time, his absence would have left a hole in their lives; they must have felt lonely and confused and disappointed. Like the hole in my pants, the reality of ordinary life can seem far away from the mystical reality Jesus promised us we would experience.

On one Ascension Sunday, I remember my grandmother telling us children, "Now, Jesus is here with us. We need to behave." As I sit here writing, I feel I am hearing my grandmother say, "Guys, Jesus is around. Watch out." This is a moment of possibility and hope, but it is also a moment of challenge. Can we rise above the dismal certainty of what we see with our physical eyes and live in the hope of the spiritual reality Jesus promised us? Will we remember that Jesus is here, suffering alongside those who are oppressed?

Recent events have taught all of us about grief and despair. As I allow myself to weep over all that has happened, I find myself remembering the women who were the first witnesses to Christ's resurrection. They didn't know it was Easter morning. For them, it was a moment of terrible sorrow and loss. They were not looking for hope when they went to the tomb; they were searching for a place to grieve. And instead, God took them totally by surprise. They encountered the Resurrection power that led to an endless ascension into a new reality, an ascension that continues even today.

Remembering those Ascension Sundays from my childhood, I can't help but smile. There was such an urgent and yet patient joy in the church's willingness to worship together for four hours at a time. The harmony of the choir and the thunder of the preaching live on in my memory, as does the spiritual resilience the members demonstrated day after day as a living community. Time after time, I saw them, in times of crisis, come together in practical ways to be a source of hope and strength for one another.

After church was done, I would go back home with my family and take off my brand-new clothes. I would take my nice black skin out of its Ascension suit and put on ordinary clothes, and then I would do my chores and my homework. In those days, I still felt quite happy and safe inside my nice black skin. I did not yet understand that one day the world would see my skin as dangerous.

I remember the innocence of those days with tears in my eyes. And yet I hear again my grandmother's voice: "Jesus is here now." Jesus is no longer confined to the story of his time on earth. Now he has flown free into the sky. He has entered my own story, and he is a part of your story as well.

Despite appearances, the presence of Christ is real. This is what gives me hope. It is what gives hope to my people as well.

Even after four hundred years of desperation, oppression, and repression, my people always find hope. We believe that something good can always come from adversity.

The weeks of protest in America in 2020 were a sign of that hope. On June 6, 2020, half a million people turned out in nearly five hundred and fifty places across the United States to make the statement that Black lives matter. Polls indicated that between 15 million and 26 million people in the United States—white, Black, Latinx, indigenous, and Asian—have participated in demonstrations over the death of George Floyd. These figures mean these protests are the largest movement in the country's history. That, to me, is a sign of hope.

Jesuit Father Timothy Brown wrote:

> Hope is not the same as that feeling that things are going well or that eagerness to invest in activities that are obviously going to succeed early on. Rather hope is the ability to work for something because it is good, it is right, not just because it is apt to be a success. It is a way to orient our lives, a way to be part of building the kingdom of God that is anchored just over the horizon and within our hearts.

After Christ's ascension, the early church defined itself by its focus on the imminent return of Jesus Christ. They were convinced they were living between the present and the future. They saw past the chronological calendar and grasped the fact that they occupied *Kairos* time, a time of immense opportunity and hope. They were not stuck in the past, constantly longing for the way things used to be, nor did they sit with folded hands, waiting for Jesus to come back to them. Instead, their hope empowered them to action. They worked relentlessly to spread the news of Christ's love and justice. When they released their hold on Jesus' physical presence, they allowed themselves to embark on an endless journey to become what they had always been called to be. For them, the Ascension was still unfinished. There was so much yet to do.

As James Baldwin said, "I really do believe that we all become better than we are. I know we can. But when?" Now is the time to ask yourself: *What does the Ascension mean to me? What does it call me to rise to? How can I be a person of hope?*

Journal

Image that you are one of Jesus' friends who have gathered to say goodbye to him. Use your journal to describe your feelings in that moment. Do you feel a sense of consolation or desolation—or both?

Now imagine what you would say to Jesus if you had this opportunity to be with him. What does he reply to you? Ask him to show you what the unfinished Ascension is calling you to today.

For Further Reflection

The movement of the Spirit of God
in the hearts of men and women
often calls them to act against the spirit of their times
or causes them to anticipate a spirit
which is yet in the making.
In a moment of dedication
they are given wisdom and courage
to dare a deed that challenges
and to kindle a hope that inspires.

—HOWARD THURMAN

Prayer

Jesus, you came to raise us up to you.
May your justice become real on earth.
You left us and told us to carry out your work.
Give us strength to build Heaven's Reign here and now.
You are hidden now from our sight.
Enable us to know the power and presence of your Spirit.
You promised to never leave us.
Help us to become the people you have called us to be.

The Grace I Keep

I ask God for the grace of hope.
May I may be strengthened to ever persevere
in the work of justice.

CONTEMPLATION OF DIVINE LOVE

The Spiritual Exercises conclude with a contemplation of God's love. Ignatius intended this to be the climax of the spiritual journey we have undergone through the Exercises. In this contemplation, he makes clear that the Divine love he describes is not something we need to earn; it is already present with us. Our goal now is to receive it consciously, allowing it to infuse our entire lives.

"God works and labors for me in all things created on the face of the earth," Ignatian wrote. The words he used here imply that the Creator is like a woman in labor, toiling and suffering to give birth to something new. Each and every atom of the universe is striving to burst into God. The Divine is being born not only in me and you but in every human being, in every plant and animal, and in every situation. Ignatius wrote:

> God dwells in creatures, in the elements, giving them being, in the plants vegetating, in the animals feeling in them, in [humans] giving them to understand: and so in me, giving me being, animating me, giving me sensation and making me to understand; likewise making a temple of me, being created in the image and likeness of His Divine Majesty.

God, said Ignatius, is both the Source of all of creation, and God is at the same time emerging from all creation, "as rays descend from the sun" and "waters from a fountain." His words here echo the vision he had on the riverbank outside Manresa, where he saw all things coming from God and at the same time returning to God.

In the words of Jesuit author Gilles Cusson,

> Any small creature could put him into contact with God, because he unceasingly and concretely perceived that nothing exists or subsists without the active and loving presence of God; and that in return every creature becomes, in its own way, a reflection and proclamation of the divine grandeur.

The Divine love that Ignatius described is not at a distance from us, existing only in some intangible spiritual realm. Instead, it constantly participates in all creation; it is active, never ceasing, incarnated endlessly throughout time and space. God's love is present in the unfolding of human history.

When Ignatius thought about the spiritual life, he always thought in terms of movement. "The laborers in the Lord's vineyard," he wrote, "should have one foot on the ground, and the other raised to proceed on their journey." He understood his own life as a pilgrimage, a process of growing and learning. The teaching he gave to his followers (and to us still today) was not a set of static prayers to be repeated or rules to be obeyed. Instead, the Spiritual Exercises, as well as Ignatius's other writings, serve as a map for our own spiritual journeys. They guide us from grace to grace, for even grace is a process.

Ignatius asks us to pray for the grace to understand all God has given to us, and then, in gratitude, to respond with "love and service." The love that Ignatius is talking about unifies all things—thought and action, spiritual and physical—as well as all people. It is a challenge to experience life in a radically new way where we encounter the Divine in everything we see and touch, everything we do and say, everything we think and feel, and in every person we encounter.

The Contemplation of Divine Love is not merely a mental activity, but rather it too is a process, a process that begins within our interior being and then moves out into the world. Since we are each so profoundly loved by God in this way, Ignatius calls us to respond with a commitment to collaborate with Jesus and his work on behalf of the Reign of God. This is not something that is forced; it's not a duty or obligation we owe in return for the love God gives us, but rather it is merely the natural outward expression of Divine Love at work within our own hearts and minds. The two things—interior knowledge and exterior service—cannot be separated from one another, for they are intermeshed in an organic whole.

This concept leads us to radical hope for our world. As God's love is actively expressed through us, it unites us with others. Jesuit author Michael Buckley described this activity as "intercommunion, personal communication, a mutual giving and receiving, an intense interchange," in which all share equally. "Love not only expresses itself but actually consists in the activity of intercommunion." Earlier in the Spiritual Exercises, Ignatius described the emptiness of material wealth, but now he reveals to us that material possessions (whether money, property, or other resources) become holy when they are shared.

What does this have to say to us within the context of the struggle against racism? I believe it tells us that the end goal of antiracism is not a world where white people give their resources to people of color to atone for the sins of the past. That plan would still allow for hierarchy and inequality. "If you have come to help me you are wasting your time," said activist Lila Watson. "But if you recognize that your liberation and mine are bound up together, we can walk together."

Divine Love calls us to a new goal: a world based on equality, where we all need each other, where we all share with each other, where we all love each other. Your freedom and mine cannot be separated. This is the reality God is calling us to make visible and tangible in our world today.

We are made for love.
We are made for togetherness....
We are made to tell the world
that there are no outsiders.

—DESMOND TUTU

DAY 1

Setting New Goals

What Is God Asking of Me?

Dear children,
let us not love with words or speech
but with actions and in truth.

—1 JOHN 3:18

Those who are too cautious
in matters relating to God
seldom do anything great and heroic;
a person who is terrified
of every little difficulty that may occur
does not undertake such things.

—IGNATIUS OF LOYOLA

To be free is not merely to cast off one's chains,
but to live in a way that respects and enhances
the freedom of others.

—NELSON MANDELA

By now you've learned that Ignatius challenges us to follow the pattern of Jesus in order to actively share in God's ongoing mission of love and justice. The personal experience of Divine Love must be expressed in the interpersonal world, where today violence and injustice are all too real. God's love demands that we do more than merely think about antiracism; we must express our antiracism actively, in constructive, practical, real-life ways.

Martin Luther King Jr. said that the majority of white Americans are suspended between two extremes: they are uneasy with racial injustice, but they are also unwilling to actively pay the price to create a more just world. They nod their heads along with antiracist rhetoric, but their voices aren't lifted in protest, their hands are still, and their feet never move. "Shallow understanding from people of good will," King said, "is more frustrating than absolute misunderstanding from people of ill will."

He also said, "True compassion is more than flinging a coin to a beggar; it is not haphazard and superficial. It comes to see that an edifice which produces beggars needs restructuring." But how do we begin to tear down the edifice? Often we have the best of intentions, but we allow ourselves to become overwhelmed by the immensity of the task and our own sense of helplessness.

How can we know the specific actions love calls us to do?

In *Christology and Whiteness,* theologian Laurie M. Cassidy asked white people to refrain from instantly leaping into action after they realize their own compromises with racism. She wrote that the urge to come up with an immediate action plan can actually express the need to still be in control. Instead, she encouraged a "willingness to be with the radical contradiction of our white everyday existence—in its pain, confusion, powerlessness, and vulnerability." Christopher Pramuk, in his book *Hope Sings, So Beautiful: Graced Encounters Across the Color Line,* also counseled against being too quick to leap into social action and political engagement. Doing this prematurely, he warned, neglects the "source of all *loving* action," the "contemplative mirror," where we sit in "silence and reverence," allowing Divine Love to blossom in our hearts until we perceive both the suffering and the beautiful "luminous differences" of people of color.

Of course, indecision and hesitation can also be excuses to avoid taking action at all. We must truly commit our hearts and minds to the Ignatian process of discernment, which is a valuable tool that allows us to sift through our multiple choices to determine the acts of love and justice God calls us to do.

Ignatius cautions us: "If you want to know what God requires of you, you must first of all put aside all affection and preference for one thing rather than another." Once we have done that, we can pay attention to both our internal feelings and external experiences, and then move on to a process of reflecting on the meaning of these feelings and experiences. Finally, we will translate the meaning into action. Through the practice of discernment, we grow in our ability to actively and helpfully express God's love.

Ignatius described this experience in a letter: "Our Lord moves and urges the soul to this or that activity. He begins by enlightening the soul; that is to say, by speaking interiorly to it without the din of words, lifting it up wholly to his divine love and ourselves to his meaning." However, Ignatius also gave this warning: "At other times, [the enemy] makes us lessen the import of the message we have received and confronts us with obstacles and difficulties, so as to prevent us from carrying out completely what had been made known to us."

Discernment is not like going to a fortune teller, nor is it a spiritual way of drawing straws. It's not a magical formula to ensure you have found *the* path—the one and only path—that God wants you to take, the path that will allow you to smugly assume you have arrived once and for all at God's perfect will for your life. Instead, like most everything in Ignatian spirituality, discernment is an ongoing process. It is not a destination to be reached but rather the way to reach that destination. We might think of it like driving a car: the constant tiny adjustments of the wheel we make as we drive are what the process of discernment looks like.

Ignatius knew from experience that the need for certainty can be paralyzing. He described an occasion when he sought to practice discernment as a "desert of any relief" when he found himself "confused with various thoughts." He fell into "desolation" because he could not see a clear way laid out before him— and then he realized that he was asking for too many signs, wanting too much certainty. What he really wanted was for everything to be "to his liking"; he wanted to feel in control. Eventually, he concluded that God would be more pleased if he could step out and act, despite not having absolute certainty. Like Rosa Parks, he found that "when one's mind is made up, this diminishes fear; knowing what must be done does away with fear."

But determining when to wait for Divine direction and when to act is a fine line to walk. This is why discernment is like the constant tiny course corrections we make as we drive a car. We constantly, daily, pay attention to our feelings, our circumstances, and the meaning of both. We might also think of discernment as being like a compass that points the way north— but it only shows us the right direction to head; it doesn't give us a precise road map.

So then we use Jesus' criterion for judgment: the fruits of our actions (Matthew 7:16) tell us whether we need to course-correct. In other words, is a specific course of action yielding practical results in the form of more justice, less racism? Is it breaking down the edifice of systemic racism—or does it turn out to be just a way for us to spin our wheels while stroking our own egos? Ignatius also gives us another criterion to use when evaluating a course of action: "Never say or do anything until you have asked yourself whether it will be pleasing to God, good for yourself, and edifying to your neighbor."

Because God is in all things, Ignatius was convinced that the Divine Voice speaks to us directly through our experiences. Nothing can be dismissed as mere coincidence or accident; instead, in each moment of our lives we can encounter God. This is how the Divine speaks to each of us individually, in unique ways all our own. Author Dan Barry said:

> In finding God in all things, we discover sacred moments in everyday life—grace-filled opportunities to encounter God. . . . In these sacred moments, we realize our

connectedness to God and how we are called to participate in the transformation of the world in both big ways
and small.

Ultimately, discernment is about humility. It's the willingness to surrender our need for certainty. It requires taking one
step at a time rather than sailing arrogantly to the head of the
line. It means we accept that we will inevitably make mistakes—
and God will use us anyway, because it's not about us. "Those
who forget themselves and their own welfare for God's service,"
wrote Ignatius, "will have God to look after them."

From the time we are conceived in our mothers' wombs,
we live in relationship with others. We need each other. "My
humanity is bound up in yours," said Desmond Tutu, "for we
can only be human together." The human need for relationship
and community is a living metaphor for Divine Love. More
than that, it is a sacrament, for it is the Eucharist present in the
interweaving of our lives. "To be human is to find our place in
these relationships and these institutions," wrote Jesuit author
J. A. Appleyard, "to take responsibility for them, to contribute
to nurturing and improving them, and to give something back
to them."

Franciscan nun Thea Bowman said, "We need to tell one
another in our homes, in our church and even in our world, I
really, really love you." How is God calling you to say, "I really,
really love you," to every person of color? And how might God
be calling you to be loved in turn?

Bowman also said that as a Black follower of Jesus, she
brought to the Body of Christ "myself, my black self, all that I
am, all that I have, all that I hope to become, I bring my whole

history, my traditions, my experience, my culture, my African American song and dance and gesture and movement and teaching and preaching and healing and responsibility as gift." Each community of color also has their own unique gifts to bring. As you think about what action God is calling you to take, you might consider: *How can I make space in the world around me so that the gifts of all people can be expressed and given shape?*

The Reign of Heaven is constantly asking to be born in our world, but no single person is expected to do the work alone of bringing this reality into being. It takes a vast network of human beings, stretching through time and space, all doing their small parts in the places where God leads them. This is what it means to be the Body of Christ. This is how Divine Love is expressed when we join contemplation with action.

Divine Love may flow out into the world through protest marches and letters to Congress. It could take the form of petitions, letters to the newspaper, or boycotts. But in the end, racism will truly be defeated when we realize how much we need one another's love. Ethicist Bryan Massingale wrote that "deep interracial friendship and love can shatter the false personal identity built upon the racialized set of meanings and values that informs American society." The person who steps into the solidarity of love and friendship, Massingale said, " is truly 'born again' and lives out of a different identity and social consciousness." He went on to say:

> Such loving and committed relationships give one the visceral outrage, courage, strength, and motivation to break free from the "rewards of conformity" that keep most whites complacent with white privilege. Transfor-

mative love, or compassion, empowers them for authentic solidarity.

As a Black man, I am holding out my hand to you, offering you my friendship. Will you take my hand? Will you join me in the struggle to make our world a safe and healthy place for all people?

Journal

As you write in your journal today, explore your reactions to today's reading. How might you begin the process of discernment in your life? What holds you back?

Often, it may be our own sense of inadequacy that gets in our way. Consider these words from Ignatius:

> A rough and unshapen log has no idea that it can be made into a statue that will be considered a masterpiece, but the carver sees what can be done with it. So many . . . do not understand that God can mold them into saints.

Put yourself in the "hands of that almighty Artisan," said Ignatius. Trust that God can and will use you to build the Reign of Heaven.

Here are a few ideas to consider as you work to discern opportunities in your life for the work of antiracism:

- Make a commitment to say something when you hear racial slurs or jokes.

- Commit to learning about different cultures in your region. Find out what groups live near you and what incidents they have experienced due to individual or systemic racism.

- Think about ways to improve your workplace to promote racial understand and equity—and then take your ideas to management.

- If you are a parent, give your child opportunities to interact with people of color.

- If you are a parent with children in school, ask to speak to teachers and administration about what is covered in history classes. If you find that stories from people of color are not included, ask what you would need to do to change that. Consider volunteering to do a history project with your child's classroom that will bring to life an event from a minority group's history.

- Document activities in your community that reflect racial prejudice or racism. Documentation will show proof that there is a problem, which you can then present at a town or city council meeting.

- Find out what groups are already part of the antiracist struggle in your community. Make an appointment to visit each one and find out what they do.

Each of these points is not a final goal—but it could help you in your journey of discernment.

For Further Reflection

To bring about change,
you must not be afraid to take the first step.
We will fail when we fail to try.

—ROSA PARKS

Prayer

Jesus, I ask that you free me from the paralysis of analysis—
wanting to make the right decision,
more than I want to be doing right in the world,
wanting to be known as a wise person,
more than I want to be a vehicle of your love.
Free me from the idolatry of assuming
there's only one perfect choice in any given situation.
Free me from making decisions primarily for my comfort
and for other's approval (or fear of their disapproval).
Free me to know that good choices don't always
lead to the easiest outcomes, especially at first.
Free me from second and
twenty-second guessing my decisions.
Free me from all that holds me back
from being useful to your Reign.
I want to work with you to bring justice to my world.

—ADAPTED FROM A PRAYER BY SCOTTY SMITH

DAY 2

Take, Lord, and Receive

Service to the Beloved

This is how we know what love is:
Jesus Christ laid down his life for us.
And we ought to lay down our lives
for our brothers and sisters.

—1 JOHN 3:16

We should value above everything else
the great service which is given to God
because of pure love.

—IGNATIUS OF LOYOLA

To say that I am made in the image of God
is to say that love is the reason for my existence,
for God is love.
Love is my true identity. Selflessness is my true self.
Love is my true character.
Love is my name.

—THOMAS MERTON

There's a story about Ignatius that goes like this: One day a young man who hoped to join the Society of Jesus came across Ignatius sweeping the floor in the Jesuit house in Rome. "Father Ignatius," the young man asked, "if you knew the world would come to an end in fifteen minutes, what would you do?"

Ignatius leaned on his broom, looked up at the young man (Ignatius was only five-foot-two), and replied, "I would go on sweeping this floor."

As the Spiritual Exercises come to an end, Ignatius tells us to ask for the grace to love and serve God in everything we encounter. This doesn't necessarily mean we keep on doing what we've always done, just with an added dollop of love. Instead, we may be asked to look beyond our usual responsibilities and see things we have previously been unable or unwilling to see. We are not to be selective about where we encounter God. On that day nearly five hundred years ago in the Jesuit house in Rome, Ignatius could have easily not even noticed the dirty floor beneath his feet. Or he might have noticed the dirt but assumed it was someone else's job to clean it. Instead, he chose to see this as an opportunity to love and serve God. "Practice the seeking of God's presence in all things," wrote Ignatius in a letter—even in a dirty floor that needs to be swept.

Finding God in all things is central to Ignatius's call to us. One of his early companions wrote that they frequently saw Ignatius

> taking the occasion of little things to lift his mind to God, who even in the smallest things is great. From seeing a plant, foliage, a leaf, a flower, any kind of fruit; from the consideration of a little worm or any other animal, he raised himself above the heavens and penetrated the deepest thoughts, and from each little thing he drew doctrine and the most profitable counsels for the spiritual life.

The thought of Ignatius holding a caterpillar in the palm of his hand as an object of contemplation makes me smile a little. But his outlook was not limited to flowers and worms or squirrels and leaves. His vision was truly all-inclusive. *Everything* spoke to him of Divine Love—and everything was an opportunity for him to participate in that love. Everything and everyone was beloved.

As we finish the Spiritual Exercises, we too are called to enter into a new relationship with the world around us. We do this not out of duty or guilt; we do it out of love. We see with new eyes. We look at one another and see the image of God. The goodness and beauty we find in each other draw us ever deeper into the goodness and beauty of God.

We seek to end racism because people of color are beloved. We stand in awe before the Divine Presence in each of them. We see their amazing beauty, their strength, their gifts, their power. We feel God's love flowing to us from them. We open our hearts to return that love. We enter into a spirit of giving that excludes no one, as we affirm that everything we have is available to God to "dispose of it entirely according" to the Divine will. We ask for the grace to grow in loving the way God loves, so that our entire being is love and we are united in love with all people. As we mutually give and receive, we grow into a deeper understanding of what it means to be the living, breathing Body of Christ.

This is reality, Ignatius said. In the sixteenth-century world of plague and violence, poverty and suffering, he still insisted that God's love was everywhere. He still believed we can live immersed in that love, participating in its active involvement in the world around us.

That's hard for me to believe some days. As I sat down to write this final chapter, I happened to see a news story on CNN. With a sick feeling in my stomach, I read about yet another incident of police brutality.

Ronald Greene was a forty-nine-year-old Black man living in Louisiana. He was a barber who had recently gone into remission after battling cancer. On May 10, 2019, he was on his way to meet his wife Florida. He never made it. Police told Mr. Greene's family he had died in a head-on collision with a tree.

And then, two years late, the Associated Press obtained forty-six minutes of body-camera footage of the events that actually led to Mr. Greene's death. The footage shows Mr. Greene sitting in a parked SUV by the side of the road. Troopers open the car door and jolt Mr. Greene with a stun gun. One trooper shoves

Mr. Greene to the ground, puts him in a chokehold, and punches him in the face. "I'm sorry," Mr. Greene screams. "I'm scared."

The troopers put handcuffs and leg shackles on him. They jolt him again with the stun gun, they grab him by his shackles and drag him face down across the ground, and then they leave him moaning, still face down, for more than nine minutes. As they wipe his blood from their hands and faces, one of them says, "I hope this guy ain't got AIDS."

The video eventually shows Mr. Greene being loaded onto an ambulance gurney. His head is battered and bloody. He appears to be unconscious. According to the crash report the troopers filed, he died on the way to the hospital.

When I began writing this chapter, I had no intention of including such an ugly story. I know you are tired of reading ugly stories. I am tired of reading them too. Every person of color in the United States is exhausted by these stories. We feel as though we cannot bear another one—and yet we have to.

So how do I find God's love here? Would Ignatius tell me God is also present in Ronald Greene's death? How can that be?

And then I remember the Third Week of the Spiritual Exercises, as we traveled with Christ to the cross. And I know that Jesus was the one who lay by the side of that road in Louisiana, face down, beaten and stunned and frightened. Jesus was treated as though he were a piece of contaminated garbage. Jesus died in that ambulance. And today, Jesus also weeps with Ronald Greene's family. Jesus holds the Black community and all people of color in his embrace, and he cries out for justice.

Justice is love in action. Injustice, on the other hand, comes from our inability to love. Love never seeks to do others harm. Love cries out for all who are beloved—for Ronald Greene and

George Floyd, Breonna Taylor and Daunte Wright, and all the countless others—and longs to not only protect them but also empower them. Love insists on their dignity and beauty. Love participates in their stories. Love seeks to heal the wounds of one more terrible death. Love does whatever it takes to make the world safe for those who are so beloved, so beautiful, so precious.

This is the love that Ignatius leaves us with at the end of the Spiritual Exercises. The very last paragraph of the Exercises calls us to "the zealous service of God our Lord out of pure love." Pure love was Ignatius's final message. It is a love that embraces all, that includes all. Love never says some people aren't worth anything or that some people should be left out. Instead, love reaches out to everyone equally. It works for connection. It creates an infinite circle of belonging.

The hatred and fear that cause injustice do just the opposite. They exclude. They say that some people aren't valuable. They create division. They put some people in a narrow space where opportunities for happiness and safety are limited. Hatred and fear make our world small and ugly.

"Step out of that shrunken way of living," Ignatius says to us through the Spiritual Exercises. "Live in the infinite space of Divine Love, a space that's big enough for everyone, a space where the beauty of each one of us will shine like the sun." Within this space, is where King's Beloved Community will thrive.

We cannot create this community with force. We can't insist that others come close enough to us that we'll feel comfortable forming connections with them. We have to surrender our control; we'd like to tell ourselves we're using our control to build a more just world, but control is always oppressive. It says, *I'm right and you're wrong.* It says, *You need to do what I say, because*

I'm better than you. Instead, love pushes us outside of our egos. Love wants you to be the best you can possibly be, no matter what that takes. Love knows that what is good for you is what is good for me.

Father Greg Boyle wrote:

> Soon we imagine, with God, this circle of compassion. Then we imagine no one standing outside of that circle, moving ourselves closer to the margins so that the margins themselves will be erased. We stand there with those whose dignity has been denied. We locate ourselves with the poor and the powerless and the voiceless. At the edges, we join the easily despised and the readily left out. We stand with the demonized so that the demonizing will stop. We situate ourselves right next to the disposable so that the day will come when we stop throwing people away.

He went on to say: "Here is what we seek: a compassion that can stand in awe at what the poor have to carry rather than stand in judgment at how they carry it."

Ignatius wrote: "The persons who receive the Exercises will benefit greatly by entering upon them with great spirit and generosity toward their Creator and Lord, and by offering all their desires and freedom to him so that his Diving Majesty can make use of their persons and all they possess in whatsoever way is according to his most holy will." This largeness of spirit, this open-hearted generosity, this willingness to surrender our own need for control are what make room for God's love to flow through us.

Then, at the end of the Exercises, Ignatius said: "Here [what I desire] will be to ask for interior knowledge of all the great good I have received, in order that, stirred to profound gratitude, I may become able to love and serve the Divine Majesty in all things." The Divine Majesty existed in Ronald Greene. America should have looked at him and been filled with gratitude for his life, for all that he contributed to the world. No matter what sins he may have committed in his life, America should have loved him and done all that it could to affirm God's Presence in him. Instead, when the trooper stunned him and beat him, they were killing the Image of God.

"All for the greater glory of God": these are the words that Ignatius repeated over and over. They are words that guide my life. That word "greater" tells us that just as with everything else in Ignatius's teaching, God's glory has no endpoint. There is always more glory to be revealed. God's glory is more love. God's glory is more justice. And God's glory is a world where no more Black men are lynched by police officers.

Thank you for coming with me on this spiritual journey. I'm ready to pick up my broom and work for the greater glory of God. Will you join me?

Journal

Use your journal to describe a scene, where you, Ronald Greene, and Jesus are sitting together. Maybe you're sharing a cup of coffee around a table, or maybe you're sitting together in a quiet and leafy park. What would you want to say to Ronald Greene? What would Jesus say?

Now think about the phrase "all for the greater glory of God." Describe what these words bring to mind. Ask God to reveal to you some small way you can create a world that has a little more room for God's glory. Make a note of any ideas that come to you and commit yourself to carrying out at least one of these as a gift of love and self-surrender.

For Further Reflection

The Exercises are, in the last analysis,
a method in the pedagogy of love—
the pedagogy, that is, of the most pure charity
toward God and toward one's neighbor.
They root out carnal and worldly love
from the human heart,
thus opening it to the beams of God's love.
A demanding love it is, calling forth in a person
a response of love and of service.
Service, which is itself love....
In the Exercises we find terms and concepts
which are logically reducible to one another:
the "glory of God," for example,
can be replaced by the "service of God."
... Only one term is final and irreducible to another:
LOVE.

—PEDRO ARRUPE, S.J.

Prayer

Take, Lord, and receive
all my liberty, my memory,
my understanding, and my entire will,
all that I have and possess.
You have given all to me.
To you, Lord, I return it.
All is yours;
do with it what you will.
Give me only your love and your grace,
that is enough for me.

The Grace I Keep

I ask God for the grace to see the Image of God
in every person I meet.
May I honor and protect the glory of every human being.

REFERENCE NOTES

Introduction

The prayer from Thomas Merton is from *Thoughts in Solitude* (New York, NY: Farrar, Straus and Giroux, 2011), p. 81.

WEEK ONE

Throughout this book I have relied on two sources for all quotes from *The Spiritual Exercises:*

Draw Me Into Your Friendship: A Literal Translation and a Contemporary Reading of the Spiritual Exercises by David L. Fleming, S.J. (Brighton, MA: Institute of Jesuit Sources, 1996).

The Spiritual Exercises of St. Ignatius translated by Louis J. Puhl (Eastford, CT: Martino, 2010).

Day 1

Quote from Deborah Cohan is from her article "Racist Like Me: A Call to Action for White Physicians" in *The New England Journal of Medicine* 380(9), 2019, p. 806.

All references to Ignatius's autobiography are from *The Autobiography of St. Ignatius of Loyola,* translated by Joseph F. O'Callaghan and edited by John C. Olin (New York, NY: Fordham University Press, 1993). The account of Ignatius's life spans the years 1521–1537; Ignatius did not write it himself but rather dictated it, and it is written in the third person.

All quotes from Robin DiAngelo are from her book *White Fragility: Why It's So Hard for White People to Talk About Racism* (Toronto, ON: Random House, 2020).

Day 2

Stokely Carmichael's quote is from *Black Power: The Politics of Liberation* (New York, NY: Vintage, 1967), p. 4.

The prayer by Mark Young is from the Denver Seminary's website (https://denverseminary.edu/racism-a-reflection-and-a-prayer/), with many thanks to Dr. Young for his gracious permission to use it here.

Day 3

Oscar Romero's quote is from his book *The Violence of Love* (Maryknoll, NY: Orbis, 2004), December 31, 1977 entry.

Quote by Desmond Tutu is from *No Future Without Forgiveness* (New York, NY: Image), p. 39.

James Martin's quote is from his *The Jesuit Guide to (Almost) Everything* (New York, NY: HarperOne, 2010), p. 8.

The fish story from Anthony DeMello, S.J. is in his book *The Song of the Bird* (New York, NY: Image, 2016).

Quote by Desmond Tutu is from his Nobel Peace Prize acceptance speech in 1984.

Day 4

Ibram Kendi's quote is from *How to Be an Antiracist* (New York, NY: One World, 2019), p. 230.

Quote by George Kelsey is from *Racism and the Christian Understanding of Man* (New York, NY: Charles Scribner's Sons, 1965), p. 69.

Quote by Richard Dyer is found in *White: Essays on Race and Culture* (Milton Park, UK: Taylor & Francis, 2013), p. 9.

The quote by Dean Brackley, S.J. is from his book *The Call to Discernment in Troubled Times: New Perspectives on the Transformative Wisdom of Ignatius of Loyola* (Chestnut Ridge, NY: Crossroad, 2020), p. 27.

Day 5

Quote by Kelly Douglas Brown is from an article in *Sojourners* magazine, July 2020.

Peggy McIntosh's "invisible backpack" is from her article "White Privilege: Unpacking the Invisible Knapsack," in S. Plous, ed., *Understanding Prejudice and Discrimination* (New York, NY: McGraw-Hill, 2003), pp. 191–196. You can also access it here: https://psychology.umbc.edu/files/2016/10/White-Privilege_McIntosh-1989.pdf.

The Ibram Kendi quote is from *How to Be an Antiracist,* p. 209.

The prayer is from the Augustinian Secretariate for Justice and Peace; midwestaugustinians.org/. Used with permission.

Day 6

The Martin Luther King Jr. quote is from a 1957 article "Advice for Living." It's available at: https://kinginstitute.stanford.edu/king-papers/documents/advice-living-1.

Quotes from Gerald M. Fagin throughout my book are from his *Discovering Your Dream: How Ignatian Spirituality Can Guide Your Life* (Chicago, IL: Loyola Press, 2013).

The James Baldwin lines are quoted in *Moments of Clarity* by Thomas L. Jackson (Bloomington, IN: Xlibris, 2002), p. 69.

Henri Nouwen's quote is from *The Inner Voice of Love: A Journey Through Anguish to Freedom* (New York, NY: Crown, 2010), p. 70.

The prayer by Karl Rahner, S.J. is from *Encounters with Silence* (South Bend, IN: St. Augustine's Press, 1999), p. 67.

Day 7

Pauli Murray's quote was first published in 1945 in an article titled "American Credo" in the journal *Common Ground*.

Kimberly Flint-Hamilton's quote is from her article "Gregory of Nyssa and the Culture of Oppression" in *Christian Reflection* (Waco, TX: Center for Christian Ethics, 2010), pp. 26–36.

Quote by Teilhard de Chardin is from *The Divine Milieu* (New York, NY: Harper Classics, 2001), p. 76.

Dr. King's quote was cited in *Martin Luther King Jr.: His Life, Martyrdom, and Meaning for the World* (New York, NY: Avon Books, 1968), p. 66.

Archbishop Tutu's quote is from his book *Made for Goodness* (New York, NY: HarperOne, 2010).

WEEK TWO

James Cone quotes throughout are taken from *The Cross and the Lynching Tree* (Maryknoll, NY: Orbis, 2011).

Day 1

James Martin's quote is from his book *Building a Bridge* (New York, NY: HarperOne, 2018).

Michelle Obama's quote is from a statement she released on May 29, 2020, in response to the killing of George Floyd.

Day 2

Quotes by Howard Thurman throughout this book are from *Jesus and the Disinherited* (Boston, MA: Beacon Press, 1996).

Day 3

W.E.B. DuBois's quote is from *The Souls of Black Folk* (Chicago, IL: A.C. McClurg, 1903), p. 2.

All quotes from Ignatius's letters are taken from *Ignatius of Loyola: Letters and Instructions,* edited by John W. Padberg, S.J., and John L. McCarthy, S.J., and translated by Martin E. Palmer, S.J. (Chestnut Hill, MA: Jesuit Sources, 2006).

Quote by Elijah Anderson is from his article "This Is What It Feels Like to Be Black in White Spaces" in *The Guardian* (June 9, 2018), https://www.theguardian.com/commentisfree/2018/jun/09/everyday-racism-america-black-white-spaces.

John Lewis is quoted as saying this in *The Shame of the Nation: The Restoration of Apartheid Schooling in America* by Jonathan Kozol (New York, NY: 2005), p. 316.

The prayer is from the booklet *Being Neighbor: The Catechism and Social Justice,* available from the US Conference of Catholic Bishops.

Day 4

Pope Francis's quote is from his April 8, 2015 general audience.

Dr. King's quote is from his "I Have a Dream" speech, given on August 28, 1963 in Washington, D.C.

Archbishop Tutu's story about the child in the resettlement camp is from a speech he gave in 1994 in Australia. You can read the whole speech here: https://www.epicenter.org/why-as-christians-we-must-oppose-racism/.

The studies cited about the health impacts of racism on children are reported in a *New York Times* article, "The Impact of Racism on Children's Health" by Perri Klass, M.D. (April 12, 2019).

Kendi's quote is from an interview he did with Colleen Walsh for the *Harvard Gazette,* "Teaching Children to be Antiracist" (July 24, 2020).

The prayer is adapted from Dennis Michno's *A Priest's Handbook* (Harrisburg, PA: Morehouse Publishing, 1998), p. 259.

Day 5

All James Tisby quotes are from *The Color of Compromise: The Truth about the American Church's Complicity in Racism* (Grand Rapids, MI: Zondervan, 2020).

The quote by James Forbes is from his TED Talk, "Compassion at the Dinner Table" (November 19, 2009).

Day 6

Archbishop Tutu's quote is from an excerpt from his book *God Has a Dream: A Vision of Hope for Our Time,* available at: https://www.spiritualityandpractice.com/book-reviews/excerpts/view/14258/god-has-a-dream.

I am quoting from Marcus Mescher's article, "Learning and Living Magis," in *Millenial* (December 11, 2018).

Material from William A. McCormick is from "A Continual Sacrifice to the Glory of God: Ignatian Magnanimity in Cooperation with the Divine," *Studies in the Spirituality of Jesuits* (Autumn 2018).

I have quoted from the Pope's address to the 36th General Congregation of the Society of Jesus (October 24, 2016).

Day 7

Both the introductory and closing quotes from Latasha Morrison are from her book *Be the Bridge: Pursuing God's Heart for Racial Reconciliation* (New York, NY: Crown, 2019), p. 220.

I quoted from Rich Villodas' article "Racial Reconciliation May Not Be What You Think It Is," *Missio Alliance* (March 10, 2016), https://www.missioalliance.org/racial-reconciliation-may-not-think/.

You can read more about H.R. 40 in Representative Lee's article on the ACLU website, "H.R. 40 Is Not a Symbolic Act. It's a Path to Restorative Justice" (May 22, 2020), https://www.aclu.org/news/racial-justice/h-r-40-is-not-a-symbolic-act-its-a-path-to-restorative-justice/.

WEEK THREE

Bishop McElroy's quote is from his homily given in San Diego on April 15, 2021. You can read more excerpts here: homily-https://www.thecompassnews.org/2021/04/crucifixions-pathway-of-radical-love-is-antidote-to-racism-says-bishop/

Day 1

The Jeannine Hill Fletcher quote is from *The Sin of White Supremacy: Christianity, Racism, & Religious Diversity in America* (Maryknoll, NY: Orbis, 2017), chapter 6.

Day 2

The Copeland quote is from *Knowing Christ Crucified: The Witness of African American Religious Experience* (Maryknoll, NY: Orbis, 2018), p. 34.

Day 3

The Mays quote is from his 1971 article, "What Is Relevant in General and Liberal Education," *Perspectives (1969–1979)* 3(1). Available at: https://scholarworks.wmich.edu/perspectives/vol3/iss1/3.

The quotes from Adam Borneman are from a post he made on *The Ministry Collaborative* on May 31, 2016, https://mministry.org/the-cross-the-body-and-the-other-what-is-reconciliation/.

All Ijeoma Oluo quotes throughout are from her book *So You Want to Talk About Race* (New York, NY: Seal Press, 2019).

Day 4

All Ignacio Ellacuria quotes are from *Systematic Theology: Perspectives from Liberation Theology* (Maryknoll, NY: Orbis, 1996).

You can read more about Janet Helms here: https://www.apa.org/members/content/race-mechanisms-inequality. This quote is from her book *A Race Is a Nice Thing to Have.*

The lengthy quote from George Aschenbrenner, S.J. is from his book *Stretched for Greater Glory: What to Expect from the Spiritual Exercises* (Chicago, IL: Loyola, 2004), p. 122.

Day 5

Pema Chodron's quote is from *The Places That Scare You* (Boston, MA: Shambhala, 2001), p. 3.

You can listen to the Resmaa Menakem interview here: https://compassioncenter.arizona.edu/podcast/resmaa-menakem

The Dalai Lama's words are quoted in *Visions of Compassion: Western Scientists and Tibetan Buddhists Examine Human Nature,* edited by R.J. Davidson and A. Harrington (New York, NY: Oxford University Press, 2002), p. 225.

Research regarding mindfulness and empathy:

"Racism and the Empathy for Pain on Our Skin" by Matteo Forgiarini, Marcello Gallucci, and Angelo Maravita, published in *Frontiers of Psychology* 2 (2011), p. 108.

"Evidence That a Brief Meditation Exercise Can Reduce Prejudice Toward Homeless People" by Stefania Parks, Michèle D. Birtel, and Richard J. Crisp, published in *Social Psychology* 45 (2014:6).

"Brief Mindfulness Meditation Reduces Discrimination" by Adam Lueke and Bryan Gibson, published in *Psychology of Consciousness: Theory, Research, and Practice* 3 (2011:1), pp. 34–44.

"How Mindfulness Can Defeat Racial Bias" by Rhonda Magee, *Greater Good Magazine* (May 14, 2015), ttps://greatergood.berkeley.edu/article/item/how_mindfulness_can_defeat_racial_bias.

"Reducing Racial Bias Among Health Care Providers: Lessons from Social-Cognitive Psychology" by Diana Burgess, Michelle van Ryn, John Dovidio, and Somnath Saha, published in *Journal of General Internal Medicine* 22 (2007:6), pp. 882–887.

Kenneth B. Clark's quotes are from "Delusions of the White Liberal," *New York Times* (April 4, 1965), https://www.nytimes.com/1965/04/04/archives/delusions-of-the-white-liberal-delusions-of-the-white-liberal.html.

The statement from the Task Force for Global Health can be found here: https://taskforce.org/tfgh-compassion-a-catalyst-for-racial-justice/.

Thich Nhat Hanh quote is from *Teachings on Love* (Charleston, SC: Booksurge, 2008), p. i.

The prayer is adapted from Digital Faith Formation's website, https://digitalfaithformation.org.

Day 6

Joseph Veale, S.J.'s article "Saint Ignatius Speaks about 'Ignatian Prayer'" was published in *Studies in the Spirituality of Jesuits*, 28 (1996:2).

The Alan Watts quote is from his book *The Book: The Taboo Against Knowing Who You Are* (New York, NY: Knopf, 2011), p. 8.

Day 7

All Ta-Nehisi Coates' quotes are from *Between the World and Me*

(New York, NY: Random House, 2015).

The Metz quote is from *Faith in History and Society: Toward a Practical Fundamental Theology*, translated by David Smith (New York, NY: Seabury Press, 1980), p. 111.

This prayer is adapted from a prayer by the prioress of St. Benedict's Monastery, https://sbm.osb.org/2020/06/02/prayer-for-justice-in-response-to-george-floyds-death/

WEEK 4

The quote by Louis M. Savary, S.J. is from his book *The New Spiritual Exercises: In the Spirit of Pierre Teilhard de Chardin* (Mahweh, NJ: Paulist Press, 2012), p. 167.

Day 1

The quote by DuBois is from his book *The Negro,* published in 1915.

Emile Mersch, S.J. quotes are from *Morality and the Mystical Body*, translated by Daniel Francis Ryan (New York, NY: P.J. Kenedy & Sons, 1939).

Elizabeth Barnes' quote is from an interview she did, reported in the *Boston Globe,* "What's up with all the body talk?" by Mark Peters (February 24, 2018).

James Baldwin's quote comes from *Conversations with James Baldwin* (Oxford: University Press of Mississippi, 1989), p. 6.

Ellison's quote is from his book *The Invisible Man* (New York, NY: Vintage, 1995).

Day 2

Father Arrupe said this in 1973 in an address he gave at a Jesuit high school in Valencia, Spain.

Father Boyle's quote is from his book *Barking to the Choir: The Power of Radical Kinship* (New York, NY: Simon & Schuster, 2017), p. 12.

The first quote from Dr. King comes from a speech he gave at Cornell University in Ithaca, New York, in 1962. The second quote is from his 1964 Nobel Peace Prize acceptance speech.

Day 2

Quote from Pope John Paul II is from his encyclical "On Social Concern," given in 1987.

Day 3

The quote by N. T. Wright is from his book *Surprised by Hope: Rethinking Heaven, the Resurrection, and the Mission of the Church* (New York, NY: HarperCollins, 2008), p. 305.

Day 4

Father Boyle's quote is from *Tattoos on the Heart: The Power of Boundless Compassion* (New York, NY: Free Press, 2011), pp. 27–28.

Quotes from Dean Brackley, S.J. are from "Expanding the Shrunken Soul: False Humility, Ressentiment, and Magnanimity," *Studies in the Spirituality of Jesuits* 34 (2002:4).

The quote by Sharon Welch is from her book *A Feminist Ethic of Risk* (Philadelphia, PA: Fortress, 1990), p. 46.

The quote by Michael Paul Gallagher, S.J. can be found in *A Jesuit Education Reader* (Chicago, IL: Loyola, 2008).

You can read more about our Superior General, Father Sosa, here: https://www.jesuitsmidwest.org/press-release/society-of-jesus-newly-elected-superior-general-fr-arturo-sosa-sj-gets-to-work/.

Day 5

Dr. Rhodes' quote is from his article "Should We Repent of Our Grandparents' Racism? Scripture on Intergenerational Sin," *The Biblical Mind* (June 19, 2020), https://hebraicthought.org/repenting-intergenerational-racist-ideology-scripture-intergenerational-sin/.

Johann Baptist Metz's quote is from his book *Poverty of Spirit* (Mahweh, NJ: Paulist, 2014).

Father Sheets' online retreat can be found here: https://onlineministries.creighton.edu/CollaborativeMinistry/Preached-30-day-Retreat/.

The prayer is from the Augustinian Secretariate for Justice and Peace, used with permission.

Day 6

The first quote by Dr. King is from his "Letter from the Birmingham Jail." The second quote is from his book *Why We Can't Wait* (New York, NY: Signet, 2000), p. 2. The final quote is from the same book, p. 74.

Quote by Teilhard de Chardin is from *The Divine Milieu* (New York, NY: Harper Classics, 2001), p. 112.

Day 7

Dan Barry, in his 2012 address at Boston College, quoted the text from Timothy Brown, S.J.

James Baldwin said these words at a Juneteenth celebration in 1986.

Contemplation of Divine Love

The quote by Gilles Cusson, S.J. is from his book *Biblical Theology and the Spiritual Exercises* (St. Louis, MO: Institute of Jesuit Sources, 1994), pp. 320–321.

Day 1

Nelson Mandela's full speech can be found here: https://www.scu.edu/mcae/architects-of-peace/Mandela/essay.html.

The first quote by Dr. King is from his "Letter from the Birmingham Jail." The second quote is from his sermon "A Time to Break Silence," given at Riverside Church in New York City in 1967.

The quote by Dan Barry is from his 2012 address at Boston College.

Appleyard quotes are from "Jesuit Education Is a Process," which you can find here: https://www.bc.edu/content/bc-web/offices/mission-ministry/publications/a-pocket-guide-to-jesuit-education/jesuit-education-is-a-process.html.

Thea Bowman's quotes are from Thea's Song: The Life of Thea Bowman, edited by Charlene Smith and John Fiester (Maryknoll, NY: Orbis, 2009).

The quote by Bryan Massingale is from his book *Racial Justice and the Catholic Church* (Maryknoll, NY: Orbis, 2010), p. 120.

Rosa Parks is quoted in *Marching Toward Coverage: How Women Can Lead the Fight for Universal Healthcare* by Rosemarie Day (Boston, MA: Beacon, 2020), p. 165.

Day 2

Thomas Merton's quote is from *New Seeds of Contemplation* (New York, NY: New Directions, 2007), p. 60.

The Father Boyle quote is another one from *Tattoos on the Heart: The Power of Boundless Compassion.*

Father Arrupe's quote is from *Pedro Arrupe: Essential Writings,* edited by Kevin Burke (Maryknoll, NY: Orbis, 2004), p. 136–137.

The final prayer is known as the "Suscipe," from the Latin word for "receive." It is a very ancient prayer that Ignatius used at the end of the Spiritual Exercises.

READING LIST

These books were of great help to me in the writing of this book.

Barbara Applebaum. *Being White, Being Good: White Complicity, White Moral Responsibility, and Social Justice Pedagogy* (Washington, DC: Lexington, 2011).

Austin Channing Brown. *I'm Still Here: Black Dignity in a Work Made for Whiteness* (New York, NY: Convergent, 2018).

Ta-Nehisi Coates. *Between the World and Me* (New York, NY: Random House, 2015).

James H. Cone. *The Cross and the Lynching Tree* (Maryknoll, NY: Orbis, 2011).

M. Shawn Copeland. *Knowing Christ Crucified: The Witness of African American Religious Experience* (Maryknoll, NY: Orbis, 2018).

Robin DiAngelo. *White Fragility: Why It's So Hard for White People to Talk About Racism* (New York, NY: Beacon Press, 2018).

Kelly Brown Douglas. *Stand Your Ground: Black Bodies and the Justice of God* (Maryknoll, NY: Orbis, 2015).

———. *The Black Christ* (Marynoll, NY: Orbis, 2019).

Jeannine Hill Fletcher. *The Sin of White Supremacy: Christianity, Racism, & Religious Diversity in America* (Maryknoll, NY: Orbis, 2017).

Willie James Jennings. *The Christian Imagination: Theology and the Origins of Race* (New Haven, CT: Yale University Press, 2011).

Robert P. Jones. *White Too Long: The Legacy of White Supremacy in American Christianity* (New York, NY: Simon & Schuster, 2020).

Francis E. Kendall. *Understanding White Privilege: Creating Pathways to Authentic Relationships Across Race* (New York, NY: Routledge, 2012).

Ibram X. Kendi. *How to Be an Antiracist* (New York, NY: One World, 2019).

Latasha Morrison. *Be the Bridge: Pursuing God's Heart for Racial Reconciliation* (New York, NY: Crown, 2019).

Ijeoma Oluo. *So You Want to Talk About Race* (New York, NY: Seal Press, 2019).

Louis. M. Savary. *The New Spiritual Exercises: In the Spirit of Pierre Teilhard de Chardin* (Mahweh, NJ: Paulist Press, 2012).

Howard Thurman. *Jesus and the Disinherited* (Boston, MA: Beacon Press, 1996).

James Tisby. *The Color of Compromise: The Truth about the American Church's Complicity in Racism* (Grand Rapids, MI: Zondervan, 2020).

Skot Welch and Rick Wilson. *Plantation Jesus: Race, Faith, & a New Way Forward* (Harrisonburg, VA: Herald, 2018).

ACKNOWLEDG-MENTS

No book comes into being out of a vacuum. This book was the result of connection and community.

In large part, this book grew from the events of 2020–2021 in America, which coincided with the five-hundred-year anniversary of Ignatius's conversion. These dual events triggered in me a deep emotional and spiritual fatigue; I experienced the pain of the struggle to *live while Black* in America. The more I prayed about my reaction, the more I found the necessity to pause, go back to Christ, and simply *be*. There, I encountered the Presence that inspired this book.

At first, though, I wanted to write an intellectual and academic volume that intersected Ignatian spirituality, the psychological thought of Jacques Lacan, and the racial dilemma in the United States. I soon realized I was too wounded to accomplish this task. I ended up writing this devotional book with Ignatius instead. It turned out to be the most consoling experience in my entire life as a Jesuit. *Thank you, Papa Ignatius.*

Sadly, I learned that the process of writing a book can trigger the loss of friends, companions, and family. Luckily, it can also be the context within which to form new connections. Both happened to me while I was writing this book. Due to the book's content, I lost some important relationships. At the same time,

I met a substantial number of good human beings who became part of my community.

In a very special way, I would like to thank Ellyn Sanna for her assistance, prayers, support, encouragement, friendship, and, of course, all her hard work as she worked with me on this book. Without her, this book would never have existed. *Mother of mercy* (as I call Ellyn), *please, receive an insignificant word of gratitude from me as a way of thanking you. God will pay you back. Mother of mercy, you evangelized me with your love and kindness through this process. Thank you very much.*

One of the pillars of the Society of Jesus is companionship. Once you become a Jesuit, you will always have faithful, trustful companions. Thus, I would like to especially thank my Jesuit companions, Fr. Daniel Hendrickson for his unconditional support, Fr. Nicky Santos, S.J., the rector of my community, and Fr. Charlie Rodriguez, S.J., for his wisdom. I extend my gratitude to my former Provincial, Fr. Brian Paulsen, S.J., for his guidance and support, and Fr. Joseph Brown, S.J., for his constant advice, guidance, and kind fraternal gaze on my formation as a Jesuit. I want to thank my friend Br. Mark Mackey for his faithful support and prayers. Also, important words of gratitude go to my friends, Br. Ralph Cordero, S.J., Br. Joe Hoover, and Fr. James Martin, S.J., for their encouragement and unconditional support. Words are not enough for me to express my gratitude to my JARS Midwest Companions: Mr. Emmanuel Arenas, S.J.; Fr. Thomas Bambrick, S.J.; Mr. Aaron Bohr, S.J.; Mr. Billy Critchley-Menor, S.J.; Mr. Patrick Hyland, S.J.; Fr. Joshua Peters, S.J.; and Mr. Damian Torres-Botello, S.J. These companions are champions in the fight of love for justice.

A big thank-you goes out to my Jesuit Community at

Creighton University. They were very patient with me. *Companions, you are one of a kind. Thank you again.*

A strong community of other friends and colleagues have also contributed to make this book possible. I want to thank Melanie Garibay, Lisa Kelly, Jill Brown, Sr. Mumbi Kigutha, Dr. Maryelle. Georgette Vonlanthen, and Georgiana Gutierrez, for their prayers and support.

Finally, words are not enough to thank Creighton University that embraces me, supports me, and gives me a home. All my students, faculty colleagues, and staff have contributed to this project in one way or another. *Thank you, Bluejays, for this unconditional love.*

Anamchara
Books

www.AnamcharaBooks.com

Made in the USA
Middletown, DE
22 May 2022